Lightly Goes The Good News

Scripture Stories For Reflection

Andre Papineau

CSS Publishing Company, Inc., Lima, Ohio

LIGHTLY GOES THE GOOD NEWS

Copyright © 2002 by
CSS Publishing Company, Inc.
Lima, Ohio

Scripture selections are taken from the *New American Bible* © 1970 by the Confraternity of Christian Doctrine, Washington, D.C., and are used with permission.

This book was originally published as two volumes: *Lightly Goes The Good News* (1989) and *Let Your Light Shine* (1990).

Library of Congress Cataloging-in-Publication Data

Papineau, Andre, 1937-
   Lightly goes the Good News : scripture stories for reflection / Andre Papineau.
     p. cm.
   ISBN 0-7880-1905-8 (pbk. : alk. paper)
   1. Bible—Devotional literature. I. Title.
   BS491.5 .P38 2002
   242'.5—dc21   2002004390

For more information about CSS Publishing Company resources, visit our website at www.csspub.com or e-mail us at custserv@csspub.com or call (800) 241-4056.

ISBN 0-7880-1905-8

To the community at Sacred Heart School of Theology for their sense of humor and compassion.
How else explain their taking me in and putting up with me for the past twenty-three years?

Table Of Contents

Introduction

G. K. Chesterton maintained angels could fly because they took themselves lightly. His remark serves as the inspiration for the title of this book. If the stories in this book "fly" it is because they are "light" reading. And they are light for four reasons.

In the first place, these stories are born from the fantasies of the writer, not the careful exegetical studies of the biblical scholar. Someone or something is fantastic when the person or thing holds a promise beyond our wildest dreams, and prompts us to ask, "How can that be?" This response to the fantastic isn't unlike Mary's response to Gabriel's "fantastic" invitation to be the mother of God.

Unfortunately, we tend to dismiss the fantastic as unsubstantial or unreal rather than as the vehicle embodying a new vision or dream of what the future holds. This dismissal of the fantastic as unreal impoverishes us because our lives are reduced solely to what is with no passion for what can be.

Secondly, these stories are light because we get enough heavy treatment of the passages on which they are based just about every Sunday from the pulpit. Far too often preachers throw us heavy verbal life rafts to save us from the perilous sin-filled waters with the promise that if we hold on for dear life we might be saved. But can't the biblical word lighten up the journey so we can sail with more ease and joy? Must we feel the boat is sinking even before we set out? Surely the Good News isn't meant to weigh us down but buoy us up and keep us moving!

Thirdly, the stories are light because they are so short. No complex plot or elaborate character development here! Like a candy bar or a cheese sandwich, they are light fare for the journey. We welcome them because they provide a needed respite for us as we ponder the outcome of the universe or shoulder the weight of the world.

Finally, the stories affirm and re-echo Jesus' challenge to us that we let our light shine, not hide under a basket. As participants in the Light, we have the potential, or God power, to illumine our world and to bring the Light of Life to others, each in our own unique way.

Lest there should be some misunderstanding, however, "lightly" doesn't mean unimportant. The Good News is important but it isn't news which we need to hear with pursed lips, a furrowed brow, and a god-awful seriousness which even God didn't possess. When the Good News comes as a gloom and doom indictment of the human race, "good" loses its meaning very fast! Life is difficult enough without making it more so by having harbingers of despair pose as angels of annunciation. Far better for God's messenger service and for us that the message is one of light and joy.

We can't really enjoy these stories, however, unless we're willing to play rather than argue the "truth" of this or that story. If we think the stories are too fanciful, and we want "objectivity," all we need do is reread many of the passages on which they are based. For example, how many people do we know who carry on conversations with angels? We accept angelic visitations in the scriptural stories because we know the imaginal realm has its own truth. The stories in this volume expand on the original imaginal situation and invite the reader to let his or her own imagination fly with the stories.

It isn't essential to read the stories in any particular order although it would be more fruitful to read the first five in the order given. The reflection which follows each story sometimes amplifies a point and at other times develops one which has hardly any connection to the story. In other words, the reflection is itself frequently a flight of fancy!

Speechless

The angel said to him: "Do not be frightened, Zechariah; your prayer has been heard. Your wife Elizabeth shall bear a son whom you shall name John." — Luke 1:13

Zech was beaming as he swung the censer in great arcs around the Temple. He hadn't felt this alive in years. And considering how old he was, that meant a lot of years. Why so alive now? Was it because he had been chosen to offer incense that evening in the Holy Place? After all, this had never happened to him before. Certainly he was filled with gratitude but this privilege didn't account for his renewed vigor or sprightly gait. Was it because he had undergone some profound religious experience? Not really. Had pleasant memories of earlier times spent in the Temple flooded his mind? Actually, no. Then what had happened which caused him to smile so broadly, swing the censer with such determination, and glide so lightly across the temple floor?

Zech sighed deeply. After twenty years of playing cribbage before they went off to sleep each night, last night he and Liz did something different; and they had fun, real fun. Zech's eyes twinkled recalling how they had gazed at one another after their second game of cribbage. "Are you thinking what I'm thinking?" he whispered to Liz as he touched her hand playfully.

"I think I am," she whispered back, lowering her eyes.

Together they giggled, "Shall we?" and together they answered, "Yehhh." And they had so much fun that night it left them speechless.

Zech decided that after last night he would give away their cribbage board. "Who needs cribbage?" he mused as he heaped more incense on the burning embers in the censer. They had taken up playing cribbage during the evening hours twenty years earlier because "it" only seemed to remind them of their continued disappointment in not being able to have children. They had earnestly performed their duty over and over but to no avail and they wondered what they had done to remain childless. And, once they became too old ever to have children, they gave up doing "it" altogether.

"But now!" Zech sighed breaking the temple silence, "Ah, sweet mystery of life!"

"Isn't that the truth?" a voice nearby chimed in.

"What?" Zech was startled as he strained to see who it was that spoke from somewhere in the cloud of incense.

"I said, 'Isn't that the truth?' — I mean the bit about life's sweet mystery. I'm just surprised it took twenty years of cribbage before you discovered it! And believe me, you'd still be shuffling and pegging if my boss, Mr. G., hadn't said, 'We've really got to do something about those two. Put a gleam in their eyes, give them a little passion for one another.' "

Zech's eyes widened as he made out the figure of a man standing close by in the haze of incense. He was dressed in a white panama suit, white shoes, and gloves. A red hankie was neatly tucked in his breast pocket.

"Who, who are yyyou?" Zech was almost speechless.

"Just call me Gabe. I hope you don't mind my being here at this time. Mr. G. asked me to drop in and give you a message. It's nice and quiet here and Mr. G. thought that since you and I are both working for him, you wouldn't feel guilty about giving me a minute or two of your time." Gabe fanned the air with his hand. "By the way, could you cool it with the censer for a minute? I'm allergic to incense and, believe me, that's bad news in my profession."

Zech immediately stayed the swinging censer with his hand. He looked warily at Gabe. His initial impulse was to make a bee-line for the temple door, clear his head with a few deep breaths of fresh air, and then reenter the sanctuary — minus the hallucination. But he didn't move. Partly out of fear. Partly out of curiosity. "You said you had a message for me?" Hallucination or not, Zech had decided to engage the stranger.

"Oh, yes, the message. Well, Mr. G. has some wonderful news for you. You and Liz are going to have a baby."

"A baby?" Zech reached for the nearest pillar to steady himself.

"Yes, a baby. See what happens when you give up cribbage for a night?" Gabe chuckled at his private joke and then continued apologetically, "I'm sorry. Those aren't Mr. G.'s words. They're my own and I take them back. But Mr. G. does want you to know that the fun you and Liz had last night was not entirely of your own making. He had a hand in it from start to finish. Because he wants you to have a baby."

"At our age?" Zech protested.

"Hey, better late than never and these are Mr. G.'s words, not mine. And what a baby this boy is going to be! He's got quite a future. Let's say he's going to be Mr.G.'s personal PR man, spreading the news about Mr. G.'s plans for his people."

By this time Zech was hugging that pillar for dear life. "But a baby at our age? He won't know whether to call us Mom and Dad or Grandma and Grandpa! He'll be pushing us in wheelchairs right after we've finished pushing him in a baby buggy. No, I think you must be mistaken. You...."

"Mistaken? Mr. G. mistaken?" Gabe sounded hurt and not a little resentful. Hands on hips, he drew a step closer to Zech. "Okay. Okay. Just so you know Mr. G. means business." Gabe shook his finger at Zech sternly. Then, less severely he continued, "Besides, the quiet will give you time to consider Mr. G.'s plans."

Zech opened his mouth to protest but nothing came out. There was a moment of astonished silence.

Then Gabe spoke slowly, deliberately. "See! Mr. G. doesn't fool around." On a lighter note he continued. "Well, I must go. We're recruiting new messengers at the office and I'm one of the interviewers. So, hang in there, Zech. You'll be hearing from me."

As Zech stood there, open mouthed, Gabe disappeared in the smoke. Loosening his grip on the pillar, Zech wondered if he had been hallucinating after all. He intended to say, "Of course," but the words would not come. Panicking, he flailed his arms, desperately trying to talk or grunt or squeak or anything. But nothing happened. He was speechless. But his mind raced from one disheartening prospect to another. How his friends would howl or wink at one another as one by one they got the news that he and Liz were going to have a baby! Liz? He had forgotten about Liz. Had Gabe told her? Zech hoped someone in Mr. G.'s messenger service had gotten to her. Because he was in no mood to explain by drawing diagrams and being called a loony by his own wife. All he needed was to have their new-found love affair end in twenty more years of cribbage! Slumping down on a temple bench, Zech propped his arms on his knees, rested his head in his hands and sat motionless for several minutes. His mind was a blank.

Then from nowhere the words "Mr. G.'s personal PR man — Spreading Plans For His People" started flashing through his mind — over and over like some electronic billboard. These words had a salutary effect on Zech. Slowly he rose to his feet, straightened himself out, and returned to the business of swinging the censer in ever greater arcs. "Hmmmm," he thought, "not just any baby. Our son is going to be Mr. G.'s personal PR man. Someone to be proud of. And ..." the censer was swinging wildly by now, "this child was the result of last night's passion when Liz and I said out of the blue, 'Shall we?' and 'Why not?' "

At that moment Zech realized no words could ever adequately express what all had happened. Even if Gabe hadn't made him speechless, he would have become so anyway. And for the time being he was satisfied to praise the Lord wordlessly in the wild eloquence of a dancing censer.

Reflection

Recall expressions like: "What can I say?" "I can't find the words." "My heart is too full to speak." Consider Zech's speechlessness following the fun he and Liz had.

We seek to convey even our inability to find the words expressing how we feel about something. A close friend dies and we want to console the widow. But all we can do is place our arm around her and shake our head. Or someone listens quietly to us as we pour out our life story. We are overwhelmed with gratitude and choke up. We cry, we laugh, embrace, pat one another on the back, or wave our hands when we all too often find we can't express ourselves in words.

"Say what you mean!" someone tells us; but we can't. Often what we mean to say cannot be said, and what we finally say is never all we really meant to say, so meaningful is that which rendered us speechless. "Ah, sweet mystery of life" is Zech's way of verbalizing an experience too profound to capture in words.

Is our speechlessness a silent safeguard which protects the truth from becoming a lie in the inadequacy of words? Is it a sign of our ultimate failure to press out the inexpressible in any and all words? Maybe if it is such a sign, it is a saving sign insofar as it reminds us of the futility of reducing realities and Reality to dogmas, creeds and formulae. For the words of a creed are no better substitutes for reality than a recipe is for a chocolate cake.

Being speechless, then, can be a brief testimony to the presence of the Silence in our lives which most often goes unnoticed but which occasionally overwhelms us.

Tradition

Now the time came for Elizabeth to be delivered, and she gave birth to a son. And her neighbors and kinsfolk heard that the Lord had shown great mercy to her, and they rejoiced with her. And on the eighth day they came to circumcise the child; and they would have named him Zechariah after his father, but his mother said, "Not so; he shall be called John." And they said to her, "None of your kindred is called by this name."

— Luke 1:57-61

Liz and Zech's relatives and friends had gathered in the living room. The occasion was their boy's circumcision. Liz called for everybody's attention. "Please, everybody! I have an announcement. I'd like you should know the name we're giving our son." Everyone quickly quieted down. "We've decided to call him John. We...."

No sooner had she spoken the name than the others gasped, "John?" In rapid succession Liz's relatives expressed dismay and astonishment.

"John? Oy vey! You want he should be called John?" Miriam clasped her hands.

"John? Since when is John his father's name?" Reuben protested. "And I might add, who among your relatives has that name?" he challenged.

"John? It's your boy, of course, but if you don't mind my saying so, isn't this a departure from tradition?" Reena objected.

"Tradition?" Liz's voice betrayed a trace of cynicism. "You're looking at a new momma in an old body and you talk to me of tradition?" She crossed her arms and tapped her right foot in irritation. "I'm waiting for an answer. Tell me how many in the tradition have become mommas at my age? Abraham's Sarah comes to mind. And that's it! So I'm in a company of two." Looking over at Zech sitting on a bench in the corner, Liz asked, "Isn't that right, Zech?"

Zech nodded his head. Out of all the people in that room, Zech knew best how he and Liz had departed from tradition. Not only had Liz conceived at an advanced age, but it took an outsider by the name of Gabe to inform them nine months earlier that they would have a baby. (Gabe had shown up nine months earlier in the Temple while Zech was offering incense during the evening service. "I've got news for you," he had announced and added solemnly as he pointed upwards, "from Mr. G." Zech almost collapsed as Gabe spelled out what Mr. G. had in mind.)

"Liz and me, parents? But we're too old. Besides it's been twenty years since...." Zech interrupted himself. He was going to say twenty years since he and Liz made an effort to have a baby. For the past twenty years it had been their tradition to play cribbage before going to bed, and that was the substance of the evening's entertainment. However, just the night before, they had looked longingly into one another's eyes over the cribbage board. "Shall we?" Zech whispered, to which Liz sighed, "Why not?" and the rest was history.

Zech had come home immediately after finishing up his work at the Temple. The other men interpreted Zech's silence and hasty departure as a sign of his deep humility. Liz wasn't quite so sure. Zech had tried to make her aware of what she could expect by drawing diagrams. Liz knew Zech had always liked to draw but she was shocked and embarrassed to have some very graphic pictures of what it takes to have a baby thrust before her eyes without a word of explanation.

"Have you been into the hootch?" Liz cried in alarm. Zech shook his head. He was beginning to wish he had as Liz wielded a heavy cast-iron frying pan in his face. "Too much incense gone to the brain? Is that it?" Again he shook his head. "You're telling me just because we missed one cribbage game we'll spend our declining years keeping Pampers in business?" Zech neither shook his head up and down nor back and forth. No. He simply shrugged his shoulders. He couldn't deny there were problems ahead. "How do I know you're not playing a game on me?" she asked skeptically. Zech counted out nine on his fingers and then curved both hands in the direction of Liz's stomach. "In nine months I'll know?" she interpreted. Zech beamed because he had finally gotten the message home to Liz.

It hadn't taken nine months, however, for Liz to confirm what was happening. A slender woman, Liz never put on weight, and when she picked up a few pounds Zech excitedly pointed over and over to the little curve on Liz's abdomen. Together they began planning for the baby's arrival. A panda bear, rocker, crib, baby buggy, tricycle, and a varied assortment of baby clothes filled the little room they had long ago set aside for the baby. The room had been sealed off twenty years earlier when their dream of having a baby failed to materialize. They had been sorely disappointed at not being able to follow the time-honored tradition of having children.

"Tradition?" Zech heard Liz challenge her guests who had gathered for the circumcision. "Don't talk to me about following tradition!"

"So you're not in favor of tradition?" Reuben raised an eyebrow.

Liz held the boy high and proclaimed, "This boy didn't come to us because of our tradition. We are not against tradition, mind you, but the tradition never prepared us for this one. Isn't that right, Zech?" Zech offered a thumbs up sign.

"But surely Zech has something to say about what the boy's name will be?" Miriam asked.

"Satisfy yourself. Ask him to tell you what the boy's name should be."

The guests looked anxiously toward the new father. "Well?" And tradition's voice waited for answer. Zech appeared to have been ready for the question. He had a writing tablet resting next to him which he now placed on his lap. Zech scribbled down four large letters. Holding the tablet in front of him where all could see he pointed to each of the letters in turn while all the guests followed in a solemn recitation, "J - O - H - N." No sooner had they said, "John," than Zech sputtered like a faucet turned on after a long period of disuse. "Jh, Jh, Jh, Jh, John. His name will be Jh—keh, Jh-keh, John and he will be Mr. G.'s personal PR Man."

"Mr. G.'s personal PR Man! Ohhhh! Really?" The guests fell silent.

"Yes, our son is going to be the advance man, traveling around the countryside, setting out Mr. G.'s plans for his people." The proud poppa flung back his shoulders and stood erect. Then, just as suddenly he plopped to his knees on the floor to play peek-a-boo with the baby. "Johnny, Johnny, cootchy-cootchy coo; cootchy-cootchy coo."

"But since he still isn't even able to stand," Liz interjected, "we have to feed John so he will grow up to be big and strong enough to tackle this job Mr. G. has in mind. And in a couple of minutes I will let you know whether his momma will break another tradition at feeding time. Zech, get up and serve the guests some tea. I'll be back shortly with our miracle baby."

And a minute later, Liz cried out joyfully from the other room, "So much for *that* tradition!"

Reflection

The past lives in us and we all live out of the past; but we are not the past. There are many persons, however, whose lives have been reduced to their pasts. "I am who I was" is a way of describing depressed people for whom there appears to be no hope because there is no future. It also aptly describes people who long for the good old days and consider the present a threat. They regard the present as a fall from better days when people presumably lived cleaner lives, worked harder, and went to church more often. "I am who I was" signals the individual's inability to be open to what is novel and surprising. But it isn't only the individual who can become a victim of the past.

Religious and political institutions fall prey to becoming identified with the past. Tradition can become a trap and a prison if it isn't open to what is different. What is tragic about the collective "I am who I was" of religious tradition is that the Unpredictable, the Mystery, the Holy cannot make an appearance unless it fits that tradition's understanding of how it should appear. In Tradition "John" doesn't fit the relatives' expectations of what the boy's name should be. They are appalled that the tradition of naming the boy after his father isn't being upheld. And in John's Gospel we read of Jesus: "He was in the world, and through him the world was made, yet the world did not know who he was" (John 1:10). John speaks of the Holy coming in a novel way; but it didn't "fit" and therefore passed unacknowledged. So today it is difficult for many persons to relate to God as Mother because, as everybody knows, God is Father!

"I am who I was" is also the fearful cry of one who is afraid of the future because it is unknown, uncertain, and uncontrollable. Liz and Zech know only too well the limitations tradition has in helping them comprehend what has happened to them. Letting go of the past and entering the future involves dying to the way things were and rising to new possibilities embodied in new vision. Flight into the past and identification with it inevitably condemn a person to be among the living dead.

A Modest Proposal

The angel Gabriel was sent from God to a town in Galilee named Nazareth, to a virgin betrothed to a man named Joseph, of the house of David. The virgin's name was Mary. Upon arriving, the angel said to her: "Rejoice, O highly favored daughter! The Lord is with you. Blessed are you among women." — Luke 1:26-28

"Can I speak to Mary?" Dressed in a white suit with a red hankie neatly tucked in his suit pocket, a young man spoke with the woman in the doorway.

"I'm Mary," she replied.

"Ah, Mary. My name is Gabe. My boss asked me to come and talk to you."

"Your boss? Who's that?"

"Mr. G. He is a very busy person, Mary. Seems to be everywhere. However, he simply couldn't be here himself. So he sent me to make you a proposal. May I come in?" Gabe had such an engaging smile with a little mole just accenting his dimpled cheek that Mary found his request impossible to resist.

"Well, only for a couple of minutes. I'm waiting for my fiancé."

"Mary, what I have to say won't take long."

"Come in then." Mary showed Gabe into the living room, pointed to a recliner for Gabe and then sat down in a rocker across from him. When Gabe had made himself comfortable, he began. "My boss, Mr. G., has been observing you for a long time."

"Observing me?" Mary puzzled.

"Yes, observing. And he's grown very fond of you."

"Fond of me?" Mary's eyes widened.

"His very words, Mary. I said to him before I left, 'Do you want me to use the word fond?' and he said, 'Oh, by all means I want you to tell her that precisely.' This means, of course, you are kind of his favorite!"

"His favorite what?" Mary grew suspicious.

"There is no one in the world like you," Gabe crooned seductively and added quickly, "his very words, not mine. Really, I'm not making them up."

By this time Mary's head was swimming. "I'm Mr. G.'s favorite? He thinks there's no one else in the world like me? Wait! I'm not sure I like this kind of attention." Mary's voice quivered as she tightened her grip on the arms of her rocker. "Quite frankly, I'm afraid. What does Mr. G. want from me?"

Gabe leaned forward in his chair and patted her soothingly on the hand. "There now, Mary, no need to fear. Mr. G. is really very gentle. He wouldn't hurt a flea. He is generous and kind towards all his workers and would do anything for them. We all think he's just — how shall I say it — ah, divine. That's it, divine! But as I told you earlier I have a proposal to make. Because you are such a favorite of Mr. G.'s, he'd like you to know that when you have your baby he's going to think of that child as his very own."

"My baby?" Mary's mouth dropped open. "Does he know something I don't know?"

"Oh, yes, a baby," Gabe repeated matter of factly. And then almost as if it were a small detail, he added, "A boy, actually. You see Mr. G. is convinced beyond a shadow of a doubt that your boy will go places. He'll be a real winner ... no doubt about it." Now Gabe paused, leaned forward even more closely and whispered conspiratorially, "In fact, on several occasions he told me personally, 'Gabe, you won't find a finer woman than that Mary. When she has a child, I'm willing to bet he'll save the whole nation!' "

"You're kidding! He said that?" Mary was having a difficult time making sense of all she was hearing.

"He did. He really did," Gabe reassured her.

"Well, he certainly seems to know more about my future than I do. But how could I possibly have a child? Doesn't Mr. G. know I'm not even married? How? What? I mean...." Mary interrupted herself, "Did he really say, 'Save the whole nation'?"

"Really. Cross my heart, Mary. Oh, and by the way, since the boy is going to be helping an awful lot of people, Mr. G. thinks 'Jesus' would be a good name for him. And he will see to it that Jesus will always have his personal backing in whatever he does and wherever he goes. He'll be with him all the way. Mr. G. has already told a number of us, 'I'll see to it that eventually Jesus gets top billing as my own son ... if it's okay with Mary.' "

Mary was silent for a moment as she carefully considered what Gabe was telling her. "I still don't understand how Mr. G. can be so sure all of this is going to happen."

"Just leave that in Mr. G.'s hands. Trust him. He has a real talent for making things happen. You could say it's his business to make the impossible possible!" Gabe paused, congratulating himself on how well he had summarized Mr. G.'s business. "Hmmm, making the impossible possible. Pretty catchy!" Then Gabe gave Mary a few tips for her future. "All you need to do is settle down and marry that young man you're engaged to. It'll work out. You'll see. Just remember one thing. You're Mr. G.'s favorite and if you believe that — you'd be surprised at what great things can happen."

Mary was overwhelmed. She had never considered herself anybody's favorite. And now this man in the white suit with the winning smile had shown up at her front door with a message from a Mr. G. whom she had never heard of before. It all seemed so incredible! Her initial impulse was to dismiss the whole thing as some practical joke. Yet, deep down, she wanted desperately to believe it. This man had made Mary feel that she was someone special, and had offered her such a marvelous vision of hope.

Finally she found the words to speak. "Please tell Mr. G. that if he thinks that highly of me, then I'm with him. I'm relying on his word."

Gabe smiled warmly. "Mary, I know Mr. G. will be delighted with your answer. I think he's already anticipated it, and intends to stage a big celebration very shortly. So, with that done I've got to be flying back to the office. But you'll be hearing from me again." Gabe rose, took Mary's hand, and kissed it gently. "And may I say, you are every bit as charming as Mr. G. led us to believe." Then without another word he made his way to the door and was gone in an instant.

"Mary, are you still asleep?"

"What?" Mary's eyes blinked open, and she found herself looking up into the face of a man gazing lovingly down at her. "Joseph? I ... uh, was I sleeping?"

"For about an hour. I was here earlier but I didn't want to disturb you." Mary didn't know whether she had been dreaming or what ... it had all seemed so real, so vivid. But if she had been dreaming, she concluded, it was certainly the kind of dream she'd have wanted to become a reality. And although the details were very hazy, Mary sensed that her future was definitely moving in a new direction.

As she got up from her rocker Mary noticed something red on the recliner. "Joseph, is that your hankie?"

"No, it isn't."

Mary rubbed her eyes. "Hmmmmm," she wondered as she reached over to pick it up. "It looks so familiar." She held it close to her heart as she pondered the meaning of all that had happened that day.

Reflection

Many of us at one time or another have been engaged to someone. But who among us has been engaged with God? Engaged with God? Can we even take the question seriously? Of course, we might say Mary was engaged with God. After all, it was through the power of God's Spirit that she became pregnant. However, maybe if we consider what engagement means we shall discover all of us have been, are, now and always will be engaged with God; and this story serves as a reminder of the meaning of engagement.

How can one be engaged with God? Consider how the word is used. Someone has an engaging personality, i.e., interesting, entertaining, charming, even seductive. Thus, Mary is drawn into conversation by Gabe who represents Mr. G. He is engaging, charming. He tells her God has a crush on her. She is a favorite of his. Then he tells her what God has in mind and she is overwhelmed and in conflict. Another meaning for the word! To engage someone is to confront and to be in conflict as when two parties engage one another in battle. "How can this be?" Mary asks. She engages and is engaged with God through the angel. Finally, she submits and places herself in God's hands; she promises herself to God. This is yet another meaning of the word engage: to promise or submit. The word has many meanings and Mary's relationship with God can be understood more deeply by understanding them all.

If we consider our own relationship with God as an engagement in the senses described above, we begin to see it in a different way. We too are engaged or seduced by God when we have a heightened sense of our own worth or value; we feel favored, important. We don't do anything to produce that awareness. It just comes over us. However, we also engage God in conflict. Like Mary we want to know, "How can this be?" Whether we are speaking about getting through the day or through a difficult period in our lives due to illness, divorce, death, etc., we are overwhelmed by what appears to be an impossible situation. So our relationship is one of conflict and darkness. But we also go along, do what we can, trust, and hand ourselves over. We become engaged, committed to whatever is in store for us. But whatever is in store is ultimately in the hands of the one Jesus called Father. We are indeed engaged with God.

And what is the result of such an engagement? Would it be too far-fetched to speak of becoming pregnant? Something of us is transformed or changed so that Jesus is incarnated, embodied, and enfleshed in engagement. The story of our engagement with Mr. G. never ends because Mr. G. always wants to become engaged.

Favorite

The angel Gabriel was sent from God to a town in Galilee named Nazareth, to a virgin betrothed to a man named Joseph, of the house of David. The virgin's name was Mary. Upon arriving, the angel said to her: "Rejoice, O highly favored daughter! The Lord is with you. Blessed are you among women." — Luke 1:26-28

Mary spent the whole day going over and over what Gabe had told her the morning before. Mr. G. was "fond" of her; she was a "favorite" of his. Favorite? Mary couldn't get over being called a favorite of Mr. G.'s. As she looked at the recliner where Gabe had sat and given her the news, she tried to recall when anyone had ever spoken of her as being favored in any way, shape, or form. As far back as she could remember she'd never been anyone's favorite. Her sisters, Ruth, Sarah, and Rachel, were all prettier than she. Mary wasn't ugly or anything like that. No, not really, but when all the girls got together, she certainly didn't stand out. Relatives and friends always had something great to say to her sisters.

"Ruth ... I just love the way you did your hair."

"Sarah ... that dress really makes you look attractive."

"Rachel ... did anyone ever tell you you have beautiful eyes?" But as for Mary it was, "... Uh ... hi, Mary!" And that was it.

And when the girls walked down the street or flirted at the neighborhood well, the boys all noticed the other girls first.

"Hey, Ruthie ... what are you doing on Tuesday night?"

"Sarah ... got anything doing on Wednesday afternoon?"

"Rachel ... there's a dance at Abe's Place tonight. Interested?"

And to Mary it was, "... Hi, Mary. Ummmmm." And that was all.

Yes, they noticed her. But she was a little on the plump side, with a shy smile that fluttered across her face whenever anyone even looked at her. Yes, they noticed her, but they never noticed anything special. Clearly, she wasn't their favorite.

And her parents? Of course they loved Mary. They loved all their daughters. But you could tell by the way they talked....

"Oh, that Ruth can really bake mile high bread!"

"What a wit our Sarah has! She's really going somewhere!"

"And Rachel ... no one has a memory like our Rachel! Photographic, really."

"Mary? Well, uh ... Mary ... will you excuse me? I think I left the water running...." Clearly she just wasn't their favorite either. No slight was ever intended, but they simply couldn't think of anything to say about her. So there was always a painful lull in the conversation whenever anyone asked about Mary.

It was understandable, then, that the other girls, the prettier ones, were engaged to be married long before Mary. Her parents just gushed over their daughters' choices.

"Ruth, we're so happy. A doctor! You're marrying a doctor. Just think. A doctor in our family."

"Sarah, he's so good looking and ... money! Not that it matters, but money! Bet you're set for life! What a match!"

"And, Rachel, you'll see the world. Who would have thought your husband would own half the boats in the Sea of Galilee?"

But Mary? Her folks were getting seriously worried. They wrang their hands. "Please, God. Is there anyone out there for her?"

So, when someone finally did come along, everybody thought it was something of a miracle. Well, not really a miracle. You see, Mary's fiancé was no great catch. It was obvious that he was never anybody's favorite either. Not much money. Not much to look at. Moreover, people had a problem remembering his name. "Don't tell me! I know you just said it a minute ago. Reuben? ... No, Simon.

Oh, yes ... Joel? ... Joshua? ... Mmmmm ... sorry about that." Mary's parents had a hard time remembering Joseph's name even after his fifth visit.

And it was a good thing he wasn't as awkward with his hands as he was with his words. If he were, he'd have been a poor carpenter indeed, not to mention missing a finger or two. "Ummmm, I'd like to ... I mean, is it all right for your Mary to be my Mary by marrying me?" No, Joseph wasn't anybody's favorite. But since Mary wasn't either, they were probably well matched. And, Mary seemed to know and understand what went on inside of him ... she could feel his hurt at being ignored or forgotten when the compliments were passed around.

She also seemed to know and understand the hurt of many of the street children, the losers, the less favored ones in the neighborhood. She'd take the kids with the big ears or noses and sit them on her lap and tell them how special they were. "I'll bet you can hear better than anyone. What a great detective you'll be!" or "Do you know how lucky you are to have that nose? Just think what you can do for the perfume industry." Even if they weren't always convinced about what Mary said, nestled on her lap they felt special for the moment and that was all that really mattered.

She also cared a lot for the old people in town who might have been someone's favorite many years ago, but weren't any longer. "I'll bring you some lemonade if you promise to tell me about your grandchildren," she coaxed them as they rocked away their lives. And then she'd spend the afternoon listening to them talk about all their grandchildren from Abimelech to Zarubabel as well as anything else that happened to pop into their minds.

Mary smiled as she caressed the red hankie she presumed Gabe had left on the chair before he returned to Mr. G. Yes, Gabe had brought her good news but very shortly he would have to pay a special visit to Joseph to clear up a misunderstanding that was growing up between them concerning all this. For not too long after her engagement to Joseph, if anyone had paid attention, they would have noticed a change in Mary.

There was now a certain radiance about her. At first no one did pay any attention to her — her sisters, her parents, her friends. After all, they had never considered her favored for anything in particular before — why should she be now? Yet, gradually they couldn't help notice something different.

"Look at that smile. Mary, you're looking great! Somebody must like you!" Oh, yes. Somebody liked her. She moved with a gracefulness that proclaimed it and she carried the child within her that announced it. And the less favored ones, the young and old alike, felt favored as never before whenever she stopped to talk with them. Exactly what had happened no one really knew. Yet the less favored ones sensed something important had taken place. Whatever it was, they sensed they all stood to gain from it. Whoever had made her his favorite was soon to proclaim that good news to them:

Rejoice, highly favored one. The Lord is with you.

Reflection

Favorite reminds us God is choosy but not in the same way as we are choosy. How do we choose? Consider what people do in the fruit and vegetable section of a supermarket. They pick, probe, and pummel produce to avoid getting the worst and ensure enjoying the best. After all, who wants pulpy peaches, lousy lemons, limp-looking lettuce, or tough tomatoes? No one. We choose the best: peachy peaches, luscious lemons, tender tomatoes.

Or think of someone choosing a puppy. A puppy lover doesn't want the runt of the litter. No way! Or when the captain of a volleyball team is choosing players. The player with the leaden feet and the clumsy hands can always count on being chosen last.

God, on the other hand, would choose the pulpy peach, the runt of the litter, and the fumbling player because God can do great things with rejects. He chose nomads with onion on their breath to be his favorites, the Baptist dressed in foul animal skins to be his advance man for Jesus, and men with the smell of fish on their

hands to be Jesus' disciples, and as we have just read, a woman
with no saving grace to be the mother of grace. Not men and women
in Brooks Brothers suits or Gloria Vanderbilt designer jeans!
The theme song of God's favorites is "You're Nobody Till
Somebody Loves You." And the good news of God's chosen isn't,
"We've got something you don't have," but, "If God loves us, he
can and does love everybody. What we've got going for us isn't
how we look, dress, work or who we know. No. We have nothing
going for us and we want everybody to know, God can raise up
somebodies out of nobodies!"

Concrete Results

*Now this is how the birth of Jesus Christ came
about. When his mother Mary was engaged to Joseph, but before they lived together, she was found
with child through the power of the Holy Spirit.
Joseph her husband, an upright man unwilling to
expose her to the law, decided to divorce her quietly. Such was his intention when suddenly the
angel of the Lord appeared in a dream and said to
him: "Joseph, son of David, have no fear about
taking Mary as your wife. She is to have a son and
you are to name him Jesus because he will save
his people from their sins."* — Matthew 1:18-21

Joseph picked up his broom and started sweeping the floor of
his little carpenter shop. He had been thinking about his dream all
morning. "What a story!" he muttered to himself. "I've heard big
ones before but this one tops the list!" He didn't know what was
funnier ... the fact that the guy in the dream had explained his
fiancée's pregnancy as the work of the spirit, or that the child she
now carried was supposed to be Israel's savior. "If someone had
come up to me and said all of this to my face, I would have known
whether he was crazy or drunk or both. But a dream? How do you
argue with a dream?"

Joseph shoved his broom around the floor distractedly, batting
at the wood shavings and sending little clouds of sawdust into the
morning air. Tightening his grip on the broom, Joseph imagined

the dream figure standing in front of him and his face flushed as he spat out: "Why wasn't I consulted? We're talking about my family, aren't we? And what's so wrong with my genes anyway? And why don't you fellows show up in person instead of in dreams? Afraid to face the music?" Joseph caught himself kicking at the pile of shavings he had just swept together. Exasperated, he flung the broom against the wall. "I've got to get hold of myself," he said anxiously as he looked out the window. "Oh," he moaned seeing Mary approach the porch steps. "I have to have this out with her. I've got to get this straightened out. Now! If I don't, I'm going to get an ulcer." Mary opened the door and walked in, beaming.

"Watch your step, Mary! There are some pretty big nails sticking out of some boards on the floor," Joseph muttered as he turned, pretending to busy himself at the work bench.

"Thanks for the warning, Joe!" Mary picked her way to the corner of the shop to which Joseph had retreated.

She had no sooner planted a kiss on Joseph's cheek than he stiffened, turned and holding her at arm's length, stared into her eyes and said, "Mary, we've got to have a talk. I mean ... we've got to have a talk!" He cleared his throat.

"For the last few months, I've noticed you putting on weight. I know I'm not all that bright, but finally I put two and two together. You're in a family way, aren't you, Mary? And I ... I had absolutely nothing to do with it, did I?" He struggled to fight back his tears. "Now I have waited ... I've waited for an explanation from you, Mary, and you haven't said anything. Not one word!" Joseph's voice broke off abruptly.

There was a long silence. "I know I should have come to you sooner," Mary confessed, "but I just didn't know how to explain the way I became pregnant."

"Mary, look, I may not be another Solomon, but I've pretty much figured out that there's only one way to get pregnant!"

The tone of his voice cut Mary to the heart. "Well, Joe, I have news for you," she shot back. "There is more than one way! You see, I had this vision and an angel came to me and...."

Joseph threw up his hands. "Oh, no! Not you too?"

Mary looked puzzled. "What do you mean, 'me too'?"

"Never mind. Finish what you were saying."

"Well, this angel came to me, introduced himself, and said, 'I have this little proposal. Would you mind being the mother of....' "

"The mother of the savior of Israel?" Joseph teased as though he had been a party to the conversation.

Mary gasped. "How do you know what he said?"

Joseph groaned and continued as though he hadn't heard Mary, "And you will conceive by the power of the spirit." He repeated these words bitterly as if each were an assault on his manhood.

Mary was excited. "Don't tell me you know Gabe too?"

"Look, Mary. This guy isn't as familiar with me as he apparently is with you." Joseph's tone was more than a little resentful. But Mary pressed on.

"Did he have a little mole on his cheek?"

"Who?"

Mary could hardly contain herself. "The person who told you about me."

Joseph searched his memory. "Well ... now that you mention it, yes...."

"That's Gabe!" Mary shouted in recognition.

"Mary, for the last couple of weeks I was ready to call it quits with you. I was really hurt and wanted nothing more than to get even. If you had come to me then with this cockamamie story, I don't know what I would have done." Joseph took a deep breath. "But last night I had this dream ... this crazy dream."

"We've both had the same dream, Joe!" Mary said as she nestled up beside him. "But I don't think it's all that crazy. And anyway I'd rather believe in a crazy dream that offers hope, than have no dream at all."

In the silence that followed, Mary twined her little fingers in Joseph's calloused hand. "You're right, Mary, at least our dream offers hope. When I look around and see so many people suffering, I guess our crazy dream or vision or whatever it is holds more promise than anything else happening today. If this child is the child of promise, the savior of Israel ... well, I would never stand in

the way of that promise." Then, smiling impishly he continued,
"On the other hand, this vision might be some big joke. And if it
is...." He reached suddenly for a large wooden board.
"And if it is...?" Mary winced.
Joseph's face broke into a wide smile as he lifted the wood
high above his head. "If it is a joke, well, at least it will have in-
spired the most beautiful baby crib in the world!" He put his arm
around Mary's waist and said, "Let's start working on that dream!"

Reflection

When we read the gospel about Joseph we tend to move too
quickly beyond his sense of betrayal to the message he receives in
the dream. Yet, that message becomes meaningful only insofar as
it is a message to one deeply in need of hearing it, and we cannot
appropriate it ourselves unless we imaginatively enter his experience.
Joseph is a man in the dark. The woman to whom he is engaged, to whom he is committed, appears to have betrayed him,
and this feeling of betrayal must be overwhelming. It is the feeling
of being played for a sucker or taken for a ride by someone close.
Joseph is a just man, we are told. But this doesn't mean he is
exempt from those bitter impulses which any betrayed man or
woman experiences.
Even the just person can want vengeance, to get even or do the
other in. Even the just person can become cynical and sneer at
once-prized ideals or reject the possibility of any future intimate
relationship. Why would the just person not want to play it safe
and just say, "Never, never again"? "I won't get my fingers burned"
is as much a temptation for the just person as it is for anyone else.
Finally, even the just person may regard shared moments of ten-
derness and concern as really moments of weakness never to be
shared again.
Joseph doesn't resort to violence; he is not a violent man. But
Joseph is hurt, and being hurt can render one all but helpless. We
don't know how long he anguished or how long he wanted to curl

up and die — the Gospel is silent. What we know is he finally decides to divorce Mary quietly. This moment must be one of despair. It is also the moment of the dream. We would be wrong to conclude in our imaginative reconstruction that the message negated all he had gone through, made everything clear, took the darkness away. What we know is the bad news slowly became good news — God with us. "Concrete Results" suggests Joseph had questions never to be answered, and answers which only raised new questions. Ultimately, trust is required.

We do not ordinarily get an explanation for betrayal in our dreams, although we dream up explanations because we have a need to understand and make sense out of these betrayals. But frequently our explanations fail to satisfy and our queries remain unanswered. "Where are you in all this?" is the cry we bring to God. It is the cry of Jesus on the cross. And all we can do is trust as Jesus did that in the silence there is an answer — waiting to be born.

Line Drawing

On one occasion a lawyer stood up to pose him this problem: "Teacher, what must I do to inherit everlasting life?" Jesus answered him: "What is written in the law? How do you read it?" He replied: "You shall love the Lord your God with all your heart, with all your soul, with all your strength, and with all your mind; and your neighbor as yourself." Jesus said, "You have answered correctly. Do this and you shall live." But because he wished to justify himself he said to Jesus, "And who is my neighbor?" — Luke 10:25-29

"Where do you draw the line?" Abe demanded. "When is enough enough? Just how far do I have to go?" Abe was a lawyer who felt compelled to know exactly what the law stipulated for every issue imaginable. "It's my training," he explained to a friend. "We lawyers are expected to spell out others' rights and responsibilities under the law. We aren't hired to give fuzzy answers. No, sir! Our clients demand precision!"

But Abe needed precision not only for his clients.

He had endless questions about his own obligations. "When I go strolling in the park, how many times should I tip my hat to a person I've passed three times in the same day? When someone wants to borrow money, how much do I have to loan them before I say, 'Enough is enough already'? How much time must I spend

36

with a friend filling me in on all his little problems? Ditto for the relatives? Just where do I draw the line?"

He consulted other lawyers. He searched and researched dusty covered tomes and scholarly periodicals for answers. And when he'd light upon one, Abe was noticeably relieved. "Ahh! If I meet someone three times a day, I tip my hat once, nod a second time, and wave a third." Or, "I loan twenty percent of a day's wage to my friend, thirty percent to my first cousin, forty percent to my brother, fifty percent to my wife, and seventy-five percent to my mother. At that point, enough is enough! Good, now I know!" Or, "Depending on how long I've known the friend, the time I must spend listening ranges from five minutes for a new acquaintance to an hour and a half for a grade school chum. Then I can draw the line and say, 'Enough is enough already.' "

True, Abe might be inconvenienced by what the law required; but inconveniences didn't matter nearly as much as knowing clearly what was expected. For example, if according to the law a friend deserved an hour's hearing whether he droned on about trivia or desperately needed Abe's attention, Abe had to listen! Only after the full hour was up could he say, "Well, enough is enough. I draw the line here." Only then could he dismiss the friend whether the friend continued to need him or not.

Needless to say, this need to know exactly what was expected of him was found to be the source of much consternation. One day as he walked down a deserted street, Abe spied a man, bruised and beaten, lying in a gutter. The man was black, dressed in a white suit, black shirt and purple tie, and barely conscious. His Panama hat and cane, broken sunglasses, and empty wallet lay scattered about the sidewalk. Abe was shocked as he approached, but stopped short. "I know him! My God, what am I going to do? It's the pimp from K Street! We've been trying to clean up his neighborhood for years. If it weren't for him and his stable of hookers, we'd have no problems! Hmmmm, he's bleeding badly. Maybe one of them clobbered him. Serves him right! But do I have to help him? Him, of all people? A pimp? The law — what does it say about helping wounded pimps? How far do I have to go? Where do I draw the line? When can I say enough is enough?"

Abe was in such a quandary that he simply wandered off without helping the man, leaving him to an uncertain fate. For the next couple of days Abe did what he always did in these situations. He searched and researched the tomes, and consulted his lawyer friends. However, he got no satisfactory answers about whether the law demanded helping pimps. Walking home from his club, still agonizing over what was expected of him, he came across a small crowd of people listening to an itinerant preacher. "It's Jesus," he muttered. "I've heard him before. Good speaker! I wonder...." Abe stood listening. When Jesus had finished speaking, much to his own surprise Abe blurted out, "Teacher, what must I do to inherit everlasting life?"

Jesus shaded his eyes, looked long and hard at Abe and asked, "What is written in the law? How do you read it?" Abe was relieved. He knew the law on that one. "You shall love the Lord your God with all your heart, with all your soul, with all your strength, and with all your mind; and your neighbor as yourself." Jesus said "You have answered correctly. Do this and you shall live." But Abe wouldn't drop the matter. That law wasn't clear enough. He needed to know exactly where to draw the line. "Who ... who is my neighbor?"

Jesus answered, "There was a man about your size, wearing a blue suit and gold rimmed glasses like yours, and carrying your kind of brown briefcase on his way from Jerusalem to Jericho. Waiting in the bushes alongside the road were three robbers. They jumped him, beat him, took his money, and then left him for dead.

"An hour passed and a man dressed in a blue suit and wearing gold rimmed glasses like yours came down the road. He also happened to be carrying a brown briefcase. When he saw the man, he stopped, opened his briefcase and removed a book called *Line Drawing*. Thumbing through it, he reached a certain page, read it, nodded confidently, closed the book, put it back into his case, and walked on.

"A half an hour later another man looking surprisingly like you came down the road, saw the man, halted, and produced a scholarly book from his briefcase. It was titled *When Enough Is Enough*. Thumbing through it several times, checking and rechecking the index and appendices, he frowned, fidgeted, and sighed. He paced up and down the road for twenty minutes deep in thought. Then, shrugging his shoulders, he walked on.

"Finally, another man came down the road. He wore a white suit, black shirt, purple tie, Panama hat, sunglasses and carried a cane. He was black. He was also the town pimp! Seeing the injured man, he ran over to him, knelt down, and exclaimed, 'What can I do for you, my man?' He took a small flask of whiskey from his suit pocket, gave the injured man a drink, got him to his feet, and practically carried him to a motel a mile down the road. There the pimp told the innkeeper, 'Watch out for my man here. I'll pay you for this cat when I come back.'

"Now I ask you, which of these three proved to be a neighbor?"

Abe was dumbfounded. "Well, not the one who consulted *Line Drawing*."

"Yes? Go on!"

"And ... uh ... not the other fella who relied on *When Enough Is Enough*."

"Who was it then?" Jesus insisted.

"The p ... p ... p ... pimp," Abe sputtered.

Jesus winked. "Then go and do likewise. Enough line drawing, okay?"

"Yeah, sure, no line drawing," Abe answered. He had learned that enough is never enough.

Reflection

"Where do I draw the line?" is not an entirely selfish question. It is an acknowledgment that we are limited in what we can and cannot do. As humans we are finite. When we constantly overextend ourselves, we are playing at being God. We need limits.

However the honest admission that we have to draw the line ought not to be turned into our life's theme.

"Where do I draw the line" as a life theme becomes a self-imposed limitation not only on what I have to be in relation to others but also on what I can become. Our concern to do only what is required blinds us to our own potential for becoming all that we can become in a variety of relationships. In terms of letting our light shine, we don't want to limit the light by asking how much we have to shine. Rather we want to realize whatever our possibilities are for shining.

If our life theme is "Where do I draw the line?" we might ask ourselves why we insist on drawing lines at all. Do we fear losing ourselves in too much caring and too much giving? Whatever the reason for our fear, only taking the step of trust in the Unbounded Light will really let us shine. Only that will enable us to say enough is never enough!

Holy Family

He went down with them, and came to Nazareth,
and was obedient to them. His mother meantime
kept all these things in memory. Jesus, for his part,
progressed steadily in wisdom and age and grace
before God and men.   — Luke 2:51-52

One day Jesus came home from school. The boy was upset. There were tears in his eyes. "Mom, mom," he cried as he ran through the house looking for Mary.

"I'm here in the living room," Mary called. "What's the matter, Jesus? You look upset," she continued as she put her arms around Jesus.

"Mom, one of the kids called me holy. I wanted to punch him in the face but he was too big. Mom, I'm not really holy, am I? Say I'm not holy, Mom, say it!" Jesus had a look of horror on his face.

Mary gazed lovingly down at Jesus, but she sounded serious, very serious. "We have to have a little talk, son. I've put this off long enough. I should have told you long ago what I'm about to tell you now, Jesus. You are different. You are holy."

"Oh, no, it's true then," Jesus said softly, trying to absorb what Mary had just told him.

"Wait, Jesus. There's more." Mary looked steadily into Jesus' eyes, both hands resting firmly on his shoulders. "Mommy and Daddy are holy too. I know this comes as quite a shock to you, but we are all holy! Jesus, don't look away from me." Jesus

41

had momentarily turned his face from Mary. "We all have to face it. We're different from the others. We're a holy trio."

"But, Mommy," Jesus pleaded, "I want to grow up and be like the rest of the kids. I don't want to be holy. I'll never be able to play hookie or have a few beers with the boys or tell off-color jokes when I grow up. I'll have to be patient and walk around with my hands folded, my eyes turned upwards, and with a sour smile on my face all the time. I don't want to! I don't want to look like I'm always sitting on a tack or sick with a bellyache!" Jesus' pouting face was wet with tears of anger.

Mary got up and walked to the window. Then she turned to Jesus and, with a note of apology in her voice, she said, "Jesus, the truth is I have myself to blame for all this. Years ago, I said, 'Yes,' and I got myself in a holy way that very instant. It certainly didn't take much! Then your father and I were married and it's been nothing but holiness ever since. Holiness, holiness, holiness! I go down the street and people whisper, 'There goes that holy Mary.' They never say this to my face, of course. They just say, 'Hail, Mary, how are you?' "

Joseph had been standing quietly in the doorway. He cleared his throat and broke the awkward silence that had fallen between mother and son. "I couldn't help overhearing. Jesus, I'm sorry we haven't had a heart to heart talk about this earlier. But as you can imagine, it isn't easy telling your only son that he's holy. I certainly didn't think when I married your mother I'd end up being so holy myself. I guess you just don't bargain for these things. I'm certainly not blaming your mother. But it's just not easy going to work and hearing the other carpenters say behind your back, 'Holy Joe! He's back again! Watch your language!' "

Then Mary said with a sigh of relief, "Well, I'm glad it's finally out in the open. Now at least we can face this together. No need pretending everything is okay when we've got this problem staring us in the face. So, what are we going to do?" They stood there silent for a moment; then Mary continued, "As far as I'm concerned, what I'd like to do is just go on living my life the way I want without letting this holiness thing get in the way."

"You mean," Jesus said excitedly, "we could really lead normal lives? You really mean it, huh?"

"I think we could give it a try, Jesus," Mary said as she smiled for the first time since they had started their little talk. "Every time you're tempted to act holy or walk around with a holy look on your face, tell yourself you don't have to act this way if you really don't want to. No matter how people treat you, no matter if they call you holy names or say your mother or your father are holy, don't let it get to you."

"Yes, son," Joseph added. "That's the last thing you want — is to let it get to you. I've seen others get called holy, and it just ate them up. They felt as if they had to act so holy all the time that pretty soon they became very boring. And of all the people I know, it is people acting holy who are the most boring. So your mother is right. Let's not let it take over our lives. Let's laugh when we want to, cry when we want to, have parties when we want to, and hang around with whatever kind of people we want to. Let's let everyone know that this family is going to live life with all kinds of people and enjoy them all to the full. And if they call that holy — well, who cares!"

The three of them laughed, embraced one another, and sat down to a game of Scrabble — free at last from the fear of being called holy.

Reflection

"Holy Family" challenges the stereotypical presentation of the holy family frequently bodied forth in sentimental holy cards and maudlin sermons. Jesus, Mary, and Joseph become too hard an act to follow once they have been sanitized and extolled as "models" of exemplary family life. Moreover, the saccharine spirituality we are called to imitate has little appeal to any family facing the problems families face today.

Stereotyping defines too narrowly the reality it attempts to describe. Certain often arbitrary standards are used to determine the basis for calling a family holy or best dressed or most likely to succeed. These standards in turn become inhibiting. That is, individuals and families feel compelled to "live up" to an idealized way of behaving which prevents spontaneity. Being oneself means having to be what is expected, e.g., Ms. Congeniality has to be smiling and the picture of politeness all the time. Becoming overly self-conscious about the "image" of holiness, people are not free to be holy in ways unique to them.

Who is the holy family? The holy family is the family which shatters the idol of holiness and seeks to put us in touch with what is unrepeatably holy and not stereotypically so in each of us.

The Last Laugh

Now Abraham and Sarah were old, advanced in years, and Sarah had stopped having her womanly periods. So Sarah laughed to herself and said, "Now that I am so withered and my husband is so old, am I still to have sexual pleasure?" But the Lord said to Abraham, "Why did Sarah laugh and say, 'Shall I really bear a child, old as I am?' Is anything too marvelous for the Lord to do?"
— Genesis 18:11-14

"Sarah, the drought has dwindled our food supply. There are difficult times ahead, but we'll survive," her mother assured her.

"Ha! Ha! Ha!" Sarah laughed until her belly ached — or did she laugh because it ached?

"Sarah, you have all the qualifications: intelligence, personality, character references. There's only one hitch. Your skin's too dark! Sorry, we'll have to hire someone else for the position," the amiable manager smiled as he walked her to the door.

"Ha! Ha! Ha!" Sarah clenched her teeth, bit her lip, and laughed her hurt away.

"Sarah, a woman belongs to her husband. She's not supposed to think for herself. And why would you want to anyway? To prove you're better than a man?" her teacher reproved her.

Sarah rapped her fingers on the desk, sailed a sigh through the air, and trailed it with laughter. "Ha! Ha! Ha!"

Sarah's response to adversity was unusual. Unlike others who cried, perspired, swore, got angry, developed migraines or ulcers, broke out in hives or cold sweat, Sarah laughed. She couldn't tell you why she laughed but one thing she knew, her laughter kept her going through thick and thin. Yes, she laughed whether she wanted to or not. It was a mixed blessing.

The same laughter which often helped relieve tension frequently created even more. For example, in the early days of married life friction flared between Abe and Sarah because Abe misunderstood her laughter. Masking the fear in her eyes, Sarah giggled uncontrollably when Abe said the Lord God commanded them to leave the security of home and country for a new land they had never seen or even heard of. "Ha! Ha! Ha!"

"I don't think it's one bit funny! We're going to a distant country, not our neighbor's tent! We need faith and lots of it, not this silly giggling," he lectured her. But his serious tone simply deepened the tension.

"Ha! Ha! Ha! Oops!" Sarah blurted, bringing both hands to her mouth in a vain attempt to stifle herself. Understandably, Abe was smarting as he stormed away wondering who the woman was he married.

But there were other times when Sarah's laughter served them well, like the time she and Abe traveled to Egypt. There had been a famine in Canaan and plenty of food in Egypt. However, while they solved one problem by going to Egypt, they came up against another once they arrived. Sarah's good looks had drawn the attention of the Pharaoh. Fearful he would lose his life if the Pharaoh discovered Sarah was his wife, Abe introduced her to the Egyptian court as his sister. Neither Sarah nor Abe knew whether the members of the court would believe their story. So, naturally Sarah was extremely nervous. But Abe had told her, "Just have faith and everything will be okay! We'll be able to stay here in Egypt."

"Most pleased to meet you, madam. You are beautiful indeed."

"Ha! Ha! Ha!" Tittering, Sarah blushed brightly.

"What do you think of our country?" he queried.

"Ha! Ha! Ha!" Sarah struggled and sputtered but couldn't speak.

Nevertheless, the courtiers were captivated. "And your laughter lightens our lives," chortled the others.

"Ha! Ha! Ha!" Surprise! Sarah's laughter impressed the court and saved the day. Or did it? She was such a hit that Sarah was "invited" to Pharaoh's chambers for the night.

Knocking warily on the chamber door that evening, she wondered what she'd do and how she'd act. "Ha! Ha! Ha!" Beside herself with fear, she laughed uncontrollably as Pharaoh greeted her with open arms.

"You're every bit the beauty they say you are," Pharaoh marveled as he drew her to his bed. "By the way, since you laugh so easily I have a joke or two for you," he winked as he sat her next to him. Wide-eyed, Sarah broke out into paroxysms of laughter whenever Pharaoh delivered his royal punch lines.

"Ha! Ha! Ha!"

He was delighted that Sarah laughed at jokes even he hadn't thought funny, much less the members of the royal household. "Now enough of mirth. Let's to bed, my love," he whispered sweetly in her ear.

As Pharaoh disrobed, Sarah doubled over with fits of laughter. "Ha! Ha! Ha! Ha! Ha! Ha!"

"Is it something about my body that strikes you funny" he asked defensively.

"Ha! Ha! Ha!" Sarah squirmed, stuffing the corner of the pillow into her mouth. His face crimson with anger, the Pharaoh scrambled for a sheet, wrapped it around himself and ordered her out of the chamber.

"Ha! Ha! Ha!" Tears streaming down her cheeks, Sarah sailed home on waves of laughter. No sooner had she arrived than Pharaoh's word overtook her and Abe. "Out! Out! Out of my country!"

"Tsk! Tsk! Tsk! Not enough faith, Sarah. That's why we've failed," Abe muttered as they left Pharaoh's land.

Back in Canaan, her troubles continued. Abe was particularly disturbed by her laughing whenever he built altars at wayside shrines. He took his relationship with God very seriously. No one was permitted a word while he meticulously piled up the stones;

and everyone was to stay completely silent whenever he performed the sacrifice.

Of course in such a super-charged atmosphere, it was inevitable that Sarah would laugh. "Ha! Ha! Ha!" she laughed one day as Abe was bowing profoundly at a wayside shrine. "Ha! Ha! Ha!"

Arching an eyebrow, Abe exploded! "Laughing during a service at a shrine! You've actually laughed! Don't you realize believing is no laughing matter? Faith and foolishness don't mix," he decreed. "What kind of a God do you think we follow anyway?"

"Ha! Ha! Ha! Surely not a God who cannot laugh," she bristled. The other members of the party weren't quite certain what to make of all this, but they secretly agreed among themselves that laughter was preferable to the unrelieved seriousness and boredom which marked Abe's worship.

Sarah's inability to conceive occasioned more bouts of laughter than anything else in her life. "Ha! Ha! Ha! I can't bear a child," she moaned. "Ha! Ha! Ha! Abe, take my servant girl Hagar and have a child by her. Ha! Ha! Ha!" Now, she suffered the double indignity of not being able to conceive and of turning to her servant for help.

She laughed through it all in spite of her tears, a response some of her friends believed helped Sarah maintain her sanity. "Ha! Ha! Ha!" Her laughter was tinged with defiance when Hagar took advantage of her pregnancy and frequently insulted Sarah.

As Sarah grew old and wrinkled, she continued to laugh in the face of difficulties which might have caused men and women half her age to weep. Getting up in the morning she'd feel arthritis aching in her hands and legs. "Ha! Ha! Ha!" She winced, but still the laughter rose to heaven. And when she'd sit and consider how she'd fare when she could no longer see or hear, she'd throw her hands up in desperation but then break into a laugh undiminished by her years. "Ha! Ha! Ha!"

One day three strangers paid Abe a visit while he stood fanning himself at the entrance to his tent. Being a hospitable man, he invited them to stay for a snack. They accepted and sat on a blanket in the shade of a nearby tree. While they got settled, Abe whispered in the tent for Sarah to bake some tea rolls for them. Then he joined his guests. After they had eaten, one of the guests dropped a bombshell. "About this time next year I'll return and when I do Sarah will have a child."

Sarah who had been eavesdropping at the entrance of the tent began to laugh. "Ha! Ha! Ha!" She couldn't stop. "After all these years, Abe at 100: no teeth, can hardly walk, barely sees and as far as I know.... Ha! Ha! Ha! And me at 90? Ha! Ha! Ha! What's Abe been giving them to drink? Ha! Ha! Ha! And the baby will be here next year? Ha! Ha! Ha!"

What Sarah didn't realize, though Abe did, was that the stranger who spoke was the Lord God. After all, who else could have made such a promise? "There is nothing the Lord can't do!" Abe thundered in anger and exasperation. "After all these years don't you have faith? I know ... it takes a lot of effort to believe but with enough will power you can do it! You...."

"Why were you laughing, Sarah?" the Lord God interrupted.

"I wasn't laughing," she said. "Ha! Ha! Ha! It's just that I ... Abe ... me ... we ... mommy and daddy.... Ha! Ha! Ha! It's wonderful!"

The Lord God could not reprimand Sarah. He remembered her history, how Sarah's laughter had gotten her this far in life. And he wasn't about to chastise her for the one thing that would have to get her through the rest. He too smiled at the thought of how old Abe and Sarah would be when they became the proud parents of their firstborn. "Ha! Ha!" he laughed. "Abe, you've got to admit, it is funny when you come to think of it."

Abe looked dumbly at the Lord God. "Am I missing the point of something?" he wondered.

And that day the Lord God thought he'd had the last laugh. He didn't. The following year, as God had promised, she had her baby. And they named the baby Isaac, which means he laughs!

Reflection

Some people come out from under the basket in times of adversity. It is then that their light really shines. We read of people who lose homes and possessions in earthquakes, tornadoes, or hurricanes, rising to the occasion and rebuilding their lives. Or we read of a college student standing his ground against a column of tanks rolling ominously towards him on a Beijing street. Or on our televisions we see ordinary people marching to protest the presence of crack houses in the inner cities.

True, the protests may appear puny considering the opposition. After all, what does the student accomplish in barring the way of tanks; what do marchers achieve in raising their voices against an immense drug problem?

But some people insist on coming out of hiding and letting their lights shine. Intimidation intensifies rather than diminishes many persons' desire to be heard and seen. In "Last Laugh" Sara's laughter is the light that breaks through adversity. During her life so many people mistake her laughter for everything but what it is, i.e., a light which cannot be overcome by any of the injustices to which she was subjected. Even Abe, the man of faith, failed to appreciate his wife's growing faith as she laughed her way through one trial after another. If laughter is the best medicine, it is also frequently the best way to let our light shine in the presence of adversity.

When have we experienced hardships which instead of diminishing the light have intensified it?

Family Ties

The crowd seated around him told him, "Your mother and your brother and sisters are outside asking for you."   — Mark 3:32

There was quite a bit of tension in the air that day. He was trying to make a point to a pretty hostile crowd. They were accusing him of being in cahoots with the head honcho of the demons. That kind of accusation hurt, particularly since he had spent so much of his time trying to heal the suffering which the head honcho had inflicted. Just as he launched into his concluding point, there was a "Pssst! Pssst! Jesus! Jesus!" At first he didn't notice. But the voice in the crowd got louder, "Jee-zuz, Jee-zuz!" When Jesus finally stopped and looked in the direction of the voice, he saw a man using one hand as a megaphone to get Jesus' attention and the other hand pointed toward the door in the back of the room.

"Your mother and your brothers and sisters are outside asking for you." Jesus' back stiffened a bit. He thought to himself, "What am I supposed to do now? Drop what I'm doing and invite them all in?"

In an instant his mind flashed back to that little incident at the wedding he and Mary had attended in Cana. He had wanted to go alone but she insisted on coming with him — to keep him company. And she did just that ... all during the ceremony and all during the reception. He had tried to get away for a couple of minutes by hiding behind some huge water jugs. But as he crouched there, servants came along and rolled the jugs away at the exact moment

Mary was scanning that part of the hall. Jesus tried to follow the
last jug but Mary caught up with him as the waiters placed it alongside the others in the rear of the dining room. He was cornered.
"Jesus, they've run out of wine. What are we going to do about
it?"
Jesus arched one eyebrow. "What are 'we' going to do about
it? Mom, this isn't any of 'our' business. And the business that I
have to attend to will come later."
Good mother that she was, Mary simply ignored what he had
just said, looked at the waiters standing by, and said, "Do whatever
he tells you." She looked at Jesus, winked, and said, "Be a good
boy, Jesus."
Jesus winced. "Mom, I'm not a boy. I'm a grown man."
"Do as he says. Do as he says," she said to the waiters and
simply ignored what she regarded as a little pouting and nothing
more. And of course he ended up making this his business. Those
jugs of water which had been of only limited help in shielding him
from his mother's constant gaze now became the vessels of a wine
that everybody hailed as a rare vintage. "Think nothing of it!" Mary
said as the headwaiter complimented Mary and Jesus on the un-
usually large supply of quality wine.   /
"Pssst! Pssst! Pssst! Jee-zuz! Jee-zuz!" The wedding scene
vanished when the shrill voice returned. "I know! I know! I can
hear you!" He loved his mother dearly. He had found it difficult to
say good-bye. But he knew that what he had to do in life would
never be accomplished if he stayed at home. Still, he had disliked
the tension his leaving created. None of his friends or relatives
wanted him to go and they had insisted that his responsibilities
were at home with his widowed mother.
Once again, he had to face the issue he thought he had already
settled. Jesus looked at the man who had told him about his mother
being outside and asking for him. He chose his words carefully,
then opened his arms to embrace the whole crowd and said, "Who
are my mother and my brothers?" And gazing around those seated
in the circle he continued, "These are my mother and my brothers.

Whoever does the will of God is brother and sister and mother to me."

He found himself caught up with emotion as he finished. He felt as though he had just taken a knife to himself. In a way he had hoped that no one would tell his mother what he had just said. Yet, he would stand by his word because this was how he had come to understand his mission. Still, he wouldn't ignore her. And knowing his mother, he knew she would never leave him. She would be with him to the end!

Reflection

The struggle for autonomy is a universal problem and it takes on added significance if we can appreciate the fact that even Jesus experienced it. We can understand what the problem is if we consider alternative ways of interpreting three song titles: "I Did It My Way," "I Gotta Be Me," "I Am What I Am." One way of looking at them is they stress the need to be one's unique, separate, distinct self. Another way is to read the titles as an expressed desire to do what one pleases. In the first case, they can express healthy self-assertion; in the second, unhealthy selfishness. The problem in the struggle for autonomy is discerning what direction one is moving.

In separating my way from their way (my expectations, hopes, ambitions, etc. from theirs), the struggle could either be in favor of affirming what is unique, distinctive, and separate or a wilfulness or self-centeredness which puts the self first at the expense of others. I want to be myself and not someone else, not my brothers, sisters, parents, or grandparents, but myself. However, in my insistence, I may separate myself from others in such a way that I deny responsibility towards them along with any legitimate claim they might have on me. As a result, "I Did It My Way" becomes more than a statement about being distinct and separate; it turns into a selfish protest.

Who's Deserving?

But the Lord sent a large fish, that swallowed Jonah and he remained in the belly of the fish three days and three nights. — Jonah 2:1

"I'll never go fishing again," Jonah promised as he straggled onto the deserted shore of Nineveh's Sin City Beach. "I've smelled enough fish in three days to last for a lifetime. And I suppose I'm the only one who knows a fish inside and out," he sniffed.

Three days earlier Jonah had all but despaired of ever seeing the light of day again, while he had floated in the cavernous belly of the whale. Fortunately the Lord must have dropped some very potent pepper in the whale's spout because it had sneezed so hard Jonah flew out of the whale and into the shallow waters of the beach.

Having caught his breath, Jonah stumbled no more than a couple of yards when he spied a message written on the sand which reminded him how he had gotten into his predicament in the first place. The message was brief. "Go to Nineveh and announce to it the message I will tell you." He scrutinized the handwriting and muttered, "Yeah, it's his all right! What choice do I have?" The handwriting was there for Jonah to see and he couldn't avoid it.

Nor had he had been able to avoid it the first time he saw it spray-painted across his front door back home. That message was also brief. "Set out for the great city of Nineveh and preach against it; their wickedness has come up before me." Jonah needed no one then to tell him that *the Lord* was responsible for that order. The peculiar slant to the letters and the uncrossed *t*'s helped him decide they were the Lord's words. It was common knowledge that that was how the Lord's penmanship appeared on the tablets which Moses had gotten from the Lord on Sinai. But what really convinced Jonah that the Lord was responsible for the graffiti on his door was the paint itself. "It's so luminous! We don't have paint that glows like that round here," he marveled.

Jonah, however, wasn't happy about having to make the trip because he suspected that the Lord would change his mind and spare the Ninevites once Jonah got there. "He likes to come off as being the tough guy, but he's a marshmallow. All anyone needs to do is shed a tear and he breaks down," Jonah told a friend. "Well, I don't want to bring these people the bad news unless it stays bad news. Those Ninevites are a sick lot and they deserve to be punished! So I'll be darned if I'm going all that distance to have the Lord go easy on them." Having given the matter serious thought, he decided to vacation in sunny southern Tarshish until the Lord reconsidered sending him to Nineveh. What Jonah hadn't expected and soon discovered was how well the Lord could play the heavy. Violent storms threatened to destroy the boat on which he was bound for Tarshish. The other passengers and crew investigated and concluded Jonah was responsible. Reluctant as they were to throw him overboard, Jonah urged them to do so. "Look, I'm already wretching terribly from seasickness. I might as *well* be dead." So they threw him overboard. But as luck would have it, a whale was in the neighborhood and just happened to be yawning when Jonah sailed right into its mouth. One gulp and Jonah's vacation plans had gone into a three-day hold!

Now, however, as he read and reread the message on the sandy beach, he realized he had to do the Lord's bidding. Shaking his head in the direction of Nineveh, he said, "Such a city. It's too big and the plumbing is bad. I hear the people hardly ever bathe. Phewww! And it's so hot this time of the year. Oy vey! I can smell it already. Why wasn't I sent in winter?" There was no answer.

Resigned to his fate, Jonah began his journey to Nineveh. He had painted black letters on a white sandwich board which announced the destruction of Nineveh in forty days. Wearing the sign, he marched down the streets shouting, "Nineveh's had it! It's all over folks! In forty days the city will be torched. Too bad! You deserve what's coming!" Jonah seemed to relish the message of gloom and doom. Smiling broadly, he preached over and over that they deserved to be punished, and whenever he got a whiff of a particularly smelly citizen, he held his nose and added, "For that alone you deserve punishment!" But punishment was not to be the order of the day.

Jonah hadn't even put in a full day's work when he came across men and women everywhere who were painting messages in black letters on white sandwich boards as *he* had done ... but with an entirely different message. "Sorry, God. We've been schlemiels. Forgive us. It's sack cloth and ashes time!"

Flailing his arms and hands, Jonah protested. "No! You can't do that! What right do you have to be sorry? You've had your fling and gotten your fun. Now you deserve to pay for it! No getting off scot free! No, sirree! Once down, always down, I say. There's no way back up!"

But still more and more people as well as cats and dogs wore the sandwich boards so that the city resembled an island of waddling penguins. And on a marquee overlooking the Palace Theater in the middle of Nineveh a neon light flashed on and off. "Repent and be saved! Tomorrow's apparel: sack cloth and ashes. Signed: The King and I." Shaking his fist at the sign, Jonah was furious. Still, his fury wasn't nearly as great as his frustration when he happened to look up into the heavens and saw skywriting which read, "All is forgiven. I love you all." Jonah tore off his sandwich board, threw it on the ground, jumped up and down on it several times and chanted, "Damn! Damn! Damn! I knew you'd be a marshmallow, Lord. Not towards me, of course. Oh, no! Me you pursued like the furies! I've had it! I've had it! I've had it, Lord! Life is not worth living when there is so much forgiveness in the land. Let me die!" As he stomped on the sandwich board he couldn't help noticing familiar scribbling in chalk on the concrete walk. "Why so angry?" it read.

"Ohhh!" Jonah groaned and marched angrily out of the city. When he had gotten on the outskirts he bought a pup tent, set it up, and wailed, "Maybe the Lord will see the error of his ways and repent of the mercy he intends to show these people. I'll wait and see." As he stationed himself at the front of his tent in the noonday sun, much to his surprise a small plant shot up through the soil and grew until it was ten feet tall. Thereupon it sprouted branches and leaves which afforded shade so that Jonah felt refreshed. "Gee, I didn't even plant the seed," he exclaimed. "What did I do to deserve this?" Then he fell into a deep sleep.

The next morning as he lay half asleep under the tree, he thought he heard a strange sound. "Chomp! Chomp! Chomp!" Opening his eyes, he was horrified. There were ten huge worms greedily devouring the leaves on the branches. "Oh, no!" he cried and within minutes the leaves were eaten. Once more he was exposed to the hot sun and burning wind. "What did I do to deserve this? I want to die," he complained. As he turned to go into his pup tent, he was startled to see a message spray-painted across the front of his tent. The penmanship and the spray paint were unmistakably the Lord's. And the message? "So who says deserves has anything to do with anything? Easy come, easy go!"

Jonah scratched his head and pondered the message. He hadn't deserved the shade tree nor had he deserved its removal. Deserve had nothing to do with it! Slowly he looked to the city of Nineveh. "Deserve has nothing to do with what's happening today," he whispered. "Nothing at all!" Again he stood for several seconds and then smiled. Picking up his sandals, he walked to the side of the tent and ... another message! "Don't worry! Be happy!" it said. Jonah decided that if he were happy, it wasn't because he deserved it. Shrugging his shoulders, he looked up into the sky and laughed, "Easy come, easy go!"

Reflection

When we catch a fish we have it on the hook. If the fish is too small or if we have one fish too many, we take it off the hook and throw it back.

Many of us play the hook game with other people. We catch people when they say something self-incriminating. "Don't lie to me! I spoke to seven people who saw you there!" Or we catch them in the act and say, "Didn't I tell you — no cookies before dinner!" We catch them cheating, making love, making faces, etc. And once we catch them, we seldom act as kindly towards them as we do towards fish. "Let them wriggle," we say. We're not going to let them off the hook. No way! They deserve to suffer for what they've done. And if someone says, "I'm sorry," or "I won't do it again," we're still not going to let them off the hook that easily. "Not so fast, Buster. You've got a lot of explaining to do," or "It doesn't work that way — you can't act as though nothing's happened!" Even if the person acknowledges hurting us and wants to make amends, we aren't going to let the sucker off the hook! We've got him right where we want him and we intend to keep him there.

Are we very different from Jonah after all? We think that people deserve what they get. Jonah's attitude contrasts sharply with God's who, in Jonah's estimation, is a marshmallow when it comes to letting people off the hook. Don't we often share Jonah's attitude? What would become of people if we let them off the hook? How would they act if we didn't let them know that we possessed the power to let them off the hook? Or if we failed to remind them daily who had let them go free? Or that they'd be on the hook again if they tried something silly?

We shudder to think what using God's gentle approach to forgiveness might release on the world! That God's light should shine on the bad as well as the good doesn't make sense to us.

Yet God's light like the sun's shines on all. If we are participating in God's light, then aren't we "cheating" God by letting our light shine on some and withholding it from others? Do we need to step out into the sun and remind ourselves that the sun has been there for us whether we've deserved it or not?

The Man Who Would Not Be King

"Go to the village straight ahead of you and as soon as you enter it you will find tethered there a colt on which no one has ridden. Untie it and bring it back."   — Mark 11:2

"They're still thinking about that?" Jesus could hardly conceal his laughter as Philip and Jude reported on what so many of his followers wanted. "They want me to be their king and run the Romans out of the country?" Then on a more sober note, Jesus added, "By this time they should know that is not what I want." Jesus searched Philip and Jude's eyes, "How can I convince them?"

After a minute in silence, his face lit up with a sly smile. "I know. I know what I will do." Jesus then stroked his beard as he chuckled to himself, leaving Philip and Jude to guess what he was up to. "They want a king, do they? And a king has to have power, doesn't he? What is more, what would a king do without subjects?" Philip and Jude knew enough not to interrupt Jesus' train of thought, but they were increasingly curious about just where this train was headed. Philip opened his mouth and was on the verge of asking, but Jesus didn't give him a chance.

"I haven't come this far to end up parading around with the very show of power I have never wanted in the first place." Jesus put his arms around Philip and Jude. "I have a favor to ask you. I want you to go to Bethany and as soon as you get there, go to Eden Street. Do you know which street I mean?"

"Sure, Eden Street," they said together.

"Well," Jesus resumed in a conspiratorial tone, "when you get to Eden Street, go to the little house opposite Abe's Deli."

"The little house opposite Abe's Deli," they repeated, making a mental note.

"There in front of the house," Jesus continued, "you will find an ass on which no one has ridden."

"An ass on which no one has ridden?" Philip puzzled as he looked at Jesus.

"Yes, an ass on which no one has ridden," Jesus repeated without explaining either how he knew the ass was there or that no one had ever ridden it. "What I want you to do is to untie it and bring it back here."

Now it was Jude's turn to look puzzled. "Untie the ass and bring it back here? For what?"

"Never mind," Jesus said. "Just do as I say." He smiled and continued, "If anyone asks you, 'Why are you doing that?' just say, 'The Master needs it, but he will send it right back.' "

Philip and Jude looked at one another and scratched their heads. Jesus' instructions seemed to be getting stranger and stranger, but they knew that any questions on their part would be answered with no more than that sly smile. So, shaking their heads, they left for Bethany and Eden Street. When Abe's Deli finally came into view, sure enough, just as Jesus had said, there was an ass tied to a post in front of the house.

"Well, I'll be...." Philip said as they eyed the scrawny beast.

"No wonder it's never been ridden," laughed Jude. "It looks like it would collapse under a child's weight." As they moved to untie the ass, it let out a hee-haw that made them both jump back a foot. In fact it let out several hee-haws before calming down. Philip looked anxiously over his shoulder as Jude untied the rope.

Just then they heard a voice from out of nowhere say, "What do you think you're doing?" Philip froze.

Jude, who by now was used to repeating whatever he heard, said, "What do we think we're doing?"

"Yes," the voice came back. "What do you think you're doing?"

Philip recovered his wits by now and repeated word for word, the instructions Jesus had given: "The Master needs it, but he will send it right back." Philip and Jude had no idea to whom they were speaking nor did they bother to find out when the voice, now relaxed and friendly, responded, "Okay, okay! See you later!"

Taking that as a sign to go ahead, Philip and Jude were in such a hurry to get out of there that they practically carried the ass back to Jesus. When Philip and Jude finally delivered the stubborn ass to Jesus, he put his arm around the animal and whispered something in its ear. The ass hee-hawed wildly as if Jesus had shared some great joke with it.

"Well, we're all set," Jesus said.

"We're all set? For what?" Jude had the feeling that he would never get out of the dark at this rate.

"We're all set to ride into the city. They want a king? They'll get one. They want a throne? I've got one that travels. They want power?" He pointed to the ass. "This is my answer to power. They want me to be serious? My trip into the city on this lovely animal is as serious as I can get over the trappings of power." He looked at the ass and said, "We're going to have a great time, aren't we? Hosanna!" To Philip and Jude's amazement, the animal brayed, "Hee-haw, hee-haw," when Jesus cried, "Hosanna!"

Then the darkness lifted for Philip and Jude. They too began laughing as Jesus mounted the ass, but their laughter was mixed with admiration because the ass seemed to carry Jesus with such grace. "Hosanna!" Jesus cried out. "Hee-haw," brayed the ass as it trotted towards the city gates. Philip and Jude added their hosannas. As they approached the city, people from all over began to fall in behind Jesus and the prancing ass. At first they couldn't believe their eyes. Then they too began to laugh and shout hosanna: "Hosanna! Blessed is he who comes in the name of the Lord! Blessed is the reign of our father David to come! Hosanna in the highest!" And all the while the ass brayed, "Hee-haw," over and over in glad celebration of the man who would not be king.

Reflection

Is it too far-fetched to suggest that Jesus wanted his disciples to have a good laugh as he rode on a donkey into Jerusalem? Not if we keep in mind his motivation, i.e., how he wanted others to view power.

On one occasion when Jesus' disciples were arguing among themselves who was the greatest, he told them the people with whom he wanted to associate had to be those who didn't get hung up on who was top banana. He wasn't impressed with people who threw their weight around, especially if others suffered as a result. There were enough heavy-handed persons around he maintained, and what he wanted were persons whose use of power was directed in the service of others. Jesus was interested in people power, that is, in helping others recognize they had the power to effect change in their lives. He wasn't interested in putting on the glad rags of power for display purposes.

The day Jesus rode into Jerusalem he may very well have been gently mocking authority and power as most of us understand it. Coming in on a donkey instead of a legionnaire's horse was like coming in on a wagon instead of an army tank. Can we imagine someone pulling the Pope into town on a hay wagon? Or asking the President to ride on the front and the First Lady on the back of a bicycle built for two? No, we think these people need limousines. We like leaders who impress.

Power makes us feel important; it gives us a thrill. Gun the engine; give orders from a big desk; tell people over a loudspeaker to quiet down; write letters dictating how people are to live their lives; yell at them; hold a gun to their heads; threaten them with the loss of soul. Control others through silent power ... the passive aggressive pouting we witness in so many people who want their way. Yes, we all like power.

But Jesus rides a donkey and in so doing reveals his attitude towards the power which makes us feel important. Jesus rides the donkey; he gets on the hay wagon. He debunks the power that destroys. Genuine power, the power that empowers others to help them make the right choices and affirms them in their choosing is the power Jesus brings.

Jesus came to use power, not to abuse it. It is he who took the instrument of power and death on Calvary and made of it an expression of powerful love.

Short On Memory

Then Peter came up and asked him, "Lord, when my brother wrongs me, how often must I forgive him? Seven times?" "No," Jesus replied, "not seven times; I say, seventy times seven times. That is why the reign of God may be said to be like a king who decided to settle accounts with his officials. When he began his auditing, one was brought in who owed him a huge amount."
— Matthew 18:21-24

The king was furious! "I want him thrown into prison — him and his whole family!" All of his advisors agreed. Ben had betrayed the king's trust and he deserved to be severely punished. Three years earlier Ben had been hired through his father's intercession. The older man had himself been a trusted advisor to the king.

"You've been very loyal to me," the king had told Ben's father. "How could I forget your loyalty? I'd be ungrateful if I denied your request." Ben was elated when he got the news of his appointment as the king's valet. Gradually he ingratiated himself through his wit and disarming manner. As valet, Ben frequently had occasion to be alone with him. He welcomed these occasions to find out as discreetly as possible what was going on in the king's personal life. Consequently, he listened attentively to every word the king spoke, and as time passed the king was deeply moved by this attention.

"We need men like you," the king commended him one day. And from that point on the king confided everything in him. It was highly unusual for a sovereign to place such trust in a commoner, but the king was extraordinarily good to Ben. Strolling together in the palace halls or the royal gardens, dining privately with the king for lunch, and horseback riding with him in the early morning hours, Ben gave an ear to all the king's problems: with his wife and children; regarding his deepest fears about himself; concerning the future of the kingdom. "I don't think of you as an advisor, Ben. I consider you my friend; I'm able to tell you secrets I don't even share with the queen."

"Thank you, majesty. I'm grateful to you for thinking of me as your friend. I would never betray a confidence. Your trust hasn't been misplaced." But what the king didn't know was that Ben was actually disclosing the nature of these private chats to whomever paid the highest price. He received large sums of money from those who needed information either to promote their own careers or to subvert the king's policies. At first Ben was very discreet in his disclosures, but as time went on, he felt more and more invincible and he grew reckless in his speech.

Then one day he bragged to an ambassador. "The King has planned a secret attack against your northern border and I can give you the details." He told him the time and place of the attack, the number of forces the king intended to use, and the king's strategy for winning the battle. What he didn't know was that the foreign official was secretly loyal to the king, and within an hour Ben was hauled into the royal courtroom.

Yes, the king's reaction was to get revenge and have him thrown into prison. Angered and deeply hurt, he cried, "How could you have done this to me?"

Terrified at the prospect of going to prison, Ben prostrated himself at the king's feet. "Majesty, I beg you, reconsider! Think of the good times we've enjoyed together. Surely your memory is not so short that you have forgotten?"

The king shook his head sadly and turned the question back on Ben. "Have you forgotten how I took you in when you had no work? Don't you remember dining at my table and drinking my wine?" Ben was silent. "I want you and your family thrown...." The king paused for a moment ... then whispered, "Wait!" Closing his eyes he said softly, "Ah yes, I remember." But what the king remembered had nothing to do with Ben.

He remembered a day long ago when, as a young prince, he had betrayed his own father, the old king, all because of some slight he thought he had received from him. He recalled foolishly gathering other young hotheads in the realm to plan a coup against his father. However, having gotten wind of the plot, his father simply reprimanded the prince and the others. He refused to hold anything against them. Rather he chalked the whole incident up to youthful folly. Remembering how overwhelmed he was by his father's mercy, the king realized that never until this minute had he been able to do for anyone else what his father had done for him. Saddened as he was by Ben's betrayal, the memory of his father's mercy prompted him to leniency. "I will not hold this against you or your family. You are free to leave."

"Thank you, thank you. I am most grateful to you," Ben blurted as he got to his knees before the king. Tears flowing down his cheeks, he cried, "I do not know how to thank you!"

"Just remember!" the king advised.

"Remember? Yes, yes," Ben agreed even though he really didn't understand what the king meant. What mattered most to him was that he was free. Rising to his feet, Ben left the royal courtroom.

No longer in the service of the king, Ben had to find other means of employment. Since he was short on funds, he decided to visit a friend to whom he had loaned a small amount of money two years earlier. "I need my money now," he demanded.

"But I can't pay you now; I barely have enough money to support myself and my family."

"I don't care about your family. I need it now! And if I don't get it — then you can spend some time in prison."

Horrified, his friend pleaded, "Ben, remember the good times we've had together! Is this the way you treat your friends?"

But Ben was short on memory. Not only had he had a memory lapse regarding the good times they had together, but he had forgotten the pardon the king had granted him. And having forgotten, he had no grateful heart to prompt him to forgive his friend. "It's off to prison, then, for you."

When news of what Ben had done reached the king, he was extremely angry. "How little Ben remembers," he thought. Once more he was tempted to throw Ben into prison. But again he remembered how gracious his own father had been towards him, and again he changed his mind. "I cannot be ungrateful," he said. So the king ordered the release of the friend to whom Ben had loaned the money.

"What about Ben?" the advisors asked. "Surely you are going to punish him?"

"No," the king answered. "He's short on memory and since he can't remember, he's locked out of his heart as well. Prison can't be worse than that!" The counselors agreed. To be short on memory is indeed a curse worse than prison itself. And so it was that Ben roamed the countryside suffering from the disease called short on memory.

Reflection

The German philosopher Martin Heidegger said that thinking is thanking. In a less philosophical vein, Bob Hope sings, "Thanks For The Memories." Remembering and thanking are closely related. Their connection is especially clear when we go to someone's wake. There we gather and share stories about our dead friend or loved one. Through these anecdotes and stories we become grateful that this person touched our lives. And being grateful can motivate us to be a bit more gracious towards others as the deceased had been towards us. However if we are short on memory, thankfulness eludes us as well and we are seldom moved to be gracious towards others.

Our story about Ben illustrates the tragedy of not remembering another's gracious actions in our lives. In this case, failure to
remember with gratitude moments of forgiveness inhibits the servant from being forgiving to others. How often when we forgive
do we remind others of how indebted they are to us for that very
forgiveness? Beneficiaries of this kind of forgiveness stand to lose
more than gain. Forgiveness given grudgingly makes us feel the
weight of guilt more intensely, whereas we feel relief if it is given
graciously.

Can we remember the people who have been gracious to us?
Can that in turn help us become more gracious in our own lives?
When we remember will we also become people of light like the
young king in the story?

Maggie

After this he journeyed through towns and villages
preaching and proclaiming the good news of the
kingdom of God. The Twelve accompanied him,
and also some women who had been cured of evil
spirits and maladies: Mary called the Magdalene,
from whom seven devils had gone out, Joanna, the
wife of Herod's steward Chuza, Susanna, and many
others who were assisting them out of their means.
                                                    — Luke 8:1-3

Seven devils? One devil is plenty. Two is more than enough. But seven? Maggie had seven devils that nagged, whined, and threatened her at every turn she took in her little house. At first there seemed to be only one uninvited guest jabbering in her head.

"Where do you get off thinking women know as much about temple politics as men?" There was an irritating nasal quality about the voice that she found almost more disturbing than the message. Every time she thought about women knowing as much as men she heard the same script coming from the same source which she had located just above her right temple. However, Maggie knew there was more than one devil in the house when she imagined herself performing the functions of the temple priests. Then her left temple throbbed as the alien voices chanted:

"Only we can wear the sacred garments.
You can mend them, hem them, gem them.
But only we can wear them."

"Who's there?" she cried out as a duet of cackling voices shattered her reverie. But there wasn't anyone there — at least not out in the room. Yet, the cackle continued.

"Only we can wear the sacred garments.
You can mend them, hem them, gem them.
But only we can wear them."

A weaker person would have consented to the devils' drivel just to get some rest. But not Maggie. She laughed defiantly as she held her hands to her head and spat out, "If we can't wear them, we won't mend them, hem them, or gem them!" The devil duo seemed not to hear her and droned on.

Fortunately, every now and then the first devil's message jammed the other two's and the garbled result brought some relief.

"Women know as much about temple politics as men."
"But only we can wear them."
"Where do you get off thinking?"
"Mend them, hem them, and gem them."

Maggie tried to carry on business as usual. She'd clean the house and prepare meals, but every now and then she'd think the thoughts that had made her vulnerable to the devils, and once more they'd be on the attack. Matters became worse for her when she told herself God certainly didn't intend to exclude women from positions of power. No sooner had the word "power" formed in her mind than she heard:

"We have all the power 'n pomp.
You get all the poop 'n pablum.
We get all the poop 'n pablum.
You get all the power 'n pomp."

Startled, Maggie dropped the dish she was wiping on the floor. Was there quadraphonic sound in the room? She perked her ears in one direction of the room and then the others as she waited for the replay of what she thought were four voices. There was silence for a moment. Then her face registered a knowing look and she thought the word "power" once more. That did it! The switch went on and she picked up the sound of four voices: two men and two women. The first two lines came from bass baritone devils and the second

two were sung by soprano devilettes. The baritones boomed bravado while the sopranos sang with sweet submission:
"We have all the power 'n pomp.
You get all the poop 'n pablum.
We get all the poop 'n pablum.
You get all the power 'n pomp."
She got the message. She knew what kind of power women could hope to expect. Bending down to pick up the broken pieces of the dish she muttered, "Without us all your power 'n pomp is nothing but poop 'n pablum." Her words started off another round from the chorus of devils and devilettes. However, this time the baritones boomed even louder and the sopranos sang even more sweetly. The increase in volume apparently triggered the other devils because the quartet's ditty was now embroidered with bits and pieces from the other devils' words.
"We have all the power 'n pomp."
"Mend them, hem them, and gem them."
"Where do you get off with"
"all the poop 'n pablum"
"thinking women know as much about temple politics as men"
"poop 'n pablum."
Maggie shook her head in a vain effort to free herself from the cacophony of demons. The only way she knew she could rid herself of those devils would be if she aligned herself with them. Sorely tempted as she was, she resisted. But her resistance only solidified and redoubled the devils' already united front.

The day after Maggie had heard the quadraphonic quartet there was an uneasy calm in her head. "Surely," she thought, "they're still around. What could they be up to? I know one of the devilettes sounded hoarse after the 25th round but their chorus capers shouldn't have stilled all of them." As Maggie stood looking out the window, she could have sworn that the house trembled. "No, that can't be," she tried to convince herself. "They're not into pulling tricks like that. That's ridiculous." But she felt the trembling again. And in an instant the house was bathed in light. "An encounter of the third kind," she gasped. "This can't be them." Her eyes widened in amazement as voices from above rang out with heavenly alleluias. Involuntarily, she fell on her knees. The alleluias reached a magnificent crescendo and then tapered off into silence.

Quietly, ever so quietly, a woman's voice gently broke the silence with:

"God is man

no wo — man.

Since that's the way it is

Since that's the way it's gotta be

Let men run the god show

And women run the home show."

Maggie was on the verge of lowering her head in reverence but she stopped and instead raised her eyes to the small opening in the ceiling where the voice seemed to be coming from. As she scrutinized the opening, the aria began again.

"God is man

no wo — man.

Since that's the way it is

Since that's the way it's gotta be...."

"I know. I know," Maggie interrupted, " 'Let men run the god show and women run the home show.' Your voice sounds familiar." Maggie picked herself up from the floor. "You wouldn't happen to be one of the sopranos in the quartet that's been visiting me, would you?"

There was no response. Then, without warning, all seven devils broke out in one ominous chorus as thunder and lightning filled the room:

"God is man

no wo — man.

Since that's the way it is

Since that's the way it's gotta be

Let men run the god show

And women run the home show."

Maggie gulped. She was impressed by the razzle dazzle but she could not be cowered into believing that these were heavenly voices. She had recognized the soprano's voice and the game was up.

After the lightning and the thunder subsided, Maggie, hands on hips, stared unflinchingly at the opening in the ceiling and challenged:
"If God is man
He came from a mommy.
And if he came from a mommy,
The god show is a home show.
So take off your shoes
You're on holy ground."

Maggie had hardly gotten the words out when she heard clamorous squealing and felt a cold breeze rush past her. All the doors and windows flew open and then all slammed shut in unison. She stood there transfixed. A door opened again and two cookies sailed through the air out of the house right before the door slammed shut again. "I was going to throw them out, anyway. They're stale," she sniffed as she looked out the window.

Maggie edged her way to the kitchen table and sat down. Cautiously she thought the thoughts that had previously made her a target for the seven devils. Nothing happened. Then she spoke her thoughts out loud. Still nothing. She spoke her thoughts aloud again, but this time with a note of celebration in her voice: a victory celebration.

She jumped up, threw open the door and shouted her thoughts for all to hear. Passersby wondered if she were mad. But one person, a young man, who happened to be walking in the neighborhood that day heard her. He delighted in what she had to say and invited her to share her message with his friends. And she did.

The seven devils had gone out for good.

Reflection

Maggie's demons aren't unknown to many of us. They are the scripts of our life story which we had no hand in writing. Many of these scripts were written for us very early in life, but some are also being written as we mature and get older. What is particularly demonic about the scripts is we have been led to believe we authored them. Bits and pieces of dialogue like "I'm no good" or "I'll never amount to much" float around in our brain and we say to ourselves, "That's me; that's what I think." But it isn't "me." It's "them" disguised as "me" telling myself it's me.

Scripting comes from parents, teachers, relatives, the church, and culture, identifying who I am, whether I'm good or bad, how I should live my life, etc. I am possessed and held in bondage by the host of demons which have taken up residence in the upper temples. Can they be exorcized?

Yes, but it takes time. The exorcism begins in differentiating their voices from my own. Whose voice is it that says, "I'm no good"? What's its origin? Somewhere in the past? Perhaps a parent scolding me, "You're no good," no matter what I did to please. Who says in me, "I can't accomplish anything right"? The voices of well-intentioned people who assumed my responsibilities because they thought me incompetent? Do they live on in me? Or, as in Maggie's situation, do the voices represent stereotypical attitudes coming from my culture? How many of these voices roam about needing to be exorcized? Whose voice is it? Mine or theirs? Answering these questions is essential in the exorcism.

Along with that task comes another: determining what I really think or feel or want to do. Not an easy determination since "they" have been telling me what to think, feel and do when I thought I was thinking, feeling, and doing. Can I listen to my own resistances, urges, and inclinations as I differentiate my voice from the others? For in the resistance, urge, and inclination I may find the clue which gives me an inkling of what I really think or feel or want.

The exorcism is never completed once and for all because there will always be demons who want to come and script my life just as I will continue to discover demons who manage to cloak themselves as "my thoughts." What is important is that the exorcism begin and I discover whose script my life story really is.

Risen

*He offered them still another image: "The reign
of God is like yeast which a woman took and
kneaded into three measures of flour. Eventually
the whole mass of dough began to rise."*
— Matthew 13:33

Her friends called her Prissy and on occasion they affectionately referred to her as Miss Prim and Proper Prissy. Priscilla Prudell
didn't mind being called Prissy by her friends in her home or in
theirs, but she insisted it was only proper she be called Priscilla in
public. "It's Priscilla," she admonished others in supermarkets, department stores, sidewalk cafes, and even on empty streets.

"But, Priscilla, there's no one else on the street except the two
of us," her friend protested.

Not only was Priscilla very proper about the use of her name,
she was also always properly preened. Her hair tightly drawn back
into a bun, she wore modest dresses which never accented her shape
in any way that might attract the least attention to herself. And she
always had the scent of Ivory soap about her because she bathed
twice a day to keep herself as clean as she could be.

Priscilla was also properly punctual. If she said she'd meet
someone at 7:00 P.M., then she'd be at the appointed place at seven
sharp. Or if she invited a friend to dinner for 8:00 P.M., the friend
knew if she came one half hour late, she could expect to be on time
for dessert and nothing more. Everything at the proper time and in
the proper place was the way Priscilla played out her life.

She even prayed properly. No outbursts of passion in her prayers! Never did she dialogue with the deity in any easy manner. God forbid! Crafting words into a careful colloquy, Priscilla demonstrated her deference to the Lord of Order and Restraint. Words like "hell" and "damn" she simply never used. She never even entertained employing such words when she addressed the divine ... or anyone else for that matter.

No wonder her friends referred to her as prim and proper. Still they loved her — for her good works, her sincerity, and her fidelity to them in times of need. But most especially they loved her for her "lapses in decorum" as she phrased it. These were the unguarded moments when she'd begin to giggle or cry or get angry in spite of herself. During these times her friends noted affectionately how free she was. Invariably, however, Priscilla apologized profusely for her aberrant behavior. "Oh, this isn't like me. I'll see it doesn't happen again." Her friends hoped that one day Priscilla Prudell would surrender some of her propriety for everybody's sake including her own. And what they hoped for, happened in a most peculiar way.

Priscilla had invited two of her friends over for a Tuesday evening dinner and she had decided to bake raisin bread for the dinner on the night before the soiree. So she marshalled all the ingredients on the kitchen counter and methodically set about mixing flour, salt, and sugar, melting butter, readying the yeast, and setting aside raisins from a cardboard container. After mixing the ingredients she thoroughly kneaded the dough until it looked the picture of perfection. "Very good," she said, "I'll give you an hour to rise. One hour," she addressed the lump of dough as she set it aside and covered it with a towel.

Exactly an hour later she returned. The dough hadn't risen — at all! Priscilla pursed her lips, swallowed hard, rapped her fingers on the counter and whispered very softly, "One more hour ... do you hear?"

Yet another hour passed. Punctually she returned. Still the dough hadn't risen, not even so much as an inch! Priscilla's face reddened. She glared at the lifeless dough. Carefully rolling up her sleeves and smoothing any wayward strands of hair, she muttered between her teeth, "Okay, okay, it's one hour more for you and then," she nodded ominously towards the wastebasket. "Get my point?"

A third time she returned. But not at the hour she had set for herself. No. She marched into the kitchen ten minutes early. Not only had the dough not risen but it looked like it had actually shrunk. "Damn! Damn! Damn! You little turd," she cried. "Why didn't you rise when I told you to rise? Do you think you're god almighty?"

Seizing the dough, she flung it against the wall over and over so violently that the bun on her head was undone and her hair tumbled freely over her shoulders. Even her stockings unrolled to her ankles. "I warned you," she cried as she grabbed the empty raisin container, shoved the dough into it, pounded the top on the container and hurled it into the wastebasket. "Damn dough," she muttered as she wiped the perspiration from her brow, reached for a glass from the cabinet, poured herself some cooking sherry, and downed the whole glass without pausing once to get her breath. Passing the basket on her way to her bedroom, she stuck out her tongue at the raisin container with its sealed contents.

Once in her room she paused to look at herself in the mirror. Any other time she would have recoiled in horror at what she saw. Now, however, she stood admiring herself for several seconds. She marveled at how she had lost her composure, but she smiled freely at feeling so very good about what had happened. Then without properly preparing herself, she plopped onto the bed and went off to sleep.

Around three in the morning Priscilla awoke and decided she wanted a glass of milk. When she walked into the kitchen, she happened to glance at the wastebasket. "Noooo!" she gasped. The top of the raisin box had popped off from the pressure of the dough which had risen during the night and was now twice its size. It spilled out of its container and filled the basket. "But it couldn't ... I mean, I didn't program it this way. It ... it ... but there it is! Well, damn, damn, damn!" Priscilla laughed until the tears came down

her cheeks. Holding high the container with its contents, she pir-
ouetted several times around her kitchen. Then she removed the
dough from the box and pushed it down on the counter for a second rising. She didn't know when the dough would rise again or
even if it would at all. This didn't matter. She had learned something precious that night and it had nothing to do with baking bread.

Reflection

Letting our light shine is not the same thing as flicking on a
light switch. Turning on the light implies control, whereas letting
the light shine suggests surrender and availability. "Letting" is not
ordering or commanding the light to appear; rather, it is being there
to receive it when it comes.

Undoubtedly being in charge or in control is a value, and we
mature by developing a strong ego whereby we can manage our
lives more efficiently. But we can be so concerned with running
our lives that the values of predictability, clarity, certainty, and orderliness become increasingly more important than what is novel,
surprising, unpredictable, or mysterious. If there is no room for
surprises in our lives, how then can we experience the Kingdom?
Thus, Priscilla's need for propriety and orderliness are so inhibiting that in the rare moments when she experiences the freedom of
the Kingdom in her own laughter and in slips of the tongue, she
quickly moves the bushel basket back into place and promises to
check any similar light moments from escaping.

However, even Priscilla can't keep the basket in place forever.
The Kingdom arrives in its own time, not hers; and her response
reveals her as a very human and lovable person.

Letting our light shine isn't a matter of calculation or control
but one of surprise. We are there to receive the light, not to manufacture it.

Can we remember moments of surprise in our life when our
light shone in unexpected ways? Might this help us be more receptive to future moments of being surprised by light?

Fishers

*Proceeding a little farther along, he caught sight
of James, Zebedee's son, and his brother John.
They too were in their boat putting their nets in
order. He summoned them on the spot. They abandoned their father Zebedee, who was in the boat
with the hired men, and went off in his company.*
— Mark 1:19-20

Poppa Zebedee approached his sons one day. He thought it
was time to talk to them about joining him in the fishing business.
But he knew it wouldn't be easy. Why? Because they hated fishing. They had always hated fishing.

"Poppa, we get seasick," Jim complained.

"And neither of us even likes to eat fish," John chimed in. "So
why do you want us to go to work for you on your boat?" Jim
queried.

"But you're my sons. Who else will take over the business
when I retire?" Poppa Zebedee pleaded. Poppa was right, of course.
Who would take over if not his two sons? He had one other child,
a daughter, and she certainly couldn't be expected to don a
fisherman's outfit and commandeer a boat full of fishermen. Besides all the men Poppa Zebedee knew turned to their sons as heirs
apparent of their daddies' fishing businesses. So why shouldn't
Poppa Zebedee expect his sons to follow suit?

The sons made one last effort to convince their dad that the
fishing life wasn't for them. "Poppa, we'd only get in the way; we

don't know one end of a boat from the other. And imagine what the other fishermen would think of us and you!" Jim pleaded.

"Yeah," John added quickly, "I can hear them now! 'There go Zeb's dummies. They can't even haul in a net without losing half the load.' Wouldn't you be embarrassed, Poppa, huh?"

Poppa Zebedee was momentarily caught off guard by the common front his sons presented. But slowly he regained his composure. "Well," he stroked his beard, "well, you'll learn. You'll learn. Just give yourselves some time." Waving his hand he stood up, bringing the discussion to a close. "No more talk about this. I've made up my mind." And there was no more talk. Once Poppa Zebedee had made up his mind, that was it.

So Jim and John joined Poppa on his boat and in the weeks that followed they tried their best to be the kind of fishermen their dad could be proud of. They tried. They really did try; but they never quite seemed to be where they were supposed to be, or do what they were expected to do — ever. "We've been waiting for you. What's taken you so long?" Poppa Zebedee snapped at his sons almost daily as he and the other fishermen waited impatiently to launch out into the deep. Invariably, Jim and John were the last men on board.

"Poppa, we stopped to tell Mrs. Borowitz how sorry we were that her dad died." And they were sorry.

"Poppa, there was a kid crying on the beach and we thought we'd cheer him up." And they did cheer him up.

"Poppa, poor Mrs. Schnickel didn't have anyone to help her carry her groceries home; so we helped her." Which was true.

Poppa Zebedee shook his head. He wondered how many excuses they'd cook up to avoid the real work of fishing.

And once on the boat? That was something else! "What's the matter with you?" Poppa Zebedee shouted as the full net of fish they had been hauling in all afternoon slipped out of his sons' hands and disappeared in the dark water.

"There's someone drowning out there! We've got to save him," they panicked pointing to an object bobbing up and down in the water about fifty yards away.

"That's just a buoy, you idiots!" Zebedee growled.

"All the more reason to save him, Poppa. He doesn't have the strength of a man to survive the current," Jim shot back.

Zebedee threw up his hands. "I don't mean a boy. I mean a marker, a buoy, telling us where we are."

"Oh!" the brothers responded feebly. Heads downcast they peered into the silent sea and pondered the cost of having tried to save a buoy that wasn't a boy. As for Zebedee, after he simmered down he resolved to chalk up this incident to inexperience. "They'll come around. They'll come around. They just need a little more time," he said half-convincingly to himself. But he couldn't justify to himself or to the hired fishermen his sons' action two days later.

Trolling from one spot to another all morning without success, suddenly they found themselves amid a school of thousands of silver bodies glistening in the water. Poppa Zebedee's eyes widened. "Drop the nets in, drop them in!" he whispered excitedly. "Incredible! Incredible!" He hadn't seen a catch like this in weeks, and could hardly contain himself. He looked out into the distance at the other fishing boats. "If they knew what was going on, they'd all be over here in a minute. But they don't. They...." He had no sooner gotten the words out when the silence was shattered.

"Over here. They're over here. C'mon. Over here!" Horrified, Zebedee saw his sons signaling to the fishermen in the other boats. Oblivious of the storm clouds gathering on their father's face, they continued, "The fish are here. Come and join us." Within seconds, boats barracudaed their way to Zebedee's boat from every direction and dropped their own nets into the teeming waters. There were choruses of "Hallelujah," and "What a great day," and "Thanks for telling us," as the men in all the boats hauled in the fish.

And although Zebedee's boat too pulled in a sizable load that afternoon, this didn't satisfy Zebedee. "How could you ... what possessed you ... what, how ... nincompoops!" Zebedee's eyes bulged and his face reddened with anger as he confronted his sons soon after the last net had been hauled in.

"Poppa, I think I know why you're upset, but we just thought it would be nice to share the good news with the others," Jim ventured cautiously.

"That's right, Poppa. The others haven't been doing so well ... so, what's a few fish among friends?" John innocently proposed. "A few fish among friends?" Poppa irrupted. "A few fish among friends? Is every fisherman in Galilee your friend?"

"We could aim for that, couldn't we?" John answered amiably.

"Ohhh!" Zebedee groaned as he hit his head with the palm of his hand. He wanted to write off this incident as inexperience too, but all he could do was shake his head in disbelief. "But they are my sons. They are my sons," he muttered, trying to prevent himself from disinheriting them then and there. "And they will be fishermen. They will be fishermen," he kept reassuring himself. "They just have to get their priorities straight!"

However, his reassurances grew harder to muster in the weeks ahead. Why were they engaging the fish in conversation? Were they apologizing for having imprisoned them in their nets? And why were chats with the hired fishermen consuming so much of their time? They seemed to spend more time spilling their guts to his sons than doing the work for which they were hired! But it wasn't until Zebedee came to board his boat one morning that he finally realized that his dream of having fishermen sons would never be.

Zebedee's boat was missing from the shore. And so were his sons. What had happened? As they waited one, then two hours, Zebedee imagined all kinds of things. Were they having an extended conversation with the fish? Were they trying to save someone? Another buoy? Were they stranded somewhere? Shipwrecked? Lost at sea? As he considered the different possibilities, one of the fishermen ran up to Zebedee and pointed to the little boat on the horizon. Zebedee's anxiety was so great he waded into the water straining to see if the boat were his. It was his all right. And as it neared the shore, Zebedee was stunned. His fishing boat was festooned from stem to stern with streamers and balloons of every color. Old men and women, street people, little kids, and an odd assortment of cats and dogs were crowded aboard. As it neared the shore, they all waved joyously to anyone in sight. "What, what is this all about?" Zebedee sputtered as the boat came to rest on the sandy beach.

"Sorry we're late, Poppa. Just thought it would be nice to give them all a ride! We had a great time!" Jim smiled proudly.

"You had a great time! You had a great time? You're not fishermen. I don't know what you are. But you're not fishermen. And you never will be." By this time a crowd of people had gathered around as Zebedee shook his finger violently at his sons. "No, all you can do is give free rides to people who can't pay, try to make friends with everybody in the country, and talk to fish about how sorry you are to catch them! So what good are you? So who needs you? Who? Anybody here?" Zebedee was almost hysterical as he swung around to the gathering crowd. "You see. No one...." He was about to say no one wanted them when a voice interrupted.

"I want them. They'll make great fishers of men." Zebedee peered into the crowd and a young man stepped forward. He had a broad smile and he looked directly at the brothers. "C'mon. Follow me. We have work to do. Much work." The man beckoned Jim and John to follow him. The brothers looked at their father and then at one another. And as if father and sons had practiced the one line they could all agree on, they sighed in unison, "Phewww! Thank God it's over!"

"No, it's just beginning," the man added quietly.

And the brothers abandoned their father Zebedee and went off in the company of the man called Jesus.

Reflection

If a stranger came along, spoke to our son or daughter about joining him as he roamed the countryside and preached God's love, how would we feel? Would we be understanding, sympathetic? Wouldn't we be concerned, upset, and worried the stranger was a cult figure mesmerizing and abducting our child?

The call stories in the gospel present Jesus as the one whose invitation, "Come follow me," evokes an immediate response as the future disciples drop whatever they're doing and follow him.

Seems like another cult story, doesn't it? What makes Jesus different from the charismatic but dangerous Jim Jones or Sun Young Moon? Of course we needn't accept these call stories as literal renditions of what happened. But granting the possibility the disciples had a little more time to ponder the invitation than is recorded in the Gospels, the question remains. What is there in Jesus and his message which prompted them to respond so readily and what makes Jesus different from cult leaders?

The first question can't be answered unless we also consider what was happening in the lives of these men which disposed them to follow him. "Fishers" gives a clue. People who are already fishers of men, i.e., compassionate, understanding, etc., resonate with Jesus' call before he even appears on the scene. What Jesus provides when he enters their lives is a clarification of and direction for their aspirations and sentiments. In other words, what they find is a home for their longing in Jesus' vision of the Kingdom. Life on the sea was never their true home, and this dissatisfaction plus the appeal of Jesus' vision quickens them to follow him.

What makes Jesus different from the cult figures is Jesus isn't forming an elite corps of persons who define themselves by what they have and others lack. Rather, Jesus calls people who in turn call out to others to recognize a shared humanity whose origin is the God whom Jesus called Abba. Better still, Jesus calls disciples to invite others whose aspirations and longing find their "fit" in his proclamation of the Kingdom. And for Jesus those aspirations are present in everybody.

Jesus' call and the disciples' immediate response can be understood, then, as the immediate fit between his vision and their aspirations whether we conceive of this recognition taking place over a day, a week, or a year.

Pearlie

"Or again, the kingdom of heaven is like a merchant's search for fine pearls. When he found one really valuable pearl, he went back and put up for sale all he had and bought it."
— Matthew 13:45

"I'm not easy. I come at a price. I'm Pearlie, your dream girl," she teased as she smiled coyly at Max.

"I know, I know," he conceded as they sat at a table in the elegant dining room of the Gem Of My Life restaurant. "I never said you were easy. And god knows you come at a price, a great price," he laughed while he scanned the list of costly entrees. Setting aside the menu, he gently took Pearlie's hands and declared, "But, Pearlie, you're the kind of girl I've always wanted to have — ever since I set eyes on you two months ago."

"To have?" Pearlie's eyes twinkled in the candlelight. Amused, she repeated, "Have?"

"Yes, have," he stated matter of factly.

Pearlie shook her head. He hadn't gotten the point of her question. Like the others she had dated, Max didn't seem to understand what he was asking of her. As she had with other men, however, she remained unruffled by his request. She knew what she had to do to enlighten him about winning her affection. Pearlie would play his game but she'd play it better than he did and maybe, just maybe the two of them would both be winners. "So you want to have me, do you? And you understand the price is high?"

"Of course, of course. I understand," he answered waving his hand impatiently. "And I'm willing to pay the price — anything for you, Pearlie."

Little did Max know how much this pearl would cost. Even if he had known, it might not have made much difference. He had always been ready to pay for whatever he wanted in life. But he had failed to notice the costliness of his need to possess, and what this had done to him. He couldn't pass a bookstore without feeling compelled to buy a book. "I want to have that book; I must have it!" And once he had the book, he stored it with all the other unread books gathering dust on shelves throughout his house. He'd frequent fashionable clothing stores and within minutes need a fix. "I love that suit. I want to have it. I'll pay anything for it." But once he owned it, the suit was tucked away in one of several closets serving as graveyards for his clothes. Always he was going on buying sprees. "That lamp! Those paintings! The mahogany dresser! I want to have them!" Store owners rushed to greet Max whenever he marched through their doors because they knew he'd be an easy mark.

Strangely, he was able to admire things before he possessed them. But once he owned something he never noticed it again. What he bought grew to occupy more and more space in his home. Paintings under beds and behind sofas. Two, three, and four lamps standing in corners like displaced persons waiting to be placed. Microwaves on top of microwaves crowding kitchen counter spaces. Statues of every conceivable size standing guard at every doorway in their house. There was so much clutter that he scarcely had room to move and breathe.

However since he met Pearlie he was forced to change his ways. Over and over she reminded him, "I'm not easy. You want to have me? Then you pay the price. Let's dine tonight at the Ritz and drink the finest champagne available!" Which is what they did. "I want to shop at chic boutiques and buy designer clothes." Which is what they did. "Let's take a trip by jet — first class — to swim in Swaziland and hunt in Kenya." And they did.

Max paid the price all right. He wanted to have Pearlie badly. Oh, he wanted her so badly that he paid her bills piled high on his desk. Sometimes he'd raise a finger and gingerly protest her spending sprees. Pearlie would simply smile, wink, and offer, "This is Pearlie you're talking to. I don't come cheap. Remember?"

How could he forget? But he had spent so much money by now that the only way he could pay her bills was by gradually selling off his possessions. Off went the books he had never read, the suits worn once at most, the furniture exiled to attic regions, and statues from every doorway.

However a strange thing happened as he got rid of what he owned. Now that he knew he would no longer own things, he delighted in them as much as before when he had impulsively purchased them. He fingered the books, opening and closing them, reading aloud from them before he placed them in boxes for the book dealers. Rediscovering long-abandoned suits, he admired them as he tried them on, paraded up and down the room before finally sending them off to this or that pawn shop. He feasted his eyes on oriental rugs as he lifted layer after layer of patterned Chinese and Persian treasures off his floors. And sinking into overstuffed chairs or sitting for a last time on mahogany benches, he sighed over and over that he had never enjoyed these things so much as now when he would no longer have them as his own.

As he continued waving good-bye to his possessions, he wondered when he'd finally have his Pearl. When he put the question to her that way, she reminded him, "This pearl is not a piece of furniture. I'm not another thing you can collect." And so she kept him in suspense. No, she wasn't easy, this precious pearl. Moreover, since he wanted to have her, he would be forced to sell everything he owned. Because he now owned very little, it wasn't long before he had nothing left except for a few clothes and household items. But to his amazement having nothing didn't seem to bother him. He could move about his house more freely and he thought he even breathed more easily now. "There's no more clutter here," he marveled. No longer in need of buying something every minute of the day, he was free to see what he had never seen before: sunrises

and sunsets; laughing children splashing water at one another in
nearby lakes; multi-colored patches of flowers in neighboring parks.
With televisions, stereos, CDs, and VCRs gone, he found himself
spending hours listening to the wind or rejoicing in the gently falling rain. He especially enjoyed the new-found time strolling with
old long-neglected friends and new acquaintances as well.

For weeks Max had seen the writing on the wall. But now he
found the courage to admit to Pearlie, "I can't keep it up. I don't
have any more money. You're too costly. I've given up everything
for you." And much to his surprise, he added, "Pearlie, I don't
need to have you anymore. Even if I could pay, I'm not certain I
would." Waves of relief came over him as the life-long burden of
needing to have was lifted from his shoulders. Looking into Pearlie's
eyes, he confessed, "I guess it's over with us."

Pearlie took his hands in hers, gently kissed him on his lips,
and whispered softly, "No, it's just beginning, Max. Pearlie is here
to be with you. What do you say we go and waltz the night away?"

Max had found the pearl of great price.

Reflection

Seeing things as they are and not as we would like them is a
way of describing contemplation. We can "do lunch" with a view
towards snagging a potential business partner, mate, enemy, etc.
We're not approaching them as individuals in their own right. More
often than not we see things in terms of our needs or their functions. We see an apple on a tree as being there for us to eat and not
as something beautiful in itself. Looking at it as food is one thing.
But regarding it apart from our need, we begin to consider its distinct shape, color, smell, and texture. We notice its proximate relationship to the branch on which it hangs as well as its more remote
relationship to the other branches and the rest of the tree.

So being contemplative means being present to people and
things in their own light and not in the light of our demands, whims,

and expectations. If we are like Max it is difficult to be contemplative. "Possessions" have no value in themselves. Their worth depends on their usefulness to us. We notice them only when they break down or no longer work. When we treat children, spouses, lovers, and friends as possessions which we must jealously guard or which are there to meet our needs, we no longer see them in their own light; we are not being contemplative.

Max was addicted to having. Fortunately, Pearlie helped Max detach himself from his need to have by leading him to believe he could have her for the right price, a price which was detachment itself. Once he became contemplative and no longer "needed" her she paradoxically became available, not as a possession, but as Pearlie.

Being contemplative enables us to experience the luminosity of Being as it shines in each and every being's own distinct way, and that is God's way of being there with us.

Is the pearl of great price something we discover in renouncing our need to have? And when does the desire for detachment itself become so intense that we become possessive in a new way? Is it possible to be so needy in our relationship with God that God becomes nothing more than a need satisfier whose being is solely to be there for us?

High Hopes

The mother of Zebedee's sons came up to him ac-
companied by her sons, to do him homage and
ask of him a favor. "What is it you want?" he said.
She answered, "Promise me that these sons of mine
will sit, one at your right hand and the other at
your left, in your kingdom."
— Matthew 20:20-21

She wasn't literally a stage mother, but Leena had shown most of the symptoms. She had had high hopes for her sons Jim and Johnny before Jesus came on the scene. As Leena sat waiting in one of the many porches of the great Temple, she tried to recapture the moment she had first laid out the future for her sons. "Oh, yes," she mused softly. It was on that warm spring day two years ago when her sons were eating aleph-a-bet soup in the kitchen. "One of you," she said solemnly, "might be the Messiah one day. I can feel it in my bones. Don't ask me how I know. I could be wrong but I will not entertain that possibility. One thing is certain." The ladle paused above the aleph-a-bet soup. "... I'm not taking any chances. Eat your food like you're in training for the position."

Leena shifted uneasily on the stone bench as the thought flashed through her mind that the instructions she had given her sons that day were just a ploy to get them to eat. She stiffened and arched her eyebrows, disdainful that such an idea should enter her mind ... that she might even be tempted to talk about messianic expectations just to get her sons to eat their soup!

90

Leena momentarily let the memory of that day fade as she shaded her eyes with her hand and scanned the temple courtyard. "I wonder where he is," she muttered. "They said he would meet me at noon and it is now five after twelve." As she squinted in the noonday sun, she remembered how positive she had been that her sons were destined for glory paths. She was so convinced that at least one of them would be the Messiah that the same day she had ordered them to go out of their way to help people. "Let people know you're there to help them. Better they should gradually come to know who it is that will save them. We don't want surprises. I don't believe in shock treatments."

But Leena was also aware of practical necessities her sons had to consider, such as supporting themselves while they were waiting for the big day. So, immediately she issued the third instruction. "Suppose you get some part-time employment. Nothing fancy, mind you, just enough work to carry you along."

"What did you have in mind, Ma?" Jim queried as he paddled his spoon in the aleph-a-bet soup.

"What do I have in mind, you ask. How about running a bank or floating a fishing fleet?" she suggested without blinking an eye.

"Hmmm. Floating a fishing fleet sounds good to me," Johnny responded without missing a beat. "Jim and I have had experience fishing. We've caught mackerel off the pier."

"Running a bank is more suited to my talents," Jim added seriously. "Finances are what I'm good at. Rabbi Schnickel is always complimenting me on being a big spender. 'Jim,' he says, 'you must be a big spender because you're always adding your two cents every minute of the day.' "

Leena smiled broadly as she remembered how she had beamed with admiration when her sons picked up on her suggestions. She had told them, "What I'm hearing fills me with pride. Not just an armada of mackerel boats but the First Jerusalem Bank, and all in our family. Such smarts you are. Who but my sons would have thought of combining the shipping and banking business in one family? What have I done to deserve such wunderkinden? I say to myself as I walk down the street, 'So, Leena, why shouldn't these people be shaking their heads at me the way they do? They know I'm the mama of boys who are going somewhere.' " In the excitement of the moment Leena had forgotten how the people who talked with her about her sons were concerned about whether her sons were going anywhere. Invariably she gave the same response. Forefinger raised high in the air, she'd say cryptically, "Somewhere," and leave her questioner dumbfounded.

The chatter of a group of tourists going through the courtyard interrupted Leena's daydreaming. "Still no sign of him," she thought as she scanned as far as she could. "No one even resembling him." It was important that she see him today because he would be off on the road the next day. And then she didn't know when she would see him again. Leena had done as much as she could for her sons. Yet, there was one thing more she intended to do and only he could help her. Only he could help her? She laughed to herself. Just two years ago she thought that by now everybody would be asking her for help or better, help from her sons. After all, she had told them to train for the position by letting everybody know they were there to help them. And that they did — very well! Frequently, men and women who didn't even know Leena came over to her while she was shopping at the market and they'd ask her why her kids were out to save the world. Leena, of course, had the answer to that question but she had to keep it to herself for the time being. She had no idea that within six months her dreams for her sons would come to an end.

She wasn't prepared for that fateful day when both of her sons came home and told her they had decided the shipping and banking businesses were simply pipe dreams. They had deceived themselves into thinking they were capable of running businesses.

"We ought to be glad we catch mackerel off the pier," Johnny said as he paddled his way through more aleph-a-bet soup at the kitchen table.

"And as for banking," Jim added, "what made us think we knew anything about financing? I haven't even earned enough money to practice keeping my own finances straight."

What she was prepared for least of all, however, was their disavowal of the messianic expectations she had for them. "What do you mean?" she asked them. "You're not training to be the Messiah? But it's our future...." she protested.

"Our future?" Jim looked at her. "Our future? I can't even seem to take care of myself. How can I think of saving others?"

"Yeah!" Johnny added. "What I need is for someone to help me. Besides I don't think a lot of the people want our help. And one more thing, Ma. We found someone who's got a message we like and he's asked us to join him. His name is Jesus...."

Once more Leena's thoughts were interrupted.

"Hello, Leena." A man in his thirties took both of Leena's hands into his as he sat next to her on the bench. He had finally arrived — this Jesus who got the position she had always thought one of her sons was meant to have. He had a kind look in his eyes, and she smiled as she remembered how angry she got every time she heard her sons mention his name, that is, until she saw the peace he brought into their lives. Now they were going somewhere, and it was he who had given them the direction. Gradually, she began to see in him something very special. Leena's way of admitting this was to tell her sons, "So maybe he's had more time to train for the position than you. I will say this much. He eats well and he's always helping people. So, who am I to complain?"

Now here he was in front of her. She had wanted to see him. If her sons couldn't get the top job, maybe ... Leena cleared her throat, "Jesus, I have a favor to ask of you."

"Yes?" Jesus said apprehensively. He knew Leena well, very well. "Promise me that these sons of mine will sit, one at your right hand and the other at your left, in your kingdom." There was a moment of silence. He had heard some wild requests before but this one beat them all. Was she serious? He studied her face. She was serious.

"Leena," Jesus started out slowly, "you just don't know what you're asking. Are your sons able to drink the cup that I have to drink?"

"Of course, of course," Leena blurted. "If they can't, I'll train them for it."

"Training or not, they will drink from the same cup," Jesus said sadly. "But sitting at my right hand or at my left isn't mine to give. That's up to my Father to decide." Leena thought it best not to press the issue. Her sons had told her she could ask Jesus this one favor, but they also told her they would accept his answer as final. Still, she didn't think it would hurt to make one last simple request. "Do you think you could put in a good word with your Father? I mean it wouldn't be too taxing for you, would it?" Jesus laughed and when he laughed there was just enough kindness in it to leave the matter open. She knew her sons would be taken care of.

Reflection

Leena's high hopes may seem an exaggeration. After all, who among us has messianic expectations for our children or ourselves? Preposterous, isn't it? Or is it? Come to think of it, most of us look to a person, place, or thing as we would to the Messiah. A lover or friend or relative becomes all important to us. We devote our energies insisting the other be everything we want and need that person to be. No longer are we capable of recognizing the friend or lover as a person with strengths and weaknesses; we see only what we need to see, i.e., the fulfillment of our expectations, a messiah.

Of course no one person is capable of being all that we need and want because, unwittingly, what we really want is all and only the All can satisfy us. Sooner or later the idols we have created begin to crumble either because the people we have forced onto pedestals don't want to be there or we finally "see" through the haze of our projections to the earthly mortal in front of us. As a result, our high hopes turn into shattered hopes. We experience disillusionment.

In "High Hopes" Jim and John see through their messianic expectations for themselves by recognizing their limitations: they can't run fishing fleets or banks. Their hopes are shattered and they are disillusioned. But disillusionment serves a purpose. It sets them free to find the Messiah who can really give them meaning and purpose for their lives. Likewise, Leena has to experience the same kind of disillusionment before she can see how Jesus gives new direction to her sons' lives.

In our own search for the Messiah we may have to be disillusioned not once but several times in order to recognize the difference between our idols and the one who is truly the Messiah.

The Treasure

"The reign of God is like a buried treasure which a man found in a field. He hid it again, and rejoicing at his find, went and sold all he had and bought that field." — Matthew 13:44

He was ecstatic! Had this happened to him? Maybe he was dreaming. But no. There was the gem box, corroded with rust, but still intact after having been buried for years in the rich soil. And the jewels in the box sparkled in the noonday sun: sapphires, rubies, diamonds, and other gems he couldn't even identify. Lester bit his lip so he wouldn't cry out for joy over his new-found discovery and arouse the suspicion of the others working in the field. Silently reviewing how he had come upon the treasure, he focused his attention on the opening in the ground. Lester had intended to drive long wooden stakes into the earth in order to establish boundaries marking off his rented portion of land from the others. What he could never have imagined was striking the metallic surface of the box with his shovel only minutes after he had begun digging.

"I'm a wealthy man! I'll never have to work again," he thought. "But I've got to calm down. The others must not see me walking off the property with this box." Lester knew that the gem box legally belonged to the landowner and there was only one way to claim the box as his own. "I'll buy the field. Yes, I'll buy the field and the box will be mine. It'll be costly. But these gems are worth fifty times the land." Addressing the box he whispered, "I'll have to bury you for a while, but I'll be back." Then he carefully replaced the box and covered it over with dirt. "And I'll draw a circle around you so I know where to find you," he confided as he traced a circle in the soil directly above the buried box. "There!" Rising to his feet, he gleefully rubbed his hands together and thought, "Wait until I tell Wanda and the kids about this!"

Lester bolted for home and on his way almost knocked over two friends.

"Les, what's the hurry?"

"Sorry, can't talk now! I've got business to take care of."

His friends looked puzzled. "That's not like Les. He's always got time to stop and talk."

But there was no stopping Lester today. Once home he announced, "We're moving out of the house. We've got to sell it!"

"What?" Wanda exclaimed.

"No time for explanations. Get the pup tent out of the garage. That'll be our home."

"But, but...."

"Just for a while," he reassured her, "a couple of days. Then we'll buy a house ten times as big as this one. See you later," he added as he left his shocked wife and hurried to the realtor.

On the way Lester came across two more of his friends, drinking buddies from the local pub.

"Hi, Les. You going to join us today?" one of them asked. "I...."

"Sorry," Les interrupted. "I've got more serious things to do now. Maybe some other time. Bye now!" And off he went.

"Les doesn't have time for a beer! That's surprising. He's always one for sitting around and having a good laugh," the friend commented.

"Yeah!" the other added. "Les is always telling us life is too short to be racing around without enjoying it." Then both of them looked on in silence as Lester disappeared down the street.

It took only two days for Lester to sell his house, get his life savings out of the bank, and purchase the land he wanted so desperately. "It's mine. The land is mine," he sighed as he kissed the deed to the land. "Now I'll get the gem box!" Lester high-tailed it to the field even though a torrential rainstorm had begun the moment he had the deed in hand. Shrugging his shoulders he muttered as he challenged the heavens, "No matter. No rainstorm can stop me." Or so he thought.

The heavy downpour coupled with strong winds had altered the landscape of the field. All of the stakes which had previously demarcated the plots were now strewn over the entire field. Arriving there, Lester was horrified. "The circle, the circle, where's the circle?" he panicked. Totally disoriented, he ran in every direction looking for the circle which had long since been washed away. "Where is it? Where is it?" he moaned. Falling on his knees, he vowed, "I'll find you. A little digging will do it. You'll see!" A little digging?

Shovel in hand, Lester attacked the earth at a point he hoped the treasure lay. But by evening he hadn't found the box. Exhausted, he leaned on his shovel and promised, "Tomorrow I'll be back with my family."

At the crack of dawn Lester, Wanda, and the kids straggled half-asleep onto the field. And they had brought with them their pup tent, food supplies, and shiny new tools. Lifting his shovel high, Lester gave the order. "Dig in! It won't take long to find the treasure but we can't fool around or laugh," he warned.

"But, Dad," one of the kids objected, "you're always telling us life is no fun if we don't have time to laugh."

"Yeah," Wanda chimed in. "He's right. Besides, do you see anyone laughing? Could anybody living in a pup tent laugh?" she cracked.

Lester waved away their questions. "Okay, okay, let's get busy!" While Lester dug enthusiastically, the others poked around half-heartedly with their shovels.

Occasionally during the day a friend or acquaintance would drop by and try to strike up a conversation with Les or Wanda or the kids. Les would raise a hand and say, "No time for small talk. Gotta keep digging." By the end of the day, they still hadn't found the box. "Well, we'll find it tomorrow," he told the tired family as they piled into their pup tent for the night.

And he told them the same thing each evening for the following two weeks as they dug and dug and dug without finding the treasure. More friends, neighbors, and relatives dropped by: sometimes to talk about the weather; sometimes to ask for advice; often to avoid being lonely. They had come to Les because in the past he had always been around to listen. But now he gave the same message to each and every person. "Can't talk! Got lotsa digging to do!" And gradually the number of visitors dwindled. Les had no time for what he considered idle chatter. "We've got to get that treasure. That's what counts. We don't have time for fooling around," he preached daily to his family as they dug and piled dirt upon dirt making small hills over the entire field.

On the morning of the third week Lester announced a new plan. "We're going to sift through all the dirt we've dug. We might have missed something."

"We might have missed something," the kids groaned. Les hadn't expected the strong reaction.

"Why, yes," he said softly.

"I'll tell you what we've missed," Wanda cried. Seizing her shovel, she hurled it as far as she could. Then she took off her shoes and socks, danced up and down the nearest hill, and then continued to do the same on the other hills.

"Yay! Yay! Yay! Go to it, Mom!" the kids chanted. Taking their cue from her, they too threw off their shoes and socks and ran in every direction onto different mounds of dirt. Sliding, tumbling, jumping, and laughing, within seconds the kids had magically transformed the morbid field into a joyous playground.

Lester was dumbfounded. He hadn't seen his children acting like children for such a long time that he didn't know what to make of it. Nor had he ever seen Wanda so carefree. His initial reaction was to order them all back to work. However he momentarily forgot himself and chuckled as he watched his wife pirouetting on a mound. He had never seen her so lovely as the sun played on her face. Before he knew it, he too had taken off his shoes and socks and was charging up a hill. "Anyone want to play King of the Hill?" he laughed. The last time he had been this happy was the day he had found the gem box hidden in that field. "The treasure," he thought. "I had forgotten about the treasure!" Then he giggled, wept, and did a jig on top the hill. "Who cares about the buried treasure! Who needs it!" Lester had found his treasure on the field!

Reflection

Where is our treasure? What are we looking for? How many miles are we willing to travel or how much time and money are we willing to spend to get what we want? And once we get what we want, will we really be satisfied? More importantly, what will we have neglected and sacrificed in our single-minded quest for our treasure?

Consider the following. A man decides to take a trip to a beautiful park that he has never seen. His map tells him that the park is fifty miles away. He must look for a sign that says, "The beginning of the park." He drives and drives, looking intently for the sign. There are beautiful trees, streams, and flowers all along the way, but he is so preoccupied in his search for the sign that he has no time for scenery. At long last he reaches a sign and it reads, "This is the end of the park. We hope you have enjoyed your visit." So intent was he on getting to the park that he didn't notice he had already been there!

We go through life looking for the treasures and we miss the treasures all along the way. We are always looking forward to some magical moment when we will find our treasure, e.g., graduation, marriage, the birth of a child, a raise in pay, etc. But our disregard or our blindness to the present moment prevents us from recognizing that the treasure is here in one another and in the events which make up our day to day living. The light is already shining in the present moment. What we need to do is open our eyes and hearts to its presence. To see the light shining now is already to have come out from under the basket.

Do we see it?

Winner

And Jesus went on with his disciples, to the villages of Caesarea Philippi; and on the way he asked his disciples, "Who do men say that I am?" And they told him, "John the Baptist; and others say, Elijah; and others one of the prophets." And he asked them, "But who do you say that I am?" Peter answered him, "You are the Christ."

— Mark 8:27-29

"He's a real winner. He's our boy!" Peter blurted.

"Did you notice the looks on their faces? Did you see their eyes? He had them. What a crowd! They were his!" Philip added gleefully.

"Had them? You're too modest! They adored him. Wouldn't let him go!" Tom insisted.

"Left on a high, singing his praises," Philip marveled.

"I'm still flying," Tom confessed.

"And I'm there with you," Peter sighed.

On a hillside sprinkled with dandelions three of Jesus' disciples were giddy, intoxicated with the crowd's reaction to Jesus' appearance hours earlier on that very hillside outside of Caesarea Phillipi. Peter looked over at Jesus resting under a tree about fifty feet away. "We're on a roll, fellas. Gotta keep the momentum going. Let's find bigger places for bigger crowds."

"Yeah," Philip agreed. "And we need advance press to start the buzz on what he's done, who he's like, what he can do. Wherever

101

we go, let's start dropping words like 'unbelievable,' 'fantastic,' 'unforgettable,' 'out of sight' in the marketplace ... small boutiques ... and in coffee houses and kosher dining rooms."

"There'll be standing room only by the time we've finished with our hype," Tom predicted. "I'd like to see him make his entrance half an hour late. Keep them waiting, keep them guessing what he's up to next."

Peter smiled shrewdly. "We could even have him come disguised — pop out of the crowd and cry, 'Surprise! It's me!' "

"And maybe even dole out prizes for guessing his disguises?" Philip added enthusiastically.

"Good idea, Phil, but we've hardly any prize money in our pockets," Peter cautioned, "unless we take up collections here and there."

"Not a bad idea, Peter," Philip concurred. "Maybe even a collection or two to smarten up his wardrobe. Nothing like a flashy tunic for turning on the crowds!"

"Not to mention sueded sandals," Tom suggested. "Maybe even a manicure to prove he's no dirty-nailed country rube."

So engrossed were they in plans for Jesus' future that they didn't notice that he had walked over to their circle and overheard much of their conversation. "Have you any idea what people are really thinking about me?" he interrupted them. Startled, the three turned and faced him.

"Jesus. We were just talking about you," Peter blushed, scrambling to his feet. "Giving some thought to your future. Very promising, you know. Nobody needs to tell you that, of course. Maybe you'd like to hear some of the ideas we have in mind for you? We...."

"Who do people say I am?" Jesus didn't appear to be interested in their plans for his future.

"Who do people say you are?" Peter looked at the others. "Did you hear that, fellas? What a great question for a billboard! 'WHO DO PEOPLE SAY I AM?' in bold letters." Peter wrote the invisible letters across a huge imaginary board. "Keeps everybody guessing, doesn't it?"

Tom extended the message for the billboard as he answered Jesus' question without addressing Jesus. " 'Some say ELIJAH has come back!' " Tom was pleased with the line. "Think of that! After all these years, Elijah charioteering back to earth. Just enough mystery in the line to make them stop and wonder."

"What about 'JOHN come back from the dead?' They've never seen Elijah but they've seen and touched John, alive and dead. And here he'd be," Philip triumphed as he pointed to Jesus, "JOHN alive and well!"

"I like that!" Peter nodded. "Old Herod believes that bit already. If we could just get him to add his endorsement, think of the crowds that signature would draw!" All three had forgotten Jesus standing there like a package waiting to be gift wrapped. Self-satisfied and having planned what they imagined was best for Jesus, they turned to him and waited for his thanks. He said nothing. An awkward silence spread among them. Something wasn't right here. What had they left out of their PR blitz? Surely they had his best interests at heart. Who else knew him as well as they did? Or so they thought.

Jesus looked at Peter, Peter his friend. "Who do you say I am?"

Peter smiled confidently. He was prepared to answer that one. Hadn't he just said Jesus was a winner? Of course he'd spell out what he meant by "winner" in a way the others hadn't. That's where he was one step ahead of the others. Peter was content to let the others call Jesus "Elijah returned" or "John reborn." That helped build suspense. As for himself, he knew the real answer to the question. "Jesus. You are the Messiah," Peter proudly proclaimed. Even Tom and Philip's admiration for Jesus hadn't prepared them for this. "Ohhh!" they gasped.

"The Messiah! Can you see that written on a billboard?" Philip whispered.

" 'The Promised One is here! The One and Only — Jesus the Messiah!' The news is bound to break attendance records," Tom whispered back. Jesus welcomed Peter's declaration but not with the joy and excitement Peter assumed his admission would evoke.

"You are the Messiah, Jesus," he repeated as if his words hadn't hit home the first time. "You're our winner. We want center stage for you, nothing less."

"Peter," Jesus interrupted. "I'd strike the word 'winner' when you talk of me. I'm going to lose a lot more before I win anything. I'll get center stage all right, but then it's curtains with no third act. Peter, you're hyping up a man who's facing a very short career."

Peter and the others stood stunned. "A loser?" Peter asked incredulously. "What have you been drinking? Talk like that will lower our morale, give you a negative image, and turn away the crowds. C'mon, c'mon. That's not in the cards if you play your hand right! Why the gloom and doom? Snap out of it! Snap...."

Jesus raised his hand. "Go to hell, Peter. What or who do you think I am? Some piece of merchandise for you to hawk in the marketplace? What do you think I'm here for? To stage a back-slapping, glad-handing road show? Grandstanding it like a prancing politician? You bet we're on the road, but it's a one-way trip to Jerusalem for me. Then it's over, finished!" Jesus drew his finger across his neck. "Finished until the real director," and he pointed above, "decides to do something about it in his own way." Heads lowered, Peter and the others stood there sheepishly. Jesus placed his arm around Peter and now spoke gently. "It's time for me to go. I'd like you and the others to be with me, but that's up to you. If you do decide, I can't promise you the reviews are going to be very favorable. That may be your plan, but I don't see the future that way." Jesus patted Peter on the back and started walking away.

Tears had formed in Peter's eyes. He thought he knew clearly who Jesus was, but obviously he had much to learn. And what he had just learned sent a shiver up his spine because his love for Jesus had implications for his own future which he was painfully beginning to realize. Chastened by what had happened, Peter turned to the others and quietly reflected, "I still don't know what he means ... this talk about being a loser. But it won't stop me from following him. Wherever he goes, I go. I'd give my life for him. And I'm willing to bet when it's all over, we'll have one word for him — Winner!"

The others nodded their heads. Together, then, they all followed Jesus on the road — the road to Jerusalem.

Reflection

There is a considerable difference between the two questions Jesus asks his disciples. "Who do people say I am?" and "Who do you say I am?" The first question is basically non-involving. It concerns who Jesus is for others. Jesus' friends can answer without being personally involved. It is only in answering the second question that the disciples involve and commit themselves. How so?

If a friend comes up and asks, "What do you think about me?" or "Who do you think I am?" my answer cannot help but affect the relationship. "I think you're a jerk" or "a cheat" or "generous" are all responses which reveal not only my perception of my friend but they also determine my behavior accordingly. For example, if I say my friend is kind and gentle, I may respond kindly or cruelly; or, if I think he is powerful and aggressive, I may submit to the aggression or become aggressive myself. The point is my perception leads to certain kinds of behavior.

This same dynamic is working in our relationship with Jesus. He asks the question, "Who do you think I am?" Is he the Infant of Prague for us? A Martin Luther King? A Superman under his Clark Kent first-century robes? Whatever our answer, we are involved in a way of relating which affects our behavior. If he is the Infant and only the Infant, then Jesus is the one we want to cuddle in our hearts. If he is the prophet, then he is the one who challenges us and doesn't let us become complacent. Is he Superman? Then does he absolve us of doing anything for ourselves?

"Who do you say I am?" is the question which is the more difficult one to answer because it is so self-involving. Because the question is more demanding, we may avoid answering it for years.

Consequently we can preach, catechize, and study about Jesus without really asking ourselves who we think Jesus is because our answer might force us to live our lives differently. So we safely proclaim what others say about Jesus. But the question Jesus asked his disciples will not go away. "Who do you say I am?"

A Fish Story

The reign of God is also like a dragnet thrown
into the lake, which collected all sorts of things.
When it was full they hauled it ashore and sat down
to put what was worthwhile into containers. What
was useless they threw away.
　　　　　　　　　　　　　　— Matthew 13:47-48

They had been dragged into a room which appeared to be an antechamber to a larger room. Fins spread apart, two brightly colored angel fish stood guard at the door to the inner room. Wearing reading glasses, a third angel sat at a desk with a stack of folders and a gavel. Raising the gavel, the angel pounded the table several times. "Order, order!" he cried. They were grumbling over how they had been caught in a net and dragged with all sorts of other creatures to this unknown destination.

"Now, now, don't take it personally, friends," the angel counseled. "Dragnets are currently the fastest way of gathering as many fish as possible."

"Boo! Boo!" His answer didn't satisfy the dog and catfish, the squid, sharks, sea squirts, bullheads, orange and blue roughys, snappers, snails, sea horses, and countless other fish in the room.

"What I want to know," snapped a sullen snapper, "is why we were hauled here in the first place?"

"I'd like an answer to that question, too," a roughy rumbled as he muscled his tattooed fins through the mess of fish to the front of the room.

Eyes bulging, a bullhead blustered, "Your reasons better be good or else!"

"Here, here!" the angel pounded the gavel. "We've dragged you here because it's time to decide who's going to fish heaven. We're going to admit some of you and we're going to send the rest back."

"Fish heaven? Hey, man, is that what's in the next room? Cool, real cool!" a catfish crooned.

"Yes, the angels at the door are prepared to open it for those who have lived good lives. And for those who haven't ... well, we have no alternative but to throw you back into the deep, dark waters."

"You mean where those mean-looking, horny-headed devil-fish hang out?" cried a frightened sea squirt.

"No, we think the devilfish only deserve one another. We wouldn't dream of sending you there. We'd just send you back to where we found you. There you could spend time getting your lives in order before we dragged you back here again," the angel explained.

"Ahhhh!" The fish were relieved. At least there was no need to worry about facing the devilfish!

However, everybody began to get excited at the prospect of going to fish heaven: some fish flipped their fins; the crabs moved forward, in reverse and sideways; the squid flailed their several arms, entangling themselves with anyone in reach; monk fish settled into chanting sea hymns; and the sea urchins grew rowdier by the minute. Only the snail-slow snails and the clams remained calm at the possibility of going to heaven. "How are you going to decide who's going to heaven? Who's going to make it and who isn't?" the fish fretted.

Pointing to the stack of folders, the angel answered, "Basically by reviewing the data on how you've behaved towards one another. For example, we note in our records that unfortunately some of the clams preferred keeping silent when they could have provided needed counseling for one of their deeply depressed sisters. On the other hand, other clams bravely clammed up when their enemy tried to pry loose information about a brother of theirs.

They preferred a clambake rather than betray a fellow clam." None of the clams commented on the angel's observations. Given their taciturn nature, that was understandable.

"I don't like what's happening here," blurted a bullhead. "We didn't have time to prepare a defense."

"Even if you had spent months preparing a defense," the angel countered, "it wouldn't have mattered in the least. You've bullied your way through life by being offensive to other fish who didn't see life as you swam it. In fact this poor shrimp next to you always suffered the indignity of your insults. Isn't that right?"

The shrimp agreed as the bullhead shook an intimidating fin at him. "Yes, the little shrimps of the world get it all the time from these fellows. We're survivors, though, and we try to support one another by looking out for one another."

"I know, I know," the angel smiled. "And because you shrimp are so supportive of one another ... well, you're going to fish heaven today!"

"Really?" The shrimp was overjoyed.

"And what about me?" snarled a shark from a dark corner of the room. Standing alone, the shark caused shivers to go up and down the backbones of the other fish as he flashed razor sharp teeth at the angel.

"A lone shark!" the angel muttered. "You've taken advantage of others, threatened, maimed, and in some instances killed them. You don't really think we consider you ready for heaven, do you?"

"Just asking, that's all," the shark answered. "By the way, you might want to have those angels at the door tail you when you go outside. It's not safe out there, you know."

"Watch your mouth, buddy," warned a deep voice from the back of the room. The shark was ready to settle accounts but as he turned and faced his challenger, he retreated into his corner. A huge whale occupied the rear of the room.

"Thank you, sir," the angel applauded. "We know you're a whale of a fellow and even though you take up a lot of room, we've got plenty of space for you in heaven because you've always been willing to carry others on your back. True, now and then, you open up your mouth and swallow a few of your neighbors. But basically, you've done all right!"

The whale gushed a geyser of gratitude while the catfish ambled over to the angel and inquired, "Hey, man, am I in or am I not? I mean am I going to swim with the best of them or am I going to end up with sharkskin Sammy there?"

The angel carried the catfish's tone and answered, "Well, man, you've done such a good job cattin' around in your swimming hole that we figured you'd like cattin' around there for a few more years."

"Hey, that's fine with me, man. I got no hurry to leave my scene anyway. Just keep Sammy boy away from me," the cat purred, pointing to the lone shark who was nibbling on some poor fish bone.

"We'll see what we can do," the angel promised.

"What about us?"

"Who's that?" The angel strained to hear the voices. He scanned the room and then it dawned on him whose voices they were. Reaching for the microphone set aside for just such an occasion, he placed it in the middle of the room.

"What about us?" they repeated. This time the voices were clear and everybody recognized the voices to be a school of minnows.

"You've had to suffer a lot," sympathized the angel. "Always being swallowed up or ending up on a nasty hook. The odds have never been in your favor. There's a place for you here where you don't need to be always on guard and where we think small is beautiful!"

"Phewww!" The minnows were relieved and presumably were dancing somewhere in the room although no one knew for sure since an anxious squid accidentally squirted an ink-like substance throughout the room temporarily darkening it.

"Dare I ask where I stand?" a barracuda asked.

"You fellows gang up on others when they can't defend themselves. Need I say more?" the angel replied curtly.

"And what about me? I guess it's back to crabbin' on my home turf," one of the crabs crabbed. "After all, nobody cares about consorting with crabs. Why should it be any different in heaven?"

Quickly reviewing the crab's records, the angel said, "Yes, just the other day you were crabbing about overcrowding in your corner. I think...."

"No, he wasn't crabbing the other day," a carp interrupted. "You're mistaking him for me. I was carpin' about the crowds in my corner. He's not to blame," the carp insisted. "I wish you people would get the records straight!"

Carefully examining the name on the folder, the angel declared, "You're right!" and then he nodded in the crab's direction, "My apologies to you." Back to the carp, "And my admiration to you for confessing carping. For that bit of honesty, you go to heaven ... on condition that you and this crab take up residence next to one another to keep each other in check. You'll make perfect partners! If he crabs, you carp and if you carp, he crabs. Okay?"

The crab and the carp sized up one another, shrugged their shoulders, and agreed to the conditions. Then the crab nudged the carp and whispered, "Maybe we can be a team, crabbin' and carpin'. We could even do a little soft shoe number since I'm a soft shell crab. I'm sure the others would love to see our act."

"I'll think it over," the carp answered thoughtfully.

On and on throughout the night the fish raised their fins and inquired about their fate. Finally, after they had all been judged, the unlucky fish were ordered back into the net and dragged to their home waters. However, the fish who had been chosen to go to heaven remained in the antechamber until the two angels who had been guarding the door slowly pushed it open. Then the angels led all the saved fish into fish heaven.

"Ohhhh!" they marveled. They had been ushered into an unbelievably huge beautiful fish bowl. There were dozens and dozens of fish bars with lovely gold bar stools throughout the fish bowl. In attendance were haloed goldfish bartenders in back of the bars waiting to serve the awestruck fish. The minnows, the shrimp, the whale of a fellow, the crab 'n carp, and all the other saved were simply overwhelmed by the splendor of their water paradise.

There was a trumpet blast and a host of angelfish streamed past the saved towards a pearl-studded door (compliments of the heavenly pearl oysters). They opened it and as the newly saved looked on in amazement a simply stunning silver-bodied fish swam through the portal. Reflecting all the room's light on his body's silvery surface, the fish was dazzling, particularly where his body bore scars from earlier wounds. Majestically surveying all the saved, the silver fish accompanied by the angels swam over and said, "Brothers and sisters, from now on you can do what you do best — drink, drink to your heart's content. Drink like a fish, my friends! And let me be the first to serve you!" Two angels tied an apron around the silver fish's waist while the saved gathered on bar stools. Then the silver-bodied fish served them.

Soon the angels brought an apron to each of the saved so they too could serve one another. Only the crab 'n carp were excepted. They were preparing their soft shoe number for the evening's entertainment. The whole evening promised to be worth a lifetime's wait ... and this was just the beginning of life in fish heaven.

Reflection

It's been said, "You are what you eat." We don't need to understand this literally to grasp the truth of the statement. We now know if we eat food high in cholesterol that our arteries get clogged. We know if people eat too many carrots, their skin turns orange. Just as there is truth in saying we are what we eat, there is also wisdom in stating that we are what we choose.

The choices we make during our lives move us in the direction of becoming certain kinds of persons. Psychologists tell us that as we age we become even more of what we had been earlier in life. Thus, if we chose to act kindly towards others earlier in the life cycle, chances are we will be kind later in life. Conversely, if we had acted meanly towards others, then we become even meaner as we age. What we end up doing through our choices is creating our own heaven and our own hell.

By heaven and hell we mean choices which expand our concern for others or contract it to a narrow self-interest. By becoming what we choose, we either see ourselves as belonging to a larger reality (the world community, cosmos, God, etc.) or we identify ourselves as the sole reality that matters. Judgment can be understood within this context as self-imposed imprisonment, a self absorption which is a living death.

The fish in this story are in some ways like people who choose to be who they are. Because of previous choices some fish go one way and the rest go to the place of light. It must seem cruel that the bullheads, the lone shark, etc., don't get to fish heaven while the whale, the crab and the carp, etc., do. Yet, it makes sense if we keep in mind that the label "bullhead" is not someone's external judgment so much as a statement of what this fish has chosen to be.

What cultural, familial, and personal predispositions have entered into shaping our destiny? Can we still make choices to enable us to come from under the basket, or must these factors isolate us from everybody else? Our choice like the fish in the story is always whether to walk into the light or remain in the darkness.

Tree Climber

Entering Jericho, he passed through the city. There was a man there named Zacchaeus, the chief tax collector and a wealthy man. He was trying to see what Jesus was like, but being small of stature, was unable to do so because of the crowd.

— Luke 19:1-3

"Here I go again, climbing a tree." That was Zacchaeus' line throughout his life. When he was a kid, he was always climbing trees to get away from the bullies who ganged up on him because he was so short.

"We're going to get you, stump!" they'd yell. And at first they were able to get him and beat him up.

"If I could just climb a tree," he said one day after he had been beaten up. "I'd be safe." So Zacchaeus learned how to climb trees. He could climb fat trees, thin trees, high trees, real leafy trees, gaunt-looking trees. You name it and Zacchaeus knew how to climb the tree. He always knew what kind of tree he needed to climb. If, for example, the other kids were very heavy, then he would run for a tree that looked very frail and couldn't bear the weight of heavier kids climbing it. On the other hand, if the kids who ran after him were squat and heavy, he would choose a tree with an enormous trunk so these kids couldn't even get their legs around the trees.

He felt more in command the further up a tree he climbed. He'd make faces at the kids on the ground or he'd moon them and tell them how dumb they were. "Boy, are you nerds down there!"

114

Of course, he'd infuriate them and they'd hang around for hours sometimes just waiting for Zacchaeus to come down. Zacchaeus wouldn't come down. He wasn't in any hurry to be beaten up. He also learned to bring books and bagels with him so he'd be able to read and eat.

Now Zacchaeus didn't stop climbing trees when he got older. Oh no! Not at all. As a matter of fact, he climbed trees more than ever. You see, he became a tax collector. That was a very nasty business to be in, but Zacchaeus had become a pretty nasty person. Since he had grown up defending himself against bullies who made fun of his size, he wanted to make sure people would see him and take note of him as an adult. His decision to become a tax collector took place one afternoon as he was thinking about how he had been treated in his life.

"They'll regret they ever made fun of me," he said as he sat on the limb of an old oak tree. "I'll let them know who's big and who isn't. They made me climb trees in the past. Well, they'll be sorry they ever did." Then Zacchaeus went to some mean Romans and made a deal. "You let me be a tax collector and I guarantee no one will get away from me when I collect the taxes."

"How do you intend to collect them?" one of the officials asked.

"First of all, I intend to climb all the trees in the neighborhoods where I'll be collecting the taxes. That way I'll be able to see into their backyards for escape routes if they try to run away from me when I visit them. I'll even be able to see into their homes as I move out on limbs close to their windows. I'll get a lay of the land that no other tax collector has ever gotten."

"You've got the job," the official said. "And if you do a good job, we'll give you a salary increase and a promotion."

"It's a deal," Zacchaeus said. "You won't be sorry." And they weren't. Zacchaeus climbed just about every tree in Jericho that year. There was a familiar line that everybody said over and over that year. "Is it a bird? Is it a kite? No, it's Zacchaeus the tax collector!" Families always felt Zacchaeus' silent presence when they ate in their backyards. Lovers didn't know if the eyes that looked at them on porches in the evening were those of a hoot owl in a tree or those of Zacchaeus.

Zacchaeus was so ambitious he even took to climbing fences and ladders as well ... yes, even trellises. He didn't care how ridiculous he looked in his pin striped suit and yellow sneakers. Zacchaeus was getting the job done to the satisfaction of the Romans. Because he got the job done, he climbed right to the top and became the chief tax collector, not to mention the fact that he became a very wealthy man.

However, Zacchaeus didn't really feel as great as he thought he would when he had gotten to the top. In fact, instead of feeling like a big man filling big shoes he felt smaller than he had ever felt before. "I don't understand why I feel so small. I've climbed my way to the top. I've seen Jericho as no one else has seen it. Yet, I really feel miserable." Zacchaeus thought and thought about how he had gotten so far up to the top that he was the only one up there. Everybody else was down at the bottom and Zacchaeus was isolated from the others.

Zacchaeus was thinking about how small he felt one afternoon as he strolled through the park when he noticed a large crowd gathering at the end of the park. Usually he stayed away from crowds because he was afraid of running into some of his clients. However, curiosity got the better of him and he walked to where the crowd had gathered. Zacchaeus could hear people talking about Jesus, the rabbi from Nazareth. "So Jesus is here," Zacchaeus thought. "Hmmm, I've heard of him. I wonder...." Zacchaeus looked at one of the trees. "I think I'll see what he has to say." Zacchaeus knew the only way he could see Jesus would be to climb a tree. He also knew he was putting himself in danger because there would certainly be some hostile clients in the crowd. "Oh, well, I've been through this before," he said as he made his way to the tree. "So I climb a tree and go out on a limb. What else is new?"

Zacchaeus climbed the tree, got out on a limb, and saw Jesus in the center of the crowd. Jesus preached and Zacchaeus listened intently. At one point Jesus looked up and saw Zacchaeus on the limb. Jesus smiled, then laughed, and turned to one of his disciples to ask about the man in the tree. Zacchaeus froze for a moment. He was afraid that Jesus would single him out to make fun of him as so many others had done. But, no! Jesus looked up at Zacchaeus, shaped his hands like a megaphone, and yelled, "Zacchaeus, come down from that tree. I want to pay you a visit at your place."

Zacchaeus' eyes opened wide. He pointed a finger at himself as he looked at Jesus. "At my place?"

"Yes, at your place." Then Jesus laughed again. "C'mon, I haven't all day!"

Zacchaeus couldn't believe someone had actually welcomed him down from a tree since he had spent so much of his life going up trees to get away from others. He was so overjoyed, he came down the tree faster than he had ever come down a tree in his life. The crowd was less than friendly.

"Sssss! Sssssss! Boooo! Booo! Jesus is going to his house? I don't believe it! Jesus is going to a sinner's house."

None of this seemed to bother Zacchaeus. He was so happy that Jesus had actually decided to visit him of all people that he felt ten feet tall. It was the very first time he had ever felt that way. "Wow! Wow!" he kept saying. When he finally made his way through the crowd to Jesus, he had made a decision. "Jesus, I'll give away half of what I own to the poor and if I've cheated any-one, I'll give that person back four times what I took."

Jesus put his arm around Zacchaeus and said, "Great! You're really talking like a true son of Abraham. Let's go to your house and have a party, Zacchaeus." Then Jesus looked down at Zac-chaeus' feet. "And take those sneakers off! You won't be needing them anymore. You're back home!"

Zacchaeus had grown to be a big man that day!

Reflection

Literally and metaphorically, "out on a limb" isn't a comfort-able place to be. It is dangerous and dead-ended. Yet, it forces the issue. Something has to give or change. Being out on a limb is a way of imaging the desperation and despair prior to a conversion or change of heart. We cry out in our helplessness; we don't know which way to turn. The self-assurance born of successfully climbing the tree or ladder has turned into defenselessness and vulnerability.

Recovering alcoholics know that only in the admission of their helplessness is there any possibility of salvation. So, too, people going through a divorce or losing a job frequently find their only salvation is in acknowledging their neediness and reaching out to others. But being out on a limb doesn't have to be so openly dramatic. Very often, people are out on a limb when they find themselves living lives without meaning. They are bored or disillusioned or depressed. So fragile is the limb, they may even contemplate suicide.

And what happens to all these people? Sometimes a friend, relative, lover, counselor, or stranger will be there to catch the person as she lets go of the limb and entrusts herself to the other. At other times the person is able to draw on some inner strength hitherto unknown. Something or someone aided the person: Jesus, God, Buddha. Tragically, still others end up broken and hurt, never to be mended. Quiet despair and death are all that remain for them. For Zacchaeus who was out on a limb and alienated from everybody, it was Jesus inviting himself to eat with Zacchaeus. Estrangement ends in belonging with ... Jesus. Can we say whatever the limb people find themselves on, it is some form of alienation from which they long to be free. And what saves is the realization they finally belong with....

The Chocolate Man

*Another time he said to his disciples: "A rich man
had a manager who was reported to him for dissipating his property. He summoned him and said,
'What is this I hear about you? Give me an account of your service, for it is about to come to an
end.' The manager said to himself, 'What shall I
do next? My employer is sure to dismiss me. I cannot dig ditches. I am ashamed to go begging. I
have it! Here is a way to make sure that people
will take me into their homes when I am let go.'"*
— Luke 16:1-4

"I can't go on this way! I've got to stop!" Lou declared. What
did he have to stop? Eating chocolates of course! "This is too much!
I've got to do something else for a living." What did he do for a
living? Managed Bonnie's Best Bon Bons Chocolate Shop. "Why
am I doing this to myself?" What was he doing to himself? At five
feet five inches he weighed in at three hundred pounds! Yes, Lou
had reason to be concerned about what had happened since he became the manager of the chocolate shop where they were made
and sold. A year earlier when Bonnie hired him, Lou weighed only
one hundred and fifty pounds.

At first the chocolates didn't tempt him. The trouble started
slowly. One day he spied an oddly formed strawberry butter cream
in a display case. "This should have been rejected," he thought as
he snatched it out from among the others. Not wanting to waste it,

he popped it into his mouth. "Ohhh! It's marvelous, simply marvelous, so smooth!" he moaned. And that did it! He was hooked!

In the days that followed he sampled all the chocolates — the creams, the pralines, the raisin and nut clusters. All of them! Hurrying to work each day, he could hardly wait to get his fix, secretly plucking freshly coated chocolates from trays and boxes. Filling his mouth, he thought, "What else is there to live for?" Very much a loner, Lou had no close friends. The routine of going back to an empty apartment each night left him feeling empty. He could hardly wait to return to work each day and be among his friends, the chocolates.

He realized he needed to be more circumspect in satisfying his craving when he noticed employees eyeing him suspiciously after they had filled the display case only to discover seconds later that all the coconut creams were missing.

What Lou couldn't conceal was his burgeoning weight. Buying bigger and bigger shirts, trousers, belts, and underwear, he thought, "This is terrible. I'm a living bon bon! I've got to stop!" But he didn't. Instead he consumed more and more chocolates on the job. And weekends were worse! Hoarding chocolates he had pilfered from the shop during the week, Lou prepared for his weekend binges. Chocolates, chocolates everywhere! Under beds, in closets, bathtubs, coffee tins, and bread boxes. The whole weekend he'd sit in his rocker and gobble them up. By Sunday night the apartment was strewn with wrappers and empty boxes.

Then the inevitable happened! Returning to the shop after another lost weekend, he was summoned to Bonnie's office. "You're fired!" she told him. Sitting at her caramel colored desk, she ticked off the times when workers saw him sneaking coconut creams. "We're not running this shop for you," she said. "As it is, we're barely breaking even. We don't even have enough money to advertise. Lou, you're killing yourself and the business! I'll let you stay two more weeks while you look for another job. In the meantime, keep your hands off the chocolates!"

Leaving her office, Lou was mortified. "What have I done? Eaten up their profits! And now I weigh a ton. People can't tell

whether I'm rolling or walking when I come down the street. And
what am I going to do? Why I can't even bend over to tie my shoe
laces. How could I do any heavy work?" As Lou agonized over his
prospects, he noticed a customer as heavy as himself wave to the
cashier. "Hmmmm," Lou wondered, "does he have a chocolate
problem too?"

"I can't pay in cash! I don't have the funds right now," the
customer was saying. "Can't you charge me once more for the
chocolates? Please?"

"He has a problem all right," Lou thought. "He's probably deep
in debt from eating so much. I feel sorry for him. I wish there were
something I could...." Lou paused, his eyes lit up, "I know! I've
got it! I've got it!" Lou waddled over to the customer and tapped
him on the shoulder. "Hey, buddy, how would you like it if we cut
your bill in half?"

"Huh? What?" The man was taken off guard. "Sure, I'd love
it! But what's the catch?"

"Well, the owner needs to advertise this place ... and I notice
you are a little on the stocky side like me."

"So...?" the customer puzzled. "So ... suppose the two of us
get sandwich boards and advertise Bonnie's Best Bon Bons in the
city square. You can work off half, maybe even more of what you
owe just by strolling through the square. People could hardly miss
seeing us and they'll sure get the point that the chocolates must be
pretty good!"

"Well...."

"And besides, we can get acquainted and get a little exercise at
the same time. It's worth a try, isn't it? So what do you say?"

"Okay, okay. I'll try it. But if I feel foolish, forget it!"

"Of course, of course. And if I find a few others like us, I'll see
if I can get them to join us."

During the next couple of days Lou managed to strike the same
deal with a few more overweight customers who couldn't pay their
bills. The next Monday at noon, six of them marched into the city
square. At first they felt silly since they practically filled the square
with their bodies. And their huge waist lines made the sandwich

boards practically stick out in front and back. Occasionally Lou had to encourage the others because some of the bystanders made nasty remarks about their weight.

"Hey, fatso — are you bon bons full of nuts or raisins or what?"

However most of the people chuckled and quite a few curious onlookers visited the chocolate shop.

More importantly, the men began sharing their concerns with one another as they walked. They talked about how they had hoped to forget their problems by eating chocolates and how depressed they were because they felt so worthless. By the third day, they had bonded and now referred to themselves as "the bon bon boys!" By week's end their discussions had been so helpful that they decided to lengthen their advertising sessions by an hour!

On Friday Bonnie called Lou into her office. "Lou, I'm amazed at what you've accomplished. At first I thought your advertising stunt was crazy and I was going to fire you immediately. Not only for parading around in the square but for reducing the bills of our biggest customers without even asking! But within the hour the number of customers had increased twenty-five percent and now we are selling more chocolates than ever. You're shrewd, Lou, very shrewd. I would like you to stay here. We need you!"

Lou smiled from ear to ear. Yes, he was shrewd but he wasn't certain he could continue working next to all the coconut creams in the shop. Yet, now he had friends who supported him and he felt he had the courage to deal with his problem. "Let me think about your offer," he said. "Maybe I'll come back but only if I can wear very heavy mittens!" he laughed. "In any case, I've got to talk it over with the bon bon boys!"

Reflection

The only way to make a figure eight is by going down, under, over, and up. There's no way but down and once down it's back up again. Once completed the figure eight makes sense. Down, under, over, and up also describes the process of conversion. We move from being on top to hitting rock bottom before we can move back up again to complete the process of transformation. Stated another way, initially we experience relative stability in our lives, then instability, confusion, and a period of being down, at our wits' end, in the pits, etc. Only then do we begin to come back up into the light of day and restabilize with a new perspective on life. Paradoxically, we come out from under the basket by first going down under, being there for a while, and then coming up from under.

However miserable Lou is, as long as he manages to get along minimally at home and at work he isn't likely to change for the better. He changes only when he is grossly overweight and is fired from his job. Only then is he able to comprehend what he has done to himself, the predicament he is in, and the necessity of changing the direction of his life. Fortunately, he is able to find support "down under" from others who share his problem.

Bonding is a special kind of support. In conversion experiences those who support us best are generally themselves in need of similar support. Alcoholics Anonymous, Sexaholics Anonymous, and Narcotics Anonymous are examples of groups who recognize the power of bonding when people are in desperate straights. Bonding is done at the "bottom" because only when we are stripped of our illusions and brought low can we share what is left to share: the empathy of our common humanity. When bonding takes place we are already on our way up from under. Why? In the bonding we discover a sense of worth, self-esteem, and the possibility of a new vision for life. However brightly our light may have shone before the conversion, the best is yet to be!

Lou faces problems in his future. He's still got a long way to go. But now he has the strength and the support of others. Against this background, his light is able to shine. And because he helped others' lights to shine, his shone all the brighter.

When have we looked to others for help? When have we been helped so that we experienced light in our lives? Could this have happened if we hadn't reached out to others? Is this the step we need to let our light shine?

Broom Bristles

Jesus entered the temple precincts and drove out
all those engaged there in buying and selling.
— Matthew 21:12

Nobody really knew where Moshe came from. Some thought he came from Galilee; others thought he came from Jericho. But one thing they all knew for certain: they'd never find out from him. Whenever he rarely talked about himself, he'd never reveal where he was from. All he would say was that he had held various odd jobs before ending up here at the temple keeping the floors clean of trash.

At times it was difficult to follow what Moshe was talking about. He had memory lapses. Frequently, in the middle of a conversation his mind seemed to jump somewhere else. Actually, most of the temple personnel paid little attention to him anyway. He had no real status or importance as far as they were concerned. He kept the floors clean. That was all he was paid for, and that was all they wanted him to do. So it upset them when he interrupted their important discussions with talk of the kind of broom bristle he preferred for sweeping the floors or the best cleaning fluid to do the job right. They were caught up in weighty matters like what brand of incense to use or the best way to wash the sacred vessels. What did they care about cleaning fluids or broom bristles? And they would lose all patience when in the middle of comparing broom bristles, Moshe would forget what he had just said and start repeating himself. Then they would tell him curtly and coldly to get on

124

with it, or they would excuse themselves for another meeting. Often, Moshe would be left chatting to himself, unaware that the others had left.

It was understandable that the others were so impatient with Moshe. After all, who wanted to be bothered with someone whose sole concern was keeping the temple floors clean? He had a single-mindedness about what he did and how best to do it that could only be described as zealous.

Yes, that is what he had, zeal! Moshe was motivated by zeal to keep God's floor clean. Some might be filled with zeal to uphold the law; still others might be filled with zeal to keep the incense pots going day and night. But Moshe's zeal was to keep the floors clean. And if you saw "slippery" signs anywhere in the temple, you could bet that Moshe was close by religiously sweeping and washing the floors.

But a little of Moshe's zeal went a long way! It was clearly his zeal which angered the temple personnel more than anything. Perhaps they were angry because Moshe seemed to regard what he did as of equal importance to what they did. Two of the temple priests could no longer contain that anger the day Moshe stopped them to complain about all the manure that was building up on the floors from the animals being sold for sacrifice. Moshe questioned the priests as to the propriety of selling these animals in the temple to begin with. "Why litter the sacred floors?" His voice rose with uncharacteristic excitement. His arms waved wildly. "And another thing...." He checked his gesture in mid-air, mumbled to himself, and then asked the others what point he was trying to make. They laughed at him contemptuously. How could he presume to tell them what was and wasn't proper in the temple? They told him he was getting carried away by his own zeal, a zeal he should limit to scrubbing the floors. Moshe lowered his eyes and said nothing.

Then from nowhere it came. Like a thunder clap, "He's right and you're wrong." Moshe and the officials turned around and standing there was a young man. He continued, "I share his zeal. You make light of him because he cleans floors. But he understands that this is God's space which he tries to keep clear of your petty dealings. He has kindled my own zeal." As he spoke, he took a long piece of rope, knotted it in several places, and began knocking over everyone and everything in sight. In a loud voice that sent everybody scurrying, he said, "Get all of this out of here; you have turned my Father's house into a marketplace." The priests ran for cover, leaving Moshe standing there to face the young man alone. Moshe didn't know what to think. On the one hand, he was terribly frightened. On the other hand, he was pleased that the point he had been trying to make, this young man had driven home in a most unforgettable way.

From a safe distance the priests demanded to know by what authority the young man did what he did. The young man moved in their direction, but after a few steps, he turned around and smiled at Moshe. "You have done well in cleaning these floors. It is the closest thing to giving God himself a bath. Don't believe for a minute that your work is any less important than theirs!" Well, that was all that Moshe needed to hear. If the others had thought his concern about broom bristles and the choice of the right detergent was nonsense, he had finally found someone who agreed with him. And he wasn't just washing God's floor — he was giving God himself a bath! He had never felt quite so proud about his work. The next time Moshe saw those temple priests, he was determined to let them know just how proud he was and what this young man had pointed out to him.

And where was this young man? Moshe could see him speaking to the temple priests at the far end of the temple, though he couldn't make out what he was saying. Moshe could only guess that this man was very close to the God whose floors he had washed daily. If Moshe had known just how close, he would have been very surprised! But for the moment, Moshe just delighted in the fact that someone thought as highly of broom bristles as he did.

Reflection

In most department stores it is possible to see signs which read "For Display Purposes Only." A camera for people to look at and admire ... but only to look at. A television for people to look at and admire ... but only to look at. A mannequin decked out in the prettiest clothes ... but only to look at. In other words, for display purposes only. The sole reason for the display is to be seen and noticed. A great idea ... unless we are talking about people for display purposes only.

In one sense "Broom Bristles" is about people who might as well carry around sandwich boards reading "For Display Purposes Only." The temple personnel are there to be noticed and seen in the liturgy. "Look at me. I can perform for you. I can smile, bow, talk, and walk for you." This type counts very much on what others think about them and their behavior is governed accordingly. What do these people lack?

They lack what Moshe possesses: integrity and genuineness. The temple personnel aren't real. They don't smile from the heart nor do they act or feel from the heart. But why speak of them? We too look to others for approval or disapproval, focusing on what we should or should not do. Politicians do. Bishops do. Business people do. Why?

We want to be liked. Who wants to be a loner? Who wants to go against the grain? We need to know we belong to the gang, the club, the tribe. But what are the consequences of being for display purposes only?

Being empty in the middle. Being hollow people. Walking mannequins. Dummies who smile and perform. Selling our souls. That is the tragedy of being for display purposes only. Jesus chastises the temple personnel because they live on the surface. Their worship is empty because they are hollow. Moshe is the man with heart, with zeal. He doesn't live for display purposes only.

Giveaway

Jesus said to his disciples: "A rich man had a man-
ager who was reported to him for dissipating his
property. He summoned him and said, 'What is
this I hear about you? Give me an account of your
service, for it is about to come to an end.' The
manager thought to himself, 'What shall I do next?
My employer is sure to dismiss me. I cannot dig
ditches. I am ashamed to go begging. I have it!
Here is a way to make sure that people will take
me into their homes when I am let go.' "
— Luke 16:1-4

"It's for you. It matches your eyes."

"Take it! It's yours. It goes with your hair."

"This will cheer you up. It fits you perfectly." What was Ted Ballows giving away? Sapsucker shirts from the Sapsucker showroom on the fourth floor of the Sapsucker Brothers Building in Chicago. Ten years ago at age fifty Ted had been hired by the brothers to promote Sapsucker shirts to prospective buyers by escorting them through the showroom where the new lines of shirts were displayed.

Ted loved his job. "I like working there because I love to meet people," he told friends. And the Sapsucker brothers were happy to have Ted as an employee because his warm, inviting smile and hearty laugh helped employees and visitors alike to feel at home.

"Ted is easy to talk to," Sam Sapsucker told his brother.

"Right, Sam!" Steve agreed. "He's a real asset to the company."

What the brothers didn't know was that Ted was making Sap-suckers a home for more people than prospective buyers. He freely gave away shirts, sweaters, and bathrobes to friends, friends' friends, relatives, and relatives' relatives. Not that any of these people had come for a handout! Oh, no. They came to Ted because they were attracted by his warm, inviting smile and hearty laugh or they had heard he listened to everyone with a sympathetic ear.

People just stopped in at the showroom. "Hi, Ted, you don't know me. I'm Bill Quick, a friend of your friend Mary Nelson. She told me to come and see you. Ahhh ... could I talk to you?" That's generally the way a story began.

Or, "Hi, Ted, I'm Joe Smith, your brother-in-law's cousin. If you have a little time, could I tell you what's bothering me? You see, I've got this problem...." And then the visitor poured out his heart and soul as Ted listened attentively. Once a visitor had told his story, Ted gave an encouraging word, a hug, and surprised the person with, "How would you like a smart Sapsucker shirt? It'll make you look snappy!"

"Why ... why, why, yes, that would be nice," the startled visitor answered. The people who came to Ted were always relieved when they left because they had found someone who listened to them. However, it didn't hurt to walk out of the building carrying the best brand in the land. A Sapsucker!

Even people who had no intention of visiting Ted were treated to a Sapsucker. Assuming many of the visitors in the building were friends' friends or relatives' relatives, Ted stopped complete strangers in hallways, elevators, waiting rooms, washrooms, or wherever and introduced himself. He disarmed them so completely with his pleasing personality that before they knew it they too were talking to him about their lives. He'd invite them to the showroom for a cup of coffee, a slice of banana yogurt bread, and cap the meeting with, "How would you like a Sapsucker?"

Over the years Ted had given away so many Sapsuckers that no one was certain when they saw someone wearing the Sapsucker label whether the person had bought the shirt or gotten it as a gift from Ted.

After Ted had been with Sapsuckers for ten years, a change occurred in his life. Years earlier when he had begun working with the company, he had gone through a difficult divorce. Badly hurt by the ordeal, Ted had periodic bouts of depression which he concealed pretty successfully. Now, however, the bouts were more frequent. More and more he neglected his appearance. Hair disheveled, trousers wrinkled, and Sapsucker shirts no longer spotlessly clean, Ted holed up in his Seventh Avenue apartment hours on end. He wanted to spend more and more time in bed. Getting up and going to work became a real chore. Life became a bore, a bummer.

All this came to a head the day Ted announced to his friends, "Well, I'm going to be fired! Wait and see. I've given away too many Sapsuckers!"

"Did the Sapsucker brothers say you were going to be fired?" they asked.

"No, but it will happen! In a couple of days," he nodded gravely. However, a couple of days passed and nothing happened. "Tomorrow, tomorrow it will happen," he solemnly assured his friends. "Yup, tomorrow is the day." But that day came and went and nothing happened.

"Why weren't you fired?" a friend asked. "They don't fire employees on St. Vitus Day," he answered. "But tomorrow ... just wait and see." But another day passed and still nothing happened.

"Why didn't the Sapsuckers fire you this time?" they asked.

"One of the Sapsucker brothers is out of town. That's why! But tomorrow when he gets back. Then it will happen."

"Oh?" His friends were growing suspicious. And they were particularly disturbed when Ted told them the Sapsucker brothers were holding off firing him until the FBI concluded its own investigation. Looking over his shoulder, he'd whisper, "They want to know how many Sapsuckers I've taken before they put the finger on me. I'm convinced they're spying. Their van is across the street from my apartment. I've seen them using binoculars to trail me."

By now his friends were very worried and they tried to persuade Ted that he needed to get rest and go into a hospital for treatment. But Ted could not be persuaded. He was convinced that the day of reckoning was right around the corner. Over and over he imagined the Sapsucker brothers confronting him. He created different scenarios as to what might happen when they spoke. "You're fired! We'll see to it that you spend the next twenty-five years at hard labor to make up for the Sapsuckers you've given away!" Or, "We'll force you to learn Korean and sew each Sapsucker by hand in our factories over there ... until you're 107!" Or, "We demand you go to all the people you've given Sapsuckers to and ask for them back."

"Oh," Ted groaned. "That would be the worst punishment of all!" He'd have to go to half the people in Chicago for that! After rehearsing all the ways he could be punished, Ted exclaimed, "What's wrong with me? Am I crazy?" His friends tried to convince him that if he didn't go to a hospital soon, not only would he be crazy but he'd drive them crazy too! Finally he agreed to enter the hospital.

Ted hadn't been there more than two days, however, and he was getting visitors from all over the city. Men and women who had met Ted at Sapsuckers lined up to see him, decked out in their Sapsucker shirts and sweaters.

"Why all the Sapsuckers?" Dr. Smucker asked a nurse.

"They're all coming to see Ted Ballows, Doctor. They're his business associates, his friends, his friends' friends, his relatives, and his relatives' relatives. It's remarkable!"

But what was even more remarkable was Ted's recuperation. No one had ever recovered as quickly in the whole history of the hospital. Why? "I found out how many people love me," Ted explained to a friend. And he no longer worried whether the Sapsucker brothers would fire him. "There will always be people who will take me into their homes. I know that now," he said. But ... surprise! The Sapsucker brothers sent Ted a bouquet of flowers that practically filled his room.

"We miss you. Come back soon," the card read.

Ted's eyes filled with tears. "The Sapsuckers want me back ... I'm going back to the Sapsuckers!" Beaming, he left his room. Passing a particularly troubled person on the stairs, Ted asked, "Do you want to talk? I'm a good listener, and ... by the way, how would you like a Sapsucker shirt? I happen to have an extra with me!"

Reflection

It's striking how Jesus' parables are so free of religious language. There is no talk of God, grace, or faith in the great stories of the Prodigal Son, the Good Samaritan, the Workers in the Vineyard, etc. And Jesus never describes characters who are good to one another "because they see God in someone" or because they are motivated by good intentions. No, he concentrates on how people deal with one another regardless of intention. What finally saves someone from destruction is how that person acts towards another human being.

Talk about purity of motive isn't an issue; results are. The unjust judge will act justly because he needs his rest and he won't get it from the nagging widow. The owner of the vineyard is good to all his workers and it is his goodness that counts, not his motives. Maybe Jesus recognizes that we can be too much concerned with motivation and too little concerned with results. His admiration for results is nowhere more apparent than in the parable of the dishonest manager. The manager knew how to "save" himself by being good to the people who could help him. We question the manager's motives and Jesus praises what he does!

Of course Ted Ballows can be faulted for his cavalier give-away program, but ... he was doing good. Perhaps even the Sapsucker brothers benefitted from the advertising! Moralists might argue about achieving a moral end through immoral means. But when lives are touched in the way Ted touched those who came to see him ... well, what can we say? The fact is — Ted Ballow's light shone all over Chicago. That ought to count for something!

Do we prevent our light from shining because others might call into question our motives for doing what we do? Isn't doing good far more important than why we do good?

Mud

With that Jesus spat on the ground, made mud with his saliva, and smeared the man's eyes with the mud. Then he told him, "Go, wash in the pool of Siloam." (This name means "One who has been sent.") So the man went off and washed, and came back able to see. — John 9:6-7

"Mud! He put mud in my eyes. Mud, mud, mud. Do you understand?" Avie had reached the limit of his patience. So many people had asked him why he was able to see. At first he was just a little annoyed. However, as time went on the questions really got to him. Strangers routinely came up to him and invariably the conversations went as follows.

"Just how did this man make mud?"

"He put spit in it."

"He put what in it?"

"Spit. S-P-I-T!"

"But that's unhealthy."

"If it's so unhealthy, why am I seeing?"

"But...."

"Look, I'm thinking about writing a book about it. Read about it when it comes out."

Of course Avie had no intention of writing a book. He simply wanted to be left alone. He pined for the days when his life had been his own, and when his only worries were scrounging for food or locating shelter for the night.

Yes, he craved anonymity so much that he took to wearing disguises! He sported a new white tunic and draped his head in a black and white checkered shawl. Never did he appear on the streets anymore without sunglasses even if the sun weren't shining or it was nighttime. Needless to say, he looked considerably different from the scraggly bearded man who only a week ago had loitered about street corners begging for food in a tattered Jerusalem gunny sack. But try as he would, the disguises never quite worked.

One morning, emerging from an alley where he had readjusted his shawl to cover even more of his face, someone spied him from across the street. She cupped her hands like a megaphone and yelled so shrilly that all the people on the sidewalk stared at Avie. "I've seen you before. Aren't you the fellow who used to stand on the corner and ask for handouts?"

Avie tried disguising his voice and squeaked, "No, not me. You must have me mistaken for someone else."

"Wait a minute. Yes, you're the one. You were blind and the man they called Jesus spit in your eyes, didn't he? Then you washed your eyes at the pool and now you can see. Isn't that right?"

Avie's passion for privacy was equaled only by his compulsion to get the record straight. "He put mud mixed with spit in my eyes; he did not spit in them. Is that clear? Mud, not spit!" Avie was quite clear. Unfortunately such public clarifications didn't enhance his possibilities for privacy. Moreover, soon his relationship with Jesus became as much a matter of public controversy as the healing itself.

But Avie knew next to nothing about Jesus other than the fact that he had taken him aside and healed him. He was grateful, but beyond this he felt no special closeness to him, just as he had never felt particularly close to anyone else. Circumstances soon changed that, however.

"Mud. I've said it over and over. Maybe it would be a good idea to paint the word in big letters on the back and front of my tunic. After all...."

"We don't care how you answer others; just tell us what we want to know." Three men had approached Avie on the street as he feigned a pronounced limp which he hoped would throw any future inquirers off the trail. It did not. In fact, if these three men were any indication, it seemed to attract some very mean people. "Jesus healed you on the Sabbath, didn't he?" one of the men asked sternly. "Why...." "And that is sinful!"

Avie soon realized that mud was no longer the issue. Mudslinging, however, was. "Now wait a minute," Avie held up his hand. "He is a prophet!" Avie clammed up suddenly. What had he said? "A prophet?" he thought. "I said, 'A prophet'?" He wasn't sure why he had said it, but now that he had he wouldn't be moved and repeated more strongly than before, "A prophet, yes, a prophet!"

The three men glowered silently. Then one of them, the meanest, spoke slowly and deliberately. "You were never blind at all, were you? This is just a game you're playing."

"A game!" Avie was dumbfounded. "A game? I am not playing any ga...." His voice trailed off as he saw his reflection in a store window immediately behind the men. Sunglasses, white tunic, checkered shawl, a limp! Slowly Avie removed his sunglasses and the checkered shawl. "Perhaps I have been playing a game, but not the kind you're suggesting," Avie said reflectively. "I'm finished talking with you. If you don't believe I was blind, then go and see my parents. They will tell you."

Without a word the three men turned on their heels and departed. Avie studied his reflection in the store window. Those men were obviously interested in nailing this Jesus who gave him his sight while he had only been interested in protecting his privacy. How could he continue this charade while others were determined to muddy the reputation of this prophet? Starting down the street, he discarded his shawl and sunglasses. He stopped the first persons coming his way and with a note of defiance in his voice said, "Mud. Jesus gave me my sight by smearing my eyes with mud. What do you think of that?"

"Mud?" The shopper puzzled.

"Yes, mud." Avie smiled. "And don't let anyone tell you that this man is anybody less than a prophet. Whoever says that is a liar!" Avie left the bewildered shopper and quickened his pace, now minus the limp, as he marched down the street. He began to feel an attachment to this man Jesus that the had never experienced before, not even on the day he had been healed.

Just how strong that attachment was became evident the following day when the three men who confronted him on the street sent a messenger demanding his presence in their office. Avie knew he had no choice but to go. These men were powerful members of the Pharisaic party. He felt weak in his knees and his stomach fluttered. He automatically reached for the sunglasses, and checkered shawl but caught himself and simply murmured, "No." He motioned the messenger to lead the way, and followed him directly to their office.

Like ravenous barracudas, the three men circled Avie and made their attack. "Give glory to God! First of all, we know this man is a sinner."

Avie started out softly. "I do not know whether he is a sinner or not. I know this much: I was blind before. Now I can see."

"Just what did he do to you? How did he open your eyes?" they shot back.

Looking directly into their eyes, Avie's voice was now tinged with sarcasm. "I have told you once, but you would not listen to me. Why do you want to hear it all over again? Don't tell me you want to become his disciples too?"

One of the men, his face reddened with anger, shouted, "You are the one who is that man's disciple. We are disciples of Moses. We know that God spoke to Moses, but we have no idea where this man comes from."

Disciple! Avie had been given an identity by Jesus' enemies. "Disciple? Why not?" he thought. "Well, this is news! You don't know where he comes from, yet he opened my eyes. We know that God doesn't hear sinners, but that if someone is devout and obeys his will, he listens to him. It is unheard of that anyone ever gave sight to a person blind from birth. If this man were not from God, he could never have done such a thing."

"What?" one of the men asked angrily as he grabbed Avie by the shoulder. "You are steeped in sin from your birth, and you are giving us lectures?" Before he knew it, Avie had been thrown out of their office bodily.

"MUD. It was MUD. He did it with MUD. And don't you ever forget it," Avie said loudly and clearly as he straightened out his tunic. "Because I'll never forget it. I'm a disciple, you know." Avie strode down the street and marveled how he had come to regard this Jesus. He marveled both because he had never felt so strongly about someone before and because he had discovered how much Jesus meant to him only in his confrontations with these men. Given what had happened in the last couple of days, Avie wondered what else could happen to him. How much more would he come to discover about this man and his relationship to him? He didn't know. He laughed to himself as the thought entered his mind that it was all clear as mud! Well, mud had brought him this far and he was relying on this mud to bring him further.

It was only a matter of time before the mud would settle out and he would find the answer to his questions.

Reflection

Getting involved, standing up and being counted, coming out of the closet, speaking out, and not remaining silent any longer are expressions which suggest the emergence of the public figure from the private. Not an easy transition as when someone casually decides to do some good deed. No. Going public is the result of soul searching and apprehension over the consequences of going public, e.g., possible loss of job or friends or prestige and in any case a certain loss of anonymity.

In some instances there seems to be an inevitability in going public. Avie would like to preserve his anonymity but can't. He is almost forced to answer questions wherever he goes. Gradually, his protest against self-disclosure becomes a protest on behalf of the truth. Obviously, what he didn't "see" he could ignore. But once he gained his sight he saw; and in seeing, he could no longer ignore without losing his integrity.

Can we say there is a point in our own lives when our standing up or our coming out is necessary because we have seen enough and because then the failure to stand up would mean the loss of our integrity? Do we reach a point where we see ourselves wearing disguises? And is this the moment when the private persona must be transformed into the public one lest it conceal rather than reveal the one who wears it. Can we also say once we have gone public there is no turning back?

Seeing cannot be followed by a real return to blindness but only to pretending not to see — like the Levite and the priest who saw the wounded man but pretended not to notice. And it is this pretense which is worse than the initial ignorance. Maybe we have a dim awareness that insight leads to behavioral changes in our lives which we'd prefer not take place; so we resist the opportunities to see! But that resistance already indicates some kind of seeing and consequently we can no longer hide behind our "ignorance." We do so at the peril of our soul.

Joanna

On one occasion when a great crowd was with Jesus, he turned to them and said, "If anyone comes to me without turning his back on his father and mother, his wife and his children, his brothers and sisters, indeed his very self, he cannot be my follower." — Luke 14:25-26

"Joanna and Chuza! They're made for one another!"

"Joanna and Chuza? The perfect couple!"

"Joanna and Chuza? A match made in heaven!"

Yes, when anyone in Herod's court spoke of Herod's finance minister, Chuza, Joanna's name was invariably mentioned. "They belong together — like two peas in a pod," a court official chortled.

"Inseparable — like Siamese twins," another added. Joanna and Chuza had been married twenty years. He had been minister to Herod for five and Herod was delighted every time Joanna accompanied her husband to the court social functions. "How charming," Herod observed on several occasions as Chuza beamed and Joanna blushed.

"See what the king thinks, Joanna, my Joanna," Chuza would say. "I'm proud of you! My Joanna, my little kitten!"

"I'm pleased as punch to make you proud," she'd purr.

"We envy you," other officials said when Chuza brought his elegant and lovely Joanna to their homes. "How witty! What class!"

"Ah yes, she's my Joanna," Chuza smiled proudly. Then he'd whisper excitedly, "Joanna, see ... see what they think of you! You're my girl, my Joanna, my pigeon!"

"Anything to please you, love," Joanna cooed.

People never tired of dishing out compliments, and as the years rolled by Chuza made certain that he always brought his Joanna with him. And Joanna? Did she ever tire of the endless round of social events and compliments? Not in the beginning. However, recently she had begun to feel bored and restless. And on one occasion after Chuza praised his Joanna for pleasing him, she snapped, "I'm not your Joanna!"

Startled, Chuza asked, "Wha ... what is wrong, Joanna?"

"Nothing ... nothing ... I don't know," she said, her eyes moistening. Chuza shrugged his shoulders and dismissed the outburst. However, the following evening at Herod's court he would do more than shrug in reaction to what Joanna did there.

Herod threw a dinner party and during the party, Salome, the daughter of Herodias, Herod's wife, danced in the king's presence. She so delighted him that he promised her whatever she desired. Salome left the room for five minutes and then returned requesting the head of John the Baptist. Surprised by her request, Herod hesitated but finally ordered the prophet's head be instantly delivered to the banquet hall. Joanna's face turned ashen white. She had never met the Baptist but she admired him for publicly speaking against Herod's illicit marriage to Herodias. She hadn't spoken of her admiration to her husband because she hadn't wanted to displease him. However, Herod's order to kill the Baptist repelled her. "I want to leave," Joanna told her husband. "Now!"

"Joanna, Joanna, we can't leave. What would the others say if we left the party before the king had gone?"

"I don't care what they'd think! I can't stomach this!"

Tightly holding her hand, Chuza said coldly, "My Joanna, I need you at my side. My elegant, my charming Joanna, how will I look without you?"

"How will you look?" Joanna's eyes widened. "Do you see that mirror?" she asked, pointing to a wall of mirrors in the entrance.

"Find out for yourself!" she cried, wrenching her hand from his. Then she darted out of the room as several persons including Herod watched.

Herod approached the embarrassed Chuza. "Where did your Joanna go?"

"Uh, she has a fever, your majesty. She had to leave."

"Oh?" Herod didn't seem convinced. "Don't you think you should be with her?"

"Yes, of course," Chuza said. He hesitated, then added, "My apologies, your majesty. With your permission I take my leave," and he made a hasty retreat from the hall.

Shortly he caught up with Joanna and demanded, "Why have you done this? Don't you realize what this can do to my career? My future?"

Joanna halted, looked intently into Chuza's eyes and answered, "I see more clearly than I ever have what being your Joanna has done to me and how it will destroy me if I keep living this way. What do you think I am? Some kind of pet or good luck charm?" Joanna winced and shook her head. "For years it gave me pleasure to please you!"

"And now? Pleasing me doesn't matter?"

"No! Not when it displeases me to see Herod destroy a man on a girl's whim! Especially a man who spoke his conscience! And all you care about is what you'll look like without me at your side. That's when I stop being your Joanna!"

Chuza's face reddened. "Oh? Is that so? Who do you think you'll be without me? Take a little time to think about what you've just said and maybe you'll reconsider!" Turning on his heels, Chuza marched off into the night.

For the next couple of days Joanna pondered what had happened. She had surprised herself. What she suspected but never clearly understood until the night she had contradicted her husband was that she was no more than an ornament in his life. But now she knew she had to lead her own life. Yet, she wondered if she was being too headstrong. "What am I doing? Being selfish? Am I out for myself? Only myself?"

Struggling with these questions, she happened upon a small crowd gathered on a street corner listening to a young man. Curious, she walked over to a woman in the group, tapped her on the shoulder, and asked who was speaking. "He's Jesus of Nazareth," she answered.

"Jesus? Another outspoken prophet," Joanna thought. "I've heard of him. He speaks his mind like the Baptist."

"Friends ..." the man said, "if any of you want to join me, I invite you to do so. But you'll have to say no to those who want to stop you. That could mean your parents, your brothers and sisters, yes, even your spouse. There's pain involved in deciding, but if you're not willing to embrace pain for the sake of the kingdom, then it's better if you stay home."

His voice was gentle but firm and his words weren't lost on Joanna. "He's read my mind," she gasped. "He knows my anguish! I must hear more!" And Joanna listened to him not only that day but she began to follow him wherever he preached. It wasn't long before she met two other women, one named Mary Magdalene and the other, Suzanna. The three followed Jesus. She was no longer Chuza's Joanna. No longer did she strive to please him. Now it pleased her to follow Jesus. She was now her own Joanna.

Reflection

Whose life are we living? Whose light is shining? We can live for years doing what others expect without ever really knowing what is in our own deepest interest. We can live not only with others but for them. As a result, we achieve no self-identity, no sense of separateness. One reason we live so attached to others is our fear of not surviving on our own. "You can't make it," or "You're helpless without me," or "Let me take care of you," are the messages we hear when we try to differentiate from our families of origin, our friends, spouses, or organizations. Unfortunately these messages never help us mature.

Maturing means achieving both communion with and separateness from others throughout the life cycle. The failure to achieve communion is a failure in intimacy while the failure to achieve separateness is a failure in identity. It isn't unusual for those of us in mid-life to realize we haven't been living our own lives. Overly dependent on spouses or others as sources of self-worth, we do whatever is in our power to please them. We must continually win approval of ourselves and of what we do. Or we become paralyzed. Overly concerned with what an elderly parent may think of us, we dare not risk offending them. In either case our excessive need to please means never really choosing what accords with our own real needs and aspirations. In other words, we live others' lives while our own light is hidden under another's basket.

Joanna illustrates a middle-aged person who takes the first, painful step out from under the basket of another's identity in order to find herself. It is painful because she feels guilty and anxious as she takes the step. Like Joanna, we sometimes have to embrace uncomfortable feelings of guilt, anxiety, and loneliness as we become the persons we are called to be. And like Joanna, we have to embrace this "cross" if we are to experience our light as our own and not as a satellite to someone else's.

Have we ever felt it vital to growing up to distinguish who we were from parents, friends, lovers, etc.? In spite of the pain, did we recognize the necessity of taking these steps if we were to experience our own light? Do we see the possibility of making similar choices in the future?

Welling Up

There came a woman of Samaria to draw water.
Jesus said to her, "Give me a drink." For his dis-
ciples had gone away into the city to buy food.
— John 4:7-8

Sarah's friends sometimes shook their heads, often laughed up a storm, and more often lectured her on how sappy she was, spilling tears for anyone or anything that came along.

"Quit your crying, Sarah! How else do you think we could catch a mouse? A trap's the only way."

"Sarah, you're a ninny. Whoever heard of crying over an unhatched bird's egg?"

"You're kidding, Sarah! Shedding tears because the rain didn't fall on ole Ezra's dried up bean patch?"

"But I can't help it. I don't want to cry. What am I to do? It just happens." Sarah was growing daily more concerned about the tears which welled up, flooding her eyes, and keeping the Kleenex folk in business. Why, she wondered, couldn't she control herself like other eighteen-year-old girls? In desperation she devised ways of holding back her tears. She'd force herself to laugh when she felt like crying. If that didn't work, she'd hold her breath when a sob seemed on the way. She even closed her eyes and bit her lip to avoid even the hint of misty eyes. And to what avail?

Her laughter always ended in tears. The first gasp to follow her marathon breath-holding was always a sob that sailed through her soul. And as for the bitten lip — just more pain to cry about!

"Get married," her relatives urged.

"You need a man," her friends advised.

"Make sure he laughs a lot," her rabbi counseled. No one was certain why a husband was the antidote to crying. But everyone agreed that something, anything had to be done. Sarah finally agreed and married a man who loved to raise the roof with jokes. Day and night he joked and carried on, keeping Sarah in stitches.

Everybody said, "See! Sarah doesn't need to wash so many hankies anymore. The problem's licked!"

What they didn't guess, and what Sarah soon discovered was her husband's chronic need to tell his jokes to other women — in other beds. Oh, yes, a real Casanova, this one! Sarah had a real eye opener. Like floodgates pressing for release, the tears flowed more freely than before. She had never been hurt so deeply as she had by this buffoon. Sarah had given her heart away and been betrayed. Night and day the tears welled up as she remembered, rehearsed, and relived her discovery of his infidelities.

Then it happened. One day the tears dried up. The well had run dry. Lips pursed and brow furrowed, Sarah determined never to feel anything for anyone again. "I don't need the hurt; I don't need the pain; I don't need." Out the door and out of her life went her quondam husband.

"Good. She's grown up," a friend nodded approvingly.

"She's nobody's fool," the wise rabbi concluded.

"A miracle! A miracle!" everybody chortled. "The tears are gone. The tears are gone," everyone congratulated everyone. "Sarah's come a long, long way."

A very long way indeed. Dressed to kill, Sarah sashayed on the scene. Mascaraed, rouged, and coifed Sarah was a Delilah reborn. She played, and played, and played some more with any man who wanted to play her game. "For keeps you say?" as she looked into her lover's star struck eyes.

"Of course, of course," he professed.

"Why not?" she purred. And within a week they were married. "Let's play with your money too, my love," she coaxed each night they bedded down.

"Of course, of course" he squealed as he held her close those first months of wedded bliss. But when the money dwindled in the second year of marriage, and when he finally protested....

"There are two beds in the house, aren't there?" she reminded him. Besides if he didn't want to play by her rules, then they weren't playing for keeps after all. "It was great while it lasted," she smiled ushering him to the door and waving good-bye. Now the tears were really flowing but they were not hers. No, her eyes were dry, oh so dry.

"My, she's composed," a friend remarked.

"What control!" another mused.

"Self-contained, I'd say," proposed yet another.

And there were more games to play. More affairs, more marriages. But always the same script.

"You want to play for keeps?"

"Oh, yes, yes. For keeps. By all means."

"Why not?" And whenever they parted the tears were never hers. Just a thin smile, a crease across her heavily powdered face.

"No feeling for him at all," a friend complained.

"Not a tear," another marveled.

"She's as dry as the desert," a third whispered ominously.

Dry as the desert to be sure. But the games were taking their toll on her. She played and played and overplayed. No fun anymore. Just going through the motions. Would the next one want to play for keeps she wondered half-heartedly. "What do I care?" she muttered as she walked the dusty road to draw water from the well that hot, dry afternoon. "Have I ever cared?" She paused. "Yes. Light years ago. It was...." She interrupted herself. "No, I mustn't think about it." Then she caught sight of the well and a man sitting on its edge. She ignored him as she approached and lowered the bucket into the water.

"Could you give me some water?" he asked.

His question startled her. This one's a winner, she thought. A man talking to her in public and not just any man but a Jew by the sound of his voice. Maybe another one who wants to play for keeps! "You want a drink of water from me? I'm a Samaritan. Aren't you afraid it'll rub off? Are you sure you really don't want something else?" she asked seductively.

"Maybe I do. Maybe I do," he answered softly.

"I'll bet you do!" she threw her head back with a hollow laugh.

"You're not very happy, are you?"

"I beg your pardon?" The question seemed an intrusion. It shocked her to wary attention.

"Have you had a good cry lately?"

"A good cry? Me? A good cry? Since when is crying good?" she shot back. "It never did me any good. The last tear I shed was years ago. And I praised the day the crying stopped because that's the day the feeling stopped — for anyone!" Sarah peered into the dark well as she began retrieving her bucket.

"Was that the same day you dried up inside?" the stranger countered.

"Dried up?" Sarah puzzled.

"Yes. The day the tears stopped flowing. The day the feeling left you."

Sarah fumbled with the water bucket. "Sharp man," she thought. "You said you wanted water? Help yourself." She handed him the ladle but he didn't take it. "Well, have you changed your mind?"

"That's not the kind of water I need or want."

"What are you talking about?" Sarah searched the man's eyes.

"This." He took the bucket from her hands and held it so the water caught her reflection.

"Oh!" she gasped.

"Wouldn't you agree it's time for a good cry?" His voice was gentle but firm.

Her fingertips slowly explored her cosmetic-caked face, and she winced. Her eyes traveled up to the stranger's face now marked by a large tear.

"Cry!" he invited her. "Let your tears bubble up like a living spring!"

The resistance of the years gave way as tears welled up in her eyes. In a moment steady streams cascaded down her cheeks. "I have been so lonely," she sobbed, "so very lonely." She continued crying but gradually smiled through her tears. "Now at least I feel alive again. Nobody ever told me crying could be so good — except for you."

The man placed his arm around her waist. "Let's say it's my gift to you — water bubbling up forever — how do you like that? Sounds good, doesn't it?"

"It's good news to me!"

"Go, tell your husband then."

"I have no husband."

"You are right. You have had five and the man you live with now is not your husband."

More tears. Her life was all there in front of her and he didn't judge her. He didn't even judge her! Waves of relief surged through Sarah's body. "I ... I must go and tell the others what has happened." As she danced away she waved to him, "Don't move, don't move until I come back! The others too must hear the good news!"

"I won't move a muscle," Jesus said as he slightly tilted his head heavenward, winked, and whispered, "Thanks!"

Reflection

Many persons will say they honestly don't know how they feel because the well of their feelings has been capped for years. These people aren't mean, insensitive, or uncaring. On the contrary, many of them are professional caregivers, e.g., nurses, psychologists, and psychiatrists. Nice, good, and pleasant are adjectives used to describe many of them. What, then, is the reason for them not knowing how they feel?

The answer may be that they have had to pay attention to one or both parents' feelings from a very early age. If sensitivity to the moods, whims, needs, and concerns of parents had been a full time occupation, it left them precious little time to tend to their own needs. Preoccupied with themselves, parents ignored their children's needs. Adult children of alcoholic parents will tell you this is true. Men and women, whose mother or father needed to be flattered (e.g., the stage mother) or whose parents demanded academic or athletic excellence of a son or daughter, will also tell you how they were forced to deny their own feelings.

And it may take years before these now-grown children dip into the well water of their own feelings. At first there may be just a trickle of resentment or anger or sadness which they experience. Merely trickles, but frightening signs since so long repressed. But then more and more feelings well up. And a well that's been capped for years yields distasteful water — muddy and stagnant — before the purer water is reached. Yet, it is necessary to reach in and let the negative distasteful feelings come up because in and through these feelings the person comes to experience himself as "I am and it is good to be myself." When this experience of "I am" happens the person has dropped the bucket deeply into her well water. But there is more.

In the experience of going deeply into one's own well is the recognition the water is funded by a source beyond itself. "I am" will not dry up because there is a power at the bottom of the well which flows into and sustains all well water. It is that power of which Jesus speaks when he tells Sarah she has a gift within. Her tears were signs of that gift because there is continuity between the simple welling up of tears and the power called the Spirit. It is important that people who don't know what they feel come to feel a feeling because it is a sacrament of God's presence at the bottom of the well.

Going Places

*For everyone who exalts himself shall be humbled
and he who humbles himself shall be exalted.*
— Luke 14:11

"Do you want to climb the ladder of success?"

"Oh, yes!"

"Do you want to be at the top?"

"Certainly!"

"Do you want to move in high places?"

"Without a doubt!"

"Then look sharp! Watch your step! Play the game! Follow the rules! Then you'll get ahead!"

As far back as he could remember, Abe had gotten advice for advancing himself socially and professionally. Since he had been so intent on moving up, he paid attention to what friends, relatives, and associates told him. "Abe, when you are with your elders, smile a lot and listen carefully. Don't interrupt when they are speaking and don't be disagreeable with them. You don't want them upset," Abe's father admonished him.

Abe smiled, listened carefully, didn't interrupt him nor disagree with him.

"You see? You see?" his dad chortled. "You are going places, believe me!"

"You want the girls should like you, Abe?" his mother asked, rocking in her rocker.

"Yeah, Ma," Abe answered eagerly.

"Then be strong, smile a lot, tell them you're crazy about the bagels they bake, but don't talk with food in your mouth! Understand?"

"Yeah, I...."

"And wear clean pants and underwear! Cover up the zits on your face, chew peppermint before kissing a girl, and — oh, yes! Don't talk with your mouth full! Understand?"

"Sure, Mom," Abe said as he looked in the mirror for telltale pimples, checked his pants and underwear, put peppermint on his must have list, returned to the mirror and practiced smiling boldly saying, "I love your bagels! I bet your little hands have been busy baking bagels for hours! I love your bagels! I bet your little hands...."

"You see? You see?" his mother beamed. "You're going places! You're going places! Wait and see!"

"You want that God should help you? That his face shine on you?"

"Oh, by all means, rabbi!" Abe said.

"Well, then, say your prayers, go to synagogue, hang around with the right kind of people, don't get smart with the elders, eat clean, be clean, check your underwear and above all, watch your mouth with you-know-who if you know what is good for you," the rabbi concluded, pointing heavenwards. "Understand?"

"Sure, sure," Abe said as he checked his underwear, muttered prayers, reviewing whether he knew enough or needed to know more.

"Should you do all I have told you, you will most certainly go places," the rabbi nodded gravely.

Abe got even more advice from comedy writers, natural food nuts, haberdashery clerks, and poise perfectionists: from comedy writers on jokes that sailed and jokes that flopped; from the food nuts on the brans he ought to eat to give nature a little help; from clothiers on the cut and color of suits calculated to advance his career; and from poise perfectionists on how to pose and be composed as he positioned himself to move to the top.

"Sure, sure," he said over and over. And over and over, the words echoed, "You've got a future. You're going places!"

Primed with so much advice and decked out in designer clothes, he ought to have successfully launched his career the day he was invited to attend a banquet at which Jesus of Nazareth was to be present. Big shot politicians and religious leaders were to be in attendance. So, too, the directors from the local community theaters! They were always looking for new talent and Abe was excited about them being present. After all, he had been acting for so many years he felt he had a good shot at getting a part in a play.

When he arrived at the home where the party was being given, he began to panic. Was he ready for all of this? Perspiring, he momentarily excused himself, went to the restroom, checked out his smile in front of the mirror, rehearsed a few prayers he had learned to impress the religious folk, checked his underwear, popped a peppermint in his mouth, rechecked his underwear, and assuming an air of nonchalance he reentered the room.

Smiling at anyone who looked in his direction, he seated himself next to an elderly gentleman. Still smiling, he cocked an ear towards the old gentleman who appeared to be whispering something to him. "What was that?" Abe asked. "Could you please speak a little louder?" The old man leaned closer to Abe but he still couldn't understand him. Straining both to keep smiling and understand the old man, Abe said, "I still can't hear you; please speak louder."

"I said," the old man yelled as everybody turned and listened, "You are sitting in the guest of honor's place. You'll have to go somewhere else! Need I say more?"

Abe was stunned, his smile froze as his face turned crimson. "I ... I ... I...." he stammered, rising to his feet and accidentally tripping on the back of the old man's robe. Quickly retreating to an open place far, far away from where he had been sitting, Abe fell into a little heap, eyes downcast, wishing with all his heart he were invisible. Mortified, he contemplated his future. Once the word had gotten around about what had happened, he couldn't possibly get to the top. He was going nowhere!

No sooner had this thought taken possession of him than someone cheerily advised, "If you really want to get to the top, why don't you sit in the kind of place you are now with the nobodies, about as far from the head table as possible? You'd be surprised what can happen. You might get invited to sit next to the somebodies. Then everybody will say, 'Somebody likes him; look where he's being seated! He must be somebody. He's really going places!'"

Abe turned his head toward a young man sitting next to him. He was nibbling a Ritz cracker. Grinning, the man continued, "Anyway the important thing to remember is if you're always trying to make it big and go to the top, you've got to play too many games. Then you're bound to feel tied up in knots, and that leads nowhere but down, down! But if you stop playing games, you can really have fun just playing at being you and not someone you're not. Sounds great, doesn't it? A line I like that sums it up nicely is, 'Those who exalt themselves shall be humbled and those who humble themselves shall be exalted!' Sounds more Chinese than Jewish, but it's true nonetheless."

The man laughed and it was so infectious that Abe laughed too! He hadn't laughed this freely in years. In fact, he hadn't been on this kind of a high ever. He realized he probably was never going to the top after today, but now that didn't seem to matter so much.

"Jesus! Jesus!" The old man who had told Abe to move was waving his hand. "Come up here! This seat is for you!"

"No, I'm just fine where I am! I'm having a great time with my friend," the man next to Abe said as he placed his arm around Abe's shoulder. Abe's mouth dropped open. This man talking to him was Jesus of Nazareth.

"Well, I'll be...." Abe cried, tears coming down his cheeks. "This fellow Jesus obviously enjoys himself wherever he's at and he has no need to get to the top!" Abe thought. He laughed. "I guess he's already there!" Then Abe sat back, relaxed, and enjoyed the view from the top with Jesus.

Reflection

Great performers are called stars; and as we know, stars shine. But the star's light is derived from a good performance, and not necessarily from the performer's personality. We can marvel at a brilliant performance by Vanessa Redgrave in *Orpheus Descending* but her performance doesn't give us a clue regarding her personal incandescence. Likewise a hack performer may radiate a personal light of which only a few close friends are aware. While the difference between a brilliant stage performance and personal brilliance may be of minor interest to most of us, the difference between the performances we deliver in our daily lives and our true stellar qualities ought to be of primary interest to all of us. Why?

Because mistaking our performances for our selves hides our light under the basket of pretense even if the performance is a good one. And many of us are performing without knowing it. Like Abe, we have been prompted from an early age on how to talk, listen, feel, and react in a variety of situations. We have been coached into acting in certain ways in public to win what we or someone else wants for us. Our scripts come from parents, friends, relatives, schools, synagogues, churches, government, etc. Often without realizing it, we are reading the lines and going through the motions determined by the script.

At some point in the life cycle it is important to consider whether the words we speak, the choices we make, and the actions we perform are our own or those of someone in performance. For however brilliant the performance, if we get lost in someone else's script, then our light will remain hidden under the basket as we live lives of inauthenticity.

The question comes down to this: Who's the shining star? The person or the performer?

Eleventh Hour

The reign of God is like the case of the owner of an estate who went out at dawn to hire workmen for his vineyard. After reaching an agreement with them for the usual daily wage, he sent them out to his vineyard. — Matthew 20:1-2

"Sure! At the eleventh hour. You might know it. At the eleventh hour they come in. Who do they think they are?" Zeke was waving one hand in the air while he counted out bagels with the other in the back room of his Hard Earned Bagel Shop. "Five cinnamon with raisin. Five raisin without cinnamon." He paused, then grumbled again, "Eleventh hour! Three raisin with diet cinnamon ... or, was it three diet raisin with cinnamon? Well, we only have the diet cinnamon, not the diet raisin. So, they get what they get," he said with a note of finality. "What do they expect? Placing their order at the eleventh hour? Other people order a day early. They don't wait until the last minute. What do these johnnie-come-latelies think we're here for? To save them from some last-minute embarrassment? We run a bagel business, not a rescue squad!"

Zeke folded the cover of the large cardboard container with such force that the bagels within appeared to sigh as whiffs of onion, garlic, cinnamon, and pumpernickel breath wafted out from underneath the descending lid. "So, if we can help people out at the last minute, why not?" Zeke's brother Ezra countered cautiously as he watched him secure the box with string with the finesse of a champion rodeo goat roper. Zeke secured the string with a quick

155

tug and turned ominously towards Ezra. "Sure, easy for you to say. If it were up to you, we'd be giving our bagels away to anyone who walked in the door. With your philosophy I'll bet you a pumpernickel buttered bagel we'd be out in the street tomorrow! Giving away bagel buns the way you do to people who don't earn them." Sniffing either out of indignation or because some cinnamon sugar had lodged in his nose, Zeke flung the cardboard box on the completed-order shelf.

Zeke was proud of his business. And he secretly gloated when he compared his success to Ezra's failure. After all, for years he had worked hard to build up his Hard Earned Bagel business whereas Ezra had come to him, hat in hand, after his own bakery called Bagels For Prodigals had collapsed. "Bagels For Prodigals indeed!" Zeke mumbled as he searched his apron pocket for a hanky. Ezra's enterprise had been doomed from the start. "How," he had asked his wife, "could Ezra expect to turn a profit by selling bagels at half price to people who had little money, most likely because they had squandered it?" Zeke had hired Ezra not because they were brothers — you can't run a bagel business based on that — but because he knew a good bagel maker when he saw one. And Ezra baked and bagged bagels with mind-boggling speed. If only he would stop passing out bagels to the widows and the beggars who snuck around to the back door whenever they knew Zeke was busy at the front counter. That drove him wild!

Yes, Zeke was proud of his business. He had gotten his money the old-fashioned way. He had earned it by working hard. But even as he congratulated himself, unforeseen events were afoot. He could not have predicted as he watched Ezra sweep the floor at the end of the day that within a couple of months a big bagel factory was to open on the other side of town. Nor could he have predicted that their cheaper bagels would eventually drive him out of business.

"From bagel master to bum," Zeke reflected as he sat on a long bench in front of the unemployment office. "How could this happen?" he muttered, head in hands. "And no one will hire me," he added despairingly. There was a glut of unemployed bakers and not even the benevolent brotherhood of bagel makers could bail him out. "What can I do? I have no other skills. Nobody is going to hire a burnt out bagel maker!"

"I need a worker to work in my wine factory today. Are you available?" An unassuming man with a wry smile stood directly in front of Zeke.

"Are you talking to me?"

"Yes."

"But I don't know the first thing about working in wine factories," Zeke confessed.

"That's okay," the man reassured him.

"And it's already late afternoon. You want me today even though it's almost quitting time?" Zeke puzzled.

"That's okay," the man said without any further explanation.

"But I'm a bagel maker. I might not really be all that good at the job you have in mind."

"That's okay. C'mon." The man smiled and motioned Zeke to follow him.

When they arrived at the wine factory, Zeke saw a faded sign over the factory door. He could make out the first letters of a man's name, Mr. P-R-O-D, but the last letters were too faded to make out. However, the words WINE FACTORY were clear. "Mr. Prod's Wine Factory," he mused under his breath. "Sign here," the man said as he pointed to a ledger at the factory entrance. Zeke signed his name, the last in a long list of names. Zeke was surprised and not a little embarrassed as he wrote his name next to the time of day he had arrived at work. It was 4:00 P.M. but in parenthesis someone had scribbled, "The eleventh hour, of course." "Come." Zeke was escorted down a corridor past several men standing in line before an open window. Zeke was stationed at the front of the line where he figured he would be getting his work instructions from whomever was in the office. But it was Mr. Prod himself who appeared at the window and handed Zeke an envelope. Then he smiled, told Zeke his wages for a full day's work were in the envelope, thanked him for coming, and asked him to sign out at the factory door. Zeke's eyes and mouth opened wide. "Quitting time," he sputtered. "But I haven't even started working yet; I...."

"That's okay" the man smiled.

"Yeh, he hasn't even started," Zeke heard the others grumble as his embarrassment deepened.

"So what?" the man shot back with a note of impatience. "That's okay!"

"But I really don't deserve this. I haven't gotten this the old-fashioned way. I haven't earned it." Zeke was really befuddled.

"That's okay," is all the man would say, and it was apparent that no further explanation would be forthcoming.

"But it's not...." Zeke wanted to protest. "It's not okay!" His philosophy, on which he had so frequently lectured Ezra, simply didn't permit this. But Zeke didn't say anything. He realized the man smiling unflustered in front of him would simply continue saying, "That's okay." So Zeke thanked the man and shuffled off, bewildered, to the factory door. As he bent down to sign the ledger, he found to his amazement that now for "time of departure" he had written, "The eleventh hour." But what amazed him even more was that someone had scribbled almost illegibly at the bottom of the page, "Mr. Prod loves eleventh hour people." Zeke dropped the pen and walked out into the fresh air.

His eyes welled up with tears as he thought about his brother Ezra and Ezra's Bagels For Prodigals business. "Maybe, just maybe," he wondered aloud, "we can get back in business, the business of baking bagels for prodigals."

And from somewhere in the factory Zeke could have sworn he heard someone say loud and clear, "That's okay!"

Reflection

Our experience tells us it pays to be an eleventh-hour person. Who wants to be a first-hour one? We've been first-hour persons so many times, we'd prefer not to think about it. Frankly, eleventh-hour people gall us. We work and study hours to prepare for an exam and a roommate studies only minutes before it. Who gets the

A? It isn't fair! Nor is it fair to stand in line in a supermarket for what seems an eternity and then watch some johnny-come-lately be first in a new line forming at a previously closed check out counter. Or recall the movie *Amadeus* in which the court musician Salieri spends so much effort writing music and Mozart comes along doing the same thing effortlessly and so much better.

Initially, we're inclined to divide the whole world up in this fashion. "We" of course are the first-hour people; the "others" are the eleventh-hour types. But is that the case? What do we do with ease that others do only through hard work? Maybe we have a winning smile or an infectious laugh. Maybe we bake mile-high bread effortlessly or enjoy the singing of a mourning dove. Maybe we can tell a joke with great ease whereas others in repeating it simply evoke groans. Yes, we may need to spend time learning the difference between north, south, east, and west or keeping our finances in order. Therefore, like the men in the parable, at times we are first-hour persons — we work and work and what do we get? At other times, however, we are eleventh-hour persons who put out little energy to do what we do and we are rewarded marvelously well.

When Jesus spoke this parable, he was commenting on the goodness of God — it isn't earned. It goes out freely. What we need to look at closely is who is the eleventh-hour person that is the recipient of God's largesse? The answer may surprise us.

New World

Martha, who was busy with all the details of hospitality, came to him and said, "Lord, are you not concerned that my sister has left me to do the household tasks all alone? Tell her to help me."
— Luke 10:40

"Mary, stop eavesdropping. What they're talking about is no concern of yours. I need you here to mash the potatoes."

"Mary. Have you got your ear against the keyhole again? What for? What they're talking about is Greek to us. Help me make the souffle."

"Mary, you've got your foot in the door again. I know what you're up to. Men folks' business is men's, not ours. Let's do the dishes and chat about the weather."

Martha shook her head. Over and over she reminded her sister that what was on the other side of the kitchen door wasn't any of their business but their brother Lazes' and the men whom he had invited to their house to discuss the heavy stuff: politics, affairs of state, religion. "We've got other things to do, you and me. Putting the Swedish meatballs side by side with cheese 'n crackers, sending our turkey and cranberries out on time and being available when we're called upon to serve second helpings or whatever else tickles their fancy."

Mary needed no reminders. But she wondered, "What's wrong with me? Why can't I be happy here in the kitchen where I belong? Why don't I delight in dicing carrots or whipping up mile-high meringues? Why can't I find the joy in cooking and celebrate cuisine? Everybody — Martha, Lazes, the girls, my rabbi — they all tell me the folly of wanting more and wanting to be more than I'm entitled to. But I do want more, so much more than compliments for doing what others say we do best — kitchen work."

That's why Mary couldn't be pressured by her sister to stay away from that door which separated them from the unknown world which only the men inhabited. Although she couldn't make out what they were saying, every now and then she overheard a word or two about who was running for an office, what interpretation a rabbi gave to a point about the law, etc. The little she heard made her eager to hear all the more.

Whenever she had an excuse to enter the room where Lazes and his friends carried on, she'd do so. "Does anyone want anything to drink?" or "Maybe I could get you more cheese 'n crackers?" or "If it's too hot in here, I can open the windows." Periodically Lazes glared at Mary and she realized she had gone too far. Retreating to the kitchen, she found no comfort from Martha.

"You don't belong there! You don't belong," Martha wagged. Humiliated by what her curiosity had prompted her to do, Mary then worked doubly hard in the kitchen: mixing even higher mountains of meringue; peeling potatoes by the bushel. But the more she applied herself to kitchen tasks the greater her passion to discover the world in the other room.

Then it happened. One day Lazes announced, "Jesus is coming. He's the popular rabbi causing all the stir these days. A few of my friends will be joining us for dinner. Prepare something special." Mary had heard of Jesus and she was overjoyed he was coming to their home. She wanted to see and hear him, but she knew she'd see and hear little unless ... unless. Mary's eyes lit up. "Yes, yes, I know what I will do," she thought.

On the day Jesus came to dinner, Mary and Martha had outdone themselves in preparing a magnificent dinner. Before the dinner, they had poured wine into a decanter and Mary quickly offered to serve the guests. No sooner had she entered the room, however, than she appeared to spill some of the wine on the floor accidentally. "Oh, I'm so sorry," she apologized profusely. "Just go on talking. I'll clean it up. It will only take a minute." She just happened to have a wet cloth with her as she got down on her hands and knees and began slowly wiping up the wine. At first no one noticed her. Jesus was talking about how the barriers between the rich and the poor had to be destroyed and that there was room for everybody around God's table.

"And I'll tell you another barrier that has to go," Mary blurted as she finished wiping the wine off the floor. Horrified, she brought her hand to her mouth. Had she said that? Slowly raising her head, she saw Lazes's face reddening and the other men harumphing and sputtering — except for Jesus. He was smiling. "What other barrier did you have in mind?" he asked. Mary slowly rose to her feet.

"I ... I...." At a loss as to what to say or do, she began to retreat towards the safety of the kitchen.

However Jesus raised his hand. "No, wait! Please come and join us. Sit with us. I would like to hear what you have to say." The other men were dumbfounded but didn't dare to protest Jesus' invitation. Warily, Mary walked a couple of feet toward where Jesus sat.

Sitting at his feet, she quietly pointed to the kitchen and said, "Why, rabbi, I mean the barrier between that room and this one."

"Ah, yes," Jesus agreed. "You are right. It has existed way too long."

No sooner had he said this than Martha barreled through the door. Her face flushed with anger, she exploded, "Rabbi, would you remind that sister of mine that there's work to be done in the kitchen."

"Calm down, Martha," Jesus said. "Mary has made her choice. She wants to be here. Let's not deny her what's better for her. If you want to come and sit down, join us. We'll all be glad to come and help you later. Right, fellas?"

The men looked at one another in disbelief. They had no idea what helping out in the kitchen would mean since they had hardly ever entered one before. But at least for that evening they too were going to take a journey to another world. Without so much as glancing up at Jesus they responded to Jesus' question by mumbling, "Right!"

But Martha could not be persuaded to remain and she marched back into the kitchen muttering, "This is where I belong."

"Now where were we, Mary?" Jesus asked. "Oh, yes, those barriers. They have to go. Have you anything else you'd like to say?"

Mary beamed. She was home.

Reflection

Many women react negatively to Mary. After all someone has to prepare the meal! They resent Jesus' apparent dismissal of Martha's complaint that Mary isn't doing her share of the kitchen duties. However, our story enables us to understand Mary's action as courageous and not as self-serving. For years her light had shone in the kitchen, but the kitchen eventually became her basket because it inhibited her from expressing another emergent dimension of herself.

The world of the kitchen can mean any man or woman's world which at one point in time enabled the person's light to shine but which at another impedes it. The impediments which prevent us from moving into new worlds are cultural, familial, and personal. We learn from our families and society what it means to be real men or real women, good or bad citizens, religious or irreligious. This acculturation process challenges us to live out certain dimensions of our selves but it can also prevent us from developing our full potentials. Feminists for example continually point out sexism in the work places and the government. Religious institutions no less than secular ones have also helped keep people under baskets by restricting what women can do.

In "New World" Martha and Mary's hospitality towards Jesus is superceded by his hospitality in inviting Mary to enter a world where her light could shine in a new way. It is also a standing invitation to all of us to explore new worlds of meaning in our own lives. We may not care to accept the invitation because it challenges us to redefine who we are. Fearing the loss of a light we already possess, we might prefer settling for safety rather than risk giving birth to the light we could become.

Can we recall those times when the light born of our risks made taking the risks well worth the venture?

The Master's Return

*Let your belts be fastened around your waists and
your lamps be burning ready. Be like men await-
ing their master's return from a wedding, so that
when he arrives and knocks, you will open for him
without delay.* — Luke 12:35-36

"It's not going to happen to me. Not if I have anything to say
about it," Larry assured himself as he peered through the newly-
installed peep hole in the large front door. "No, it won't happen to
me," Larry repeated thoughtfully. "Now that The Master is on his
way to the wedding I've got to prepare. They didn't prepare. No,
sir! If those five silly girls had been prepared, they wouldn't have
run out of lighter fluid that night. Imagine that! No fuel for their
torches. And instead of being ready to greet the bridegroom, torches
burning brightly, they were off looking for lighter fluid! Silly! Silly!
Silly! Well, I've already taken care of that little matter. The fellas
know they better have their buckets of lighter fluid and torches
ready at all times."

Larry smiled self-assuredly as he walked from the door to the
window and peered out into the distance to one of the stately elms
on the property. "With the alarm system that I've rigged up out
there, I can detect The Master's Return from a block away. I dare
him to reach this door without the alarm going off. And when it
does, everybody will know it. It goes wooo-wooooo-woooo in every room including the johns." Larry paused to admire his own
foresight. "And just to give me a little extra time to be prepared for

The Master I dug a couple of holes around the mansion to keep him from reaching the door too quickly. Nobody's going to call me silly, silly, silly." All there remained for Larry to do was to drill the servants one more time. Larry went over and sounded the alarm.

From all corners of the mansion the ten servants assembled breathlessly. Each carried a torch in one hand and a bucket of lighter fluid in the other. "Attention," Larry cried, and all the servants save one clicked their heels while holding lamps and buckets in readiness close to their sides. "What's wrong with you, Neville? You're never ready." Larry reprimanded the servant who held his torch haphazardly upside down with the wick brushing the floor.

"Hey, relax, man," Neville said calmly as he righted his torch. "Don't get so uptight. Who do you think we're working for? Genghis Khan?" The other servants giggled as Larry tried his best to ignore Neville.

"Men," he intoned striding before them like a general reviewing his troops, "we've got to keep our eyes and ears open. All we'd need is for The Master to come and find us unprepared. I want to run through the torch lighting procedure once again."

The servants groaned in unison, "Again?"

"At the count of three, I want you to light your torches as quickly as possible. There can be no delay. Do you understand?" They all looked at one another, then at Larry, heaved a sigh of resignation, and agreed they understood. "Good," Larry beamed. "Get ready, get set! 1, 2, 3." In a matter of seconds all of them had their torches burning brightly. All that is, except Neville.

Neville took his time as he admired his torch, running his fingers first gently over the wick, and then down the torch's thin oak stem. Finally he lit the lamp and held it before his eyes, awestruck by the little orange flame flickering heavenwards.

"And just what do you think you're doing?" Larry was visibly upset.

"Hey, man. Just enjoying the torch. Take it easy. I'm not a pyromaniac like those guys!"

"Ooooh!" Larry tried to ignore Neville, but he couldn't help mutter, "Never-ready Neville," under his breath. "Okay, fellas, you can snuff the torches. Now, here's your instructions. When you hear the alarm go off, grab your torches wherever you are, and don't waste any time getting here. That way, we'll all be sure to be prepared for The Master's Return. Understand?" Again, they looked at one another, then at Larry and agreed they understood. "Good. Off you go, then." Larry clicked his heels and they all stood at attention, all that is except Neville who was still enraptured with the dancing flame on his torch. "Dismissed," Larry shouted and they all filed out of the room.

No sooner had the servants resumed their various duties when the alarm went off and the wooo wooo wooo echoed throughout the mansion. The sounds of tools dropping, chairs overturning and toilets flushing throughout the building were replaced with the patter of feet racing through the halls as the servants, torches in hand, came rushing down the stairs and into the front room. Everyone stood at attention; all that is, except Neville who strolled into the room, enjoying an apple he couldn't bear leaving behind. He stepped casually into line, lit his torch from the torch of the fellow next to him and continued munching.

Larry faced the door, rigidly attentive, waiting for The Master to order the door to be opened. But all they heard was a faint scratch, scratch, scratch. Puzzled, Larry slowly opened the door, and he discovered not The Master but a small shivering mutt of a dog.

"Ohhh!" the servants groaned disappointedly as they lowered their torches. Larry was flabbergasted! He was about to take his frustration out on the dog when Neville stepped forward and said, "Hey, relax, man. It's only a little puppy. Maybe it's hungry or something." Then Neville got on his knees and called "Here, mutt! Come on. I'll take care of you." Before Larry could say anything, Neville had taken the dog into his arms and left the room. The other servants followed Neville's lead and Larry soon found himself alone.

Hardly had Larry begun considering how to fix the alarm system to screen out unwanted animals when suddenly the alarm went off again. As before, feet raced down the halls and within seconds all the servants were once more in the main room standing at attention with torches burning. Neville, of course, was late as he came nursing the little mongrel with milk from a baby bottle. This time he stood in line without his torch.

Standing more or less at attention, they heard a sharp rap, rap, rap on the door. Larry heaved a sigh of relief. "Thank God, it's the Master," he winked at the servants, as he stepped forward to open the door. But his relief turned instantly to anger when he saw not The Master but a bum darkening the great doorway. "What do you want?" Larry yelled. "Just a bed for the night," the man answered sheepishly. "For you? Are you kidding? We're waiting for The Master, not for you." He was about to slam the door shut when Neville intervened and calmly stayed Larry's hand. "Relax, man. He can use my bed. No big deal. He's tired. Let him sleep. Come on in, buddy." He took the bum inside and the three of them, Neville, the dog, and the bum headed upstairs. The other servants mumbled and glowered at Larry, extinguished their torches and broke ranks.

Larry hoped this was the end of unwanted visitors. Unfortunately for him and the other servants it wasn't. All through the night and into the wee hours of the morning the alarm sounded. Again and again the servants dragged their lighted torches to the door with diminishing enthusiasm. Again and again Larry opened the door only to discover an unbelievable assortment of people, ranging from a hooker who was drawn by all the red lights she saw in the windows to the milkman who was making his early morning delivery. Invariably Larry tried to get rid of the visitors while Neville kept inviting them in.

"Relax," he'd say. "Let them in. We're having a little party upstairs." The other servants grew so exhausted from false alarms, that one by one they fell asleep in their rooms. Larry, on the other hand, was so enraged that The Master hadn't shown up according to his own plans, he finally decided to shut off the alarm system altogether. He threw open the door, ran out of the house, and turned off the switch some one hundred feet from the mansion. However, as luck would have it, on his way back he fell into one of the holes he had dug and momentarily went unconscious.

Meanwhile back inside the mansion Neville had come down the stairs to replenish the salami tray when he noticed the front door standing wide open. And who should be standing there but (you guessed it) ... The Master.

Neville waved. "Hi, boss. We've been waiting for you. Nice to see you're back. We've got a little party going on upstairs in your honor. Come on up and join us."

The Master smiled, pleased that at least someone was there to welcome him. And a party in his honor ... nice touch! "Thanks, Neville. I'd be glad to join you but where's Larry? I thought for sure he'd be waiting for me."

"Larry? I guess he got tired and went to bed, boss."

"Well, I'll have to talk to him in the morning. After all, I don't pay him to sit around and do nothing."

"Relax, boss. He's just a little burned out. It happens to the best of us."

"Burned out?" The Master was puzzled but didn't press the issue as he and Neville went upstairs to the party. And Larry? He had regained consciousness but not all his wits. He remained standing in the hole, glazed eyes riveted on the road leading to the mansion, waiting for The Master's Return.

Reflection

Is it possible to be too prepared? Perhaps the answer to the question depends on what we mean when we speak of being prepared. We have been told since we were children we ought to be prepared by planning ahead, putting something away for a rainy day. We are cautioned not to be caught off guard or with our pants down. We have also been warned to watch our tongue and listen carefully. We mustn't daydream but stay awake. We have to have a clear head and pay attention. After all, one false move and ... and what?

We won't be in control of our future, ourselves, the situation, etc. Preparation frequently means control. We want to be prepared and being prepared means being in charge or on top of things. We don't want things to get out of hand. Larry embodies this kind of preparation. He also embodies a paranoia that goes along with it. He is fearful and suspicious even of the master. Larry goes so far as to dig a trench to catch the master because he doesn't want the master to sneak up on him; he doesn't want anything unpredictable to happen.

But the unpredictable does happen. Life is unpredictable, full of surprises and ultimately uncontrollable. It is frequently messy, muddy, and murky, and attempts at reducing life to the manipulable are not only ultimately futile, they make life unenjoyable. It is in those moments when we lose control and surrender ourselves that we are filled with awe and joy. We lose our breath at the sight of a beautiful sunset or a newborn baby; we are overcome with gratitude at kindnesses bestowed, and we are taken up by someone's unexpected thoughtfulness. Ecstasy is losing ourselves and finding ourselves in communion with something larger than ourselves. It is only when we are willing to surrender ourselves over to whatever is happening that we are really prepared. Then we become like Neville.

Neville is available to what happens. He is prepared to be as available to the stem of his lantern as he is to the puppy dog. Preparation is availability to the predictable and the unpredictable. It is the willingness to be surprised rather than the wilfulness to control and do away with all surprise.

If we are too controlling we shall miss out on the thousand and one ways in which God comes to us. The Master returns but we may have so determined ahead of time how and when the Master will come that we miss him when he actually arrives. *Semper Paratus* is a nice slogan, but taken to the extreme it means *Never Prepared*.

Our Kind

They came to Gerasene territory on the other side of the lake. As he got out of the boat, he was im- mediately met by a man from the tombs who had an unclean spirit ... "What is your name?" Jesus asked him. "Legion is my name," he answered. "There are hundreds of us." — Mark 5:1-2, 9

"We've got to live with our own kind." Whenever Lem said this to Fanny and the kids, they knew they would repeat the famil- iar pattern of packing their belongings, selling their home, and re- locating to a different part of the city.

"But, Lem," Fanny pleaded, "I'm tired of moving. Why do you want to move this time?"

"Too many divorced people in the neighborhood," he answered. "They're a bad influence on the kids." Fanny shook her head sadly. The first time that Lem said he wanted to be with his own kind he was referring to his kind of skin color. "Too many of 'them' in the neighborhood," he whispered, pointing to a Latino walking down the street. "They have a strange way of talking. Not like us!" The second time he decided to be with his own kind, he meant some- thing else. "They don't make my kind of money," he confided to Fanny. "The value of our property is going down because their kind is moving in."

And now they were moving again. "This had better be the last time," Fanny warned. But it wasn't. Within the next year and a half they moved three more times and always because the people in the neighborhood were not Lem's kind. Their worship or politics or clubs weren't like his. They didn't dress or eat or dance as he did. Lem and his family moved to more and more exclusive sections of the city where Lem thought their kind lived. Finally, Fanny had had enough. She gave an ultimatum. "Lem, if you want to move, go ahead. But the kids and I are staying here. We've had it!"

"But, but ... don't you want to be with our own kind?" Lem was shocked that Fanny could think otherwise.

" 'Our kind'? Are you looney? We hardly have any friends left because you keep finding reasons why they're not really our kind. From now on find your own kind on your own because I've decided you're not my kind!"

"Well ... if, if that's the way you want it," he sniffed, "I don't need your kind." A week later Lem moved out of the house into an apartment.

"I'll be fine, just fine," he thought as he looked out of his second floor window on to a neighborhood populated with folks he was certain were his own kind. After all, he had chosen it because the men there wore his kind of suits, they drove his kind of car, voted his kind of politics, and shopped in his kind of supermarket. "Ah, yes, I'm contented here. They're all like me. I think I'll take a little walk down the street."

Lem left his apartment and began his tour of the neighborhood. Humming "My Kind Of Town," Lem hadn't walked more than two blocks when he found himself looking into the window of a liquor store. "Hmmm, I think I'll go in and get a bottle of scotch." Inside he scanned the shelves for his favorite brand. Becoming more and more agitated because he couldn't find his kind, Lem's face reddened and his eyes rolled back so that only the whites were visible. Turning on his heels, he faced the proprietor and screamed, "Where is our kind?"

Startled, the owner asked, "Our kind of what?"

"Where is our kind?" Lem shouted again.

"Sir, your kind of...."

"Where is our kind?" Again the same question but now the sound of Lem's voice was so ominous that frightened customers fled the store. Going berserk, Lem began clearing the shelves of all the bottles. "We want our kind!" he howled. The owner cowered behind the counter to avoid the flying bottles. Shortly the police arrived with a straitjacket and Lem was taken away to a distant place called The Tombs. The Tombs were dreary cells in the psychiatric ward of a hospital on the outskirts of the city. There Lem didn't need to worry about living with other kinds of people because only his kind would ever dare to live there. And what kind was that?

"Our name is Legion!" the voices babbled. "But don't worry, you're our kind of guy! You think, act, and talk like us! Who could ask for anything more?" Lem knew the voices were right. And he was so weary that he wished he could die. In fact several times he had attempted suicide by banging his head against the walls of his padded cell.

"I'm sick of my kind," he cried. "It's a living hell — living only with my own kind. What can I do? Will no one help me?"

"Hey, man, I will," a voice said softly.

"Wha...?" Lem spun around and spied a small, brown-skinned man standing in the doorway. Lem's eyes opened wide. What was this fellow doing here? He wasn't Lem's kind in any sense. He fell to his knees and blurted, "Jesus, Son of the Most High God! What do you want with our kind? Don't punish us!"

"Hey, man, don't get excited. Who do you think I am? My name is Jesus Jimenez [hay-sus he-men-ez]. I'm jes the orderly. You used to live in our neighborhood. Remember? Then you pick up and leave one day, you and your family. Too bad — we was jes getting to know you, man. What did you say your name was now?"

"Legion is our name! There are many of us, but we're really all one of a kind. Please, please help me, Jesus!"

"Jesus, man, not Jesus," he said. "You're in bad shape, man." Jesus knelt down, placed his arm around Lem, and gently rocked him in his arms for a minute. "It's not so bad now, is it?" he said. His voice was soothing, but Lem's body was still shaking. Jesus asked, "Do you wanna stay with me and my family for a while? We got a spare room."

"With you? You? Jes ... I mean Jesus?"

"Yeah!"

"Oh, yes! Yes! Jesus! Jesus!"

No sooner had he said, "Yes, Jesus," than his body quieted down while in a nearby field a herd of pigs were going wild.

Jesus laughed. "I guess they got their own kind of problems ... looks like a pig race!" Lem smiled at Jesus. He was beginning to find his kind of people.

Reflection

When we think of "exclusive" neighborhoods, are we offended? Maybe not. We have heard "exclusive" used so often in relation to beautiful suburbs with expensive homes, perfectly manicured lawns and gardens, BMWs, Cadillacs, Lincoln Continentals, well-heeled and well-dressed people that we may never reflect on the meaning of the word itself. Exclusive comes from the Latin *ex claudere*, which means to shut out, reject. "Our Kind" live in exclusive neighborhoods and "any other kind" is shut out, rejected.

Of course, the people who live in these neighborhoods don't ordinarily exert any physical force to shut out "the other kind." But they probably assume that whoever comes into their neighborhoods had better be able to keep up with their Joneses (if they know what is good for them). Living in an exclusive neighborhood or associating exclusively with certain kinds of people encapsulates us in a very small world. It keeps us under the basket, shielding us from people who have different ideas, tastes, aspirations, and problems. Finally, our passion to be exclusive becomes an affliction. It leads us to reject whatever is different and alien within ourselves. We are afraid of the "inner stranger" who doesn't speak our language, think our thoughts, or share our feelings — but who preys upon us in our moods, our strange desires, impulses, dreams, and obsessions. We are left with our demons, and they are many.

And how can we be saved? By being inclusive. Jesus is the brown-skinned alien who includes, draws in, embraces, and is finally included in Lem's life. To be inclusive is to invite others into our lives. It is to own our inner stranger — our shadow, as Jung named it. We are inclusive when our kind is hospitable toward every other kind.

Are we porchlights welcoming only a select few into our lives? Or are our lights burning brightly for people coming from all walks of life? Could something as simple as driving our car in neighborhoods we rarely if ever visit be our first step in becoming the porchlight, the sign that all visitors are welcome at our front door?

Big Daddy

*The reign of God may be likened to a king who
gave a wedding banquet for his son. He dispatched
his servants to summon the invited guests to the
wedding, but they refused to come.*

— Matthew 22:2-3

"What?" Big Daddy yelled as he gripped the arms of his throne.
"But that's impossible! How could they say no at the last minute?
They told me two months ago they'd be able to attend." Big Daddy's
voice echoed through the royal throne room. He was upset, very
upset. He and Big Momma had sent out wedding invitations months
ago and had quickly gotten replies from practically everybody.
Handwritten notes like "wouldn't miss it" or "can hardly wait" or
"what a privilege" appeared on virtually all the RSVP cards. Everybody knew when Big Daddy threw a party, the place to play
was the Palace. In fact, all the other places closed on Palace days.
Even if some misguided proprietor thought to keep a place open,
no one would show up because the food, the drinks, the entertainment, and the company didn't measure up to what was at the Palace. "Are you certain the royal reminders we sent to the invited
guests haven't garbled their messages?" Big Daddy searched the
chief steward's eyes.

"Our reminders have been trained at the Royal Academy to
listen carefully, Big Daddy," the chief steward replied.

"But why would anyone want to turn down the only bash in
town? When we play the Palace there isn't any other life around!"

Big Daddy tipped his crown forward, scratched the back of his head, and nudged the crown back in place.

"I know. I know," the steward agreed.

"I'd like to know why they're going back on their word — now — of all times? Doesn't it matter to them how we've already gone out of our way to make this a big day for them as well as for Junior?"

"You'd think so," the steward nodded.

"Yes, you'd think so," Big Daddy said softly as he rose and walked a few paces from his throne. "Stu, I know our royal reminders have had special training in correctly giving and receiving messages, but I want to be certain all the people we invited are aware how much time and effort Big Momma and I have spent on this party. Send out the royal reminders once more. Tell them we've got the food and drink ready. Not cheap hamburger but filets. Not low-grade scotch but Crown Royal. Not the Buzz Boys but the Royal Philharmonic. Let them know Big Momma and I will be at the Palace door to greet each one of them. And that we'd really miss not seeing them." By this time Big Daddy's eyes teared up as he repeated in a hushed voice, "We'd really miss not seeing them."

"Big Daddy, I will send out the royal reminders immediately," the steward said as he bowed and left the royal chambers.

The royal reminders set out that very day. Each and every invited guest was reminded exactly as Big Daddy intended. The Palace would be the only place to play ... it would be dullsville everywhere else ... Big Daddy and Big Momma personally would be there to greet them, etc., etc. Little did Big Daddy realize the kind of reaction his reminders would receive.

"Work is more important than playing at the Palace," one invited guest said as he pursed his lips and clenched a fist. "I agreed to go to the Palace before I realized that work is what life is all about. When Big Daddy decides to change the Palace into a stock exchange, maybe then I'll show up."

Another reminder had a problem with someone who didn't even want to open his door when the reminder knocked. "Leave me alone," the voice said. "Who needs parties? Who needs crowds of people? Who needs people? Tell Big Daddy I must have been crazy when I said I'd come to the Palace. I don't wanna be where there's people. You can't trust them. Leave me alone." The reminder stood silently for a moment, wondered what life, if any, there was behind the door. Sadly shaking his head he walked away. The reminder didn't know how fortunate he was to be able to walk away unharmed. Other reminders weren't so lucky.

"Big Daddy is up to something! I don't know what it is but he can't be up to any good. He's got to have an angle. Don't tell me anybody can be that good — throwing a party and serving filets? Hamburgers, maybe, but not filets!" The big man muscled the reminder against the corner of a building. "Listen, buddy. If he's up to no good, you aren't either." Thereupon the man pushed, punched, pommeled, and knocked the reminder to the ground. Leaving the reminder in a pool of blood, the man marched off.

When the chief steward reported to Big Daddy what had happened to all the reminders, Big Daddy was very sad. "They will never be invited here again. Ever. If someone wants to make life one big job, fine. If someone else wants to seal herself off from everybody else, good. And if another chooses to misinterpret my intentions and cast a cynical eye on everything good, then let it be. They have all made their choices. But that will not stop me or Big Momma. Nobody is going to stop us from playing the Palace and throwing our party for Junior." Big Daddy put his arm around the steward, smiled broadly and continued, "Stu, I want you to send the reminders out again, this time to anyone they come across — bag ladies, hookers, winos, exhibitionists, skid row derelicts, gays, lesbians, transvestites, flop house roomers, welfare mothers, unwed mothers, the divorced and remarried and redivorced. Let them know the Palace is the place to be, the only place to really be! Big Momma and I will be waiting for them. Oh, yes! Big Daddy and Big Momma will let them know they belong here — playing the Palace like it was their own. Got the message, Stu?"

The chief steward nodded, bowed, and left the royal chambers. That very day the reminders went out into the byroads and rounded up everyone they met, bad as well as good. And they all played the Palace with Big Daddy and Big Momma like they never played before!

Reflections

"Excuses, excuses!" runs the expression and it could be an alternate title for Big Daddy. On one level the excuses are for not attending the party at Big Daddy's Palace. On a deeper level they are excuses for not participating in life.

What are our excuses and why is it they keep us from being involved in life? Some people will not answer the door when someone knocks. They prefer to watch television or pretend they aren't home. Other persons don't want to risk venturing forth. Too much effort! Too scary! Too little self-confidence! Still others prefer to comment negatively on the involvements of friends, relatives, and neighbors without becoming involved themselves.

But we have been invited to the banquet. We are meant to live our lives fully; and life lived in depth is the discovery of the pearl of great price: the Kingdom. Sad to say, there are those who profess to be in search of that pearl but who refuse to pay the price, which is to live life fully. They say it is the afterlife they look forward to, but this is nothing but a thinly-disguised refusal to live this life in depth.

Thank God the invitation goes out again and again. The story is told and retold and each time we receive a renewed invitation. How many times do we turn it down before it isn't offered again? Or is the offer ever finally withdrawn? Whatever the answer, we waste precious moments by refusing the invitation. Big Daddy is playing the Palace. It's time to go.

Broken Promise

On that same day two of Jesus' followers were go-
ing to a village named Emmaus, about seven miles
from Jerusalem, and they were talking to each
other about all the things that had happened.
— Luke 24:13-14

"Life is a broken promise now that Jesus is dead," Cleo complained to his friend Eli as they walked on the road to Emmaus.
"What's there to live for? Now everything has fallen apart." Twenty-
five years earlier, Cleo had had such high hopes. "My future's promising," he had boasted. "It's looking great! I'm going to find me a
good-looking gal. We'll get married, settle down, and have bright
kids who'll really go places. And I'll own a business that will make
me a mint." A promising future? That's what he thought twenty-
five years ago. But now at age forty-five, it was a different story.

Cleo had gotten married but not to the girl of his dreams. True,
she had pale blue eyes, ruby lips, and a winning smile, but she also
had a nose bent just slightly to the left. She cooked a good meal,
but she couldn't sew a button on a shirt if her life depended on it.
She had a good ear for listening, but she wasn't much for talking.
Humming was her long suit, but she sang with a twang.

As for their marriage, sometimes they'd chirp along, but just
as often they'd growl. Smiling one day, they snarled the next. All
in all the marriage wasn't bad, but Cleo had had such high hopes
— and now life seemed a broken promise.

And his children? The kids who'd eagerly listen to Mom and Dad's words of wisdom? The bright kids who were really going places? One was smart in math but dumb in spelling; the other was smart in spelling but dumb in math. They weren't bad-looking, but they had their mother's nose which bent just slightly to the left. As for listening to their parents' words of advice, they listened all right. Then they'd scratch their heads, shrug their shoulders, and do whatever they wanted. Both of them moved to the other side of town and worked in the local glue factory. It didn't take much to make them happy. But Cleo had had such high hopes for them, and now life seemed a broken promise.

And the promising career? Cleo owned and operated a bagel bakery. Not the smallest business in town, but not the biggest. His bagels weren't bad, but they weren't the best either. He made money, but not the mint he said he'd make. All in all, his was a modestly successful business. But Cleo had had such high hopes, and now life was passing by. It seemed a broken promise.

As if to prove that "there's no fool like an old fool," well into his forties Cleo got suckered in again. This time he pinned his high hopes on Jesus of Nazareth. "Surely he won't let me down," Cleo thought. "Jesus is the one. He's the wave of the future. He's our promise. A real winner! Here! His power base is here and he's going to drive the bully boys away. He'll make this a land of promise again and we'll be on the move." But the promised one was nailed to the tree and left to die a broken man. Hardly a winner and no one's future. Just another broken promise. And for Cleo, the last straw.

"I just don't understand," Cleo complained as he and his friend Eli walked the dusty road to Emmaus. "What went wrong? He wasn't supposed to die. That wasn't in the cards. Where's the winner we were promised? I'll tell you ... nowhere! Sure, a couple of women report he's alive but that's absurd, impossible!"

"May I join you?"

"Wha...?" Cleo and Eli turned to see a man walking a few feet behind. "May I join you? I don't like walking this road alone."

"Suit yourself," Cleo said. "We were just talking about Jesus of Nazareth."

"Oh? What about him?"

"You mean you haven't heard the news?"

"I've been away for three days."

"Well, he's not what we'd thought. Just another flash in the pan, another broken promise." And Cleo proceeded to tell the man all that had happened not only to Jesus, but to all the disappointments in his own life as well.

"Hmmm," the man stroked his chin. "Your story sounds vaguely familiar. About three years ago I was convinced that all of us — my friends, the people I talked to, myself — that we all had a promising future. Changes in our lives were to take place overnight. The day would dawn when people from all over would sit around one table and enjoy each other's company. We knew we'd have to overcome certain obstacles. But we'd win out! We'd triumph! Life seemed so promising!" The stranger paused.

"And?" Cleo waved a hand.

"Well ... not everyone shared our enthusiasm. In fact, some people were downright hostile! Even the friends we counted on most betrayed us." His voice grew raspy. "And worst of all, the one whose support and love I relied on most seemed to have abandoned me when I needed him most!"

"Really?" Both Cleo and Eli's eyes widened.

"Yes, when I was just hanging there, hurting, I said, 'Where are you when I need you?' And, you know, he said nothing. Nothing!"

"No kidding! So what did you do?" Eli asked.

"At first I thought, 'That's it! There goes the future! Promises, promises! Right out the window!' I felt wretched and in a lot of pain. But then I thought, 'So there's a change of plans. So it's not working out according to my expectations! I can't do anything about that. I'll just hang in there, wait, and trust it will all work out. What else can I do?' "

"And what happened?"

"I think I died."

"I know the feeling well," Cleo sighed.

"You what?" Eli was all in a muddle.

"I think I died," the stranger repeated, looking off into the distance.

"But ... you're here. How...?"

"I'm here but ... all I know is that the one whom I thought had abandoned me pulled me through. And now I'm alive in a new way. Even my friends aren't going to recognize me right away. It's a changed ball game, believe me! Just when you think, 'It's over. My life is just a heap of broken promises....' Surprise! Back alive in a way no one expected!"

"Hmmm, I never thought of it that way," Cleo said. Turning to the man he asked, "Have we met before? Your voice ... your smile...."

"Maybe I resemble someone you know."

"Could be. Could be," Cleo said, trying without success to re-call who this engaging young man resembled. However they had reached Emmaus and the stranger told them he had to continue on his way. But Cleo and Eli persuaded him to join them at the bagel factory for a light lunch.

When they arrived, Cleo spread a white tablecloth over a work bench and placed on it a small loaf of bread, a carafe of wine, and three goblets. Once they sat down Cleo invited the stranger to do the honor of breaking the bread. Taking the bread into his hands, the man ran his fingers over the small loaf. "Nice texture! Did you bake it?"

"Yes," Cleo answered. "This morning."

"Ah, freshly risen," he whispered, "and it smells so good." No sooner had the stranger spoken the word "risen" than Cleo's heart began beating faster. He remembered the stranger's words about coming alive in a new way, and it struck Cleo how closely this man's experience paralleled Jesus' — his hopes, his betrayal, his death, and now? Both Cleo and Eli's eyes were riveted on their guest as he broke the bread and shared the cup. When they had finished the meal the man said, "We know each other better now, don't we? I hope you will remember me whenever you break bread together."

"Yes," Cleo said softly. "We will." The stranger rose.

"It's time for me to go. I have much to do. I have many friends with whom I'll be breaking bread. Thank you for your hospitality. Please stay sitting. I'll let myself out." And the man left the house.

"It's him," Cleo whispered.

"I know," Eli said.

Cleo rose, went to the window, and watched the stranger as he disappeared over the horizon. "He's come back, Eli. He's come back!"

Reflection

"Hangin' in there" expresses how we are getting along: how we're handling a job; working through a relationship; doing in school. For some of us hangin' in is not particularly difficult. We're pretty confident that we'll do all right; we'll manage. However, for others, hangin' in there means being painfully helpless. We're not really sure if we'll survive a difficult time: a mid-life transition or the loss of a loved one. The pain of just hangin' in there can reveal just how broken we are in body, mind, and spirit.

The times of just hangin' in there are frequently dark and depressing, hardly times we'd expect to experience any light. Yet, as our story suggests, hangin' in can also mean trusting and waiting. We wait and wait. For what? For something new to develop. For a break through brokenness. For transformation. For new life.

Trusting and waiting doesn't mean that after a period of hangin' in there we finally figure a way out. It means we have reached an impasse and cannot find any way to stop hanging in. All we can do is trust that there is One who is with us as we hang, and that, as in Jesus' hanging and dying, this One will be with us.

Hangin' in there, then, is both a sign of our helplessness and the medium through which we can experience transformation from death to life, not because this has to happen but because we believe that the One who raised Jesus from the dead has promised it will happen.

As the medium of transformation, hangin' in there is paradoxically darkness and light; it is a blinding light. We do not see a way out of our predicament and because we are blind we wait in the dark to "see" in a new way. Is waiting itself the first necessary step we need to take to experience light in a new way?

The Sinner

*He then spoke this parable addressed to those who
believed in their own self-righteousness while holding everyone else in contempt.*   — Luke 18:9

"Sinner — SINNER — that's what I am. A sinner. Rotten to
the core — to the CORE." From the place where Percy invariably
sat in the very back of the Temple he began his confession ... first a
slight bow of the head, then a profound bow of torso and head, and
finally a very deep grovel. Long ago, he had decided that if anyone
deserved to be labeled as sinner, he did. He had spent the following years bad mouthing himself, confessing to God how sinful he
was. And the very thought that God took Percy's immeasurable
sinfulness as seriously as he did caused his spine to tingle. "Ohhh,"
he'd moan, "what a sinner I am!"

Finishing his first round of self-accusations Percy looked up.
"I love it back here," he reveled as he ran his fingers over the worn
surface of the dark pew on which he was sitting. "It's as far back in
the Temple as anyone can get. Whoever would come walking in at
this minute would certainly say, 'Hey! That Percy must be one
mean guy. Look where he's sitting. Way in the back where all the
big time sinners sit.' " Percy's daydreams were cut short when he
noticed a man coming into the Temple. "Pssst! Over here," he
whispered. The man glanced at Percy, took a couple of steps towards the front of the Temple, hesitated, then came over to Percy.

"Yes? You wanted me?" the man asked warily.

"Do you know," Percy said slowly and deliberately, "do you know what *this* pew is reserved for? Huh? Do you?"

The man looked puzzled. "No, I ... I can't say I do. What is it reserved for?"

Percy smiled enigmatically and looked the man straight in the eyes as he hissed, "Sinners."

The man was nonplussed, not so much by what Percy had told him, but by the almost diabolical delight he took in saying it.

"Yup." Percy stared transfixed. "It's for sinners. And I'm the biggest of them all. I've worked at it for years." Then he leaned forward, beat his breast several times, struck his head on the pew, and wailed aloud, "They don't come as bad as I do." The stranger began to panic as Percy continued, "And it's being a real sinner — that is the difference between you and me, buddy." Percy raised his hand as if to forestall any objection. "I know, I know. You're going to tell me you stink too. You might even tell me you stink a lot." Percy dismissed the thought with a wave of his arm. "But you could never stink as much as I do."

The man was positively intrigued by Percy's insistence on his own perversity. He'd never heard of anyone ecstatic over being so sinful. Percy continued on, almost oblivious to the young man enthralled at his delivery, "... and it's admitting you're utterly depraved that really makes you acceptable to God. Own up to your evil inclinations and you're already a winner! But nowadays everyone is ignorant of how wretched, miserable, and unlovable they are. Why, they don't even feel guilty anymore! And where do you think we'd be in this world without guilt?" Percy stopped short after the word "guilt" as if obedient to an internal clock. "Excuse me a minute!" he mumbled. Then leaning forward as he beat his breast resolutely, he finished, waited a couple of seconds, and then pounded himself three more times for good measure before turning back to the young man.

"As I was saying," he continued, "without guilt, who'd come to the Temple? A lot of preachers would be out of jobs. They need sinners to keep them in business. Sinners. Sinners. Sinners. Sinners...." Percy seemed hypnotized by the word and kept repeating it until the other man snapped his fingers in Percy's face. He started and skipped like a phonograph needle, "Yes, our preachers do a thriving business on us louts. They remind us that the world and everything in it is going to hell. Now I ask you. What right do we have to disappoint them? Who are we to claim anything better than being the worst? They've got to make a living too, you know."

"Wait! Wait a minute." The man had heard enough. "It seems to me that if you think you're so bad, you'd suffer quite a bit too!"

"Of course I would." Percy was growing impatient. "Suffering is good, goooood for us — good for the soul. It lets you know you're alive. Like a pinch on the cheek or a slap on the buttocks. And the more you suffer, well, the happier you'll be some day."

"I see. I see," the man said. He didn't see, but he didn't intend to get caught up any further in Percy's vision of salvation. "If you'll excuse me...." The man started backing away, "I want to go and pray for a couple of minutes."

"Sure." Percy gestured, having already delivered the sum of his wisdom. He beat his breasts a couple more times and then fixed his eyes on the temple door anxious for whoever might enter next.

In the meantime the young man had sat down alone in the front pew and prayed in silence. "I'm not perfect, Lord, but neither am I a piece of dirt in your creation. Basically, I think I'm pretty good. And while I've done some things I'm not proud of, my middle name isn't Guilt. My desires sometimes take me where I don't want to go, but they also move me to do what I had never dreamed possible; and more importantly they lead me here to you." Then he glanced back at Percy and with a sigh of relief concluded, "And one more thing, if you don't mind me saying so, I sure as hell am glad I'm not that fella back there."

Then there was silence — occasionally punctuated with the sound of a fist pounding on a breast somewhere in the back of the Temple.

Who do you think went home justified?

Reflection

Isn't it odd someone would be so elated about being bad? Maybe even perverse? It really isn't odd if by that we mean exceptional or unusual; nor is it perverse if we understand the perverse as evil. The truth is, very many people feel good about feeling so bad. Self-deprecation is a covert way of asserting one's importance. How can this be?

All we need to do is watch some of the religious programs on television. There we see a preacher haranguing his congregation over how sinful the world is and how wicked they all are. "Filthy, filthy, filth–ee! The whole world and everybody in it is filthy!" may be an exaggeration of what is preached but not too much. Given the authority of the preacher, what can the assembled do but nod their heads and say, "Amen, brother, we are a dirty lot who deserve the worst!" If anyone in the congregation were to protest and say, "Wait a minute. I don't think I'm that bad. I'm not perfect, but I'm no piece of junk, either," that person would no longer belong; he or she would be ostracized. The rest of the faithful, however, could take a certain amount of pride in having sufficiently beat their breasts and confessed their wickedness. They could feel good about feeling so bad.

All this would be humorous were it not for the fact that the message, "You are no good; you are dirt," is the only message many have ever received about themselves. They were taught to believe that their salvation depended on observing rules and regulations established first by parents and later by other authority figures. If they failed to comply, they were made to feel even worse. Only through punishment could they experience acceptance, but an acceptance conditioned on observance of the rules. Inevitably, the rules would be broken and the cycle of feeling bad, guilty, doing penance, and experiencing a conditioned acceptance was repeated.

It is important we don't read the parable of the pharisee and the publican as an exhortation to confess our wickedness, because this kind of a message gives rise to what has just been described. There are already too many persons whose sense of self is very low. What many need is self-affirmation, not self-denigration. Why we make the good news bad news is sad news since we are left with so many Mr. Bads in the world.

The Topbanana Tree

Now the serpent was the most cunning of all the animals that the Lord God had made. The serpent asked the woman, "Did God really tell you not to eat from any of the trees in the garden?"
— Genesis 3:1

"Either she's not gotten around to getting her wardrobe or she's so naive it hasn't occurred to her that she needs one," Mr. S. wisecracked to himself as he spied on Eve from behind one of the many green bushes in the garden. "I'll wager she is naive. She doesn't seem the least bit embarrassed sitting there sipping tea, naked as a newborn babe except for that silly garden hat she's wearing," he observed. "Hmmmm ... I'll bet Mr. G. would like to keep her an infant too. It would be far too messy for him if she and her husband woke up from their dream of innocence. Then he'd really have his hands full."

"For starters, she'd want a wardrobe. That would lead to agonizing over what to buy, getting Adam upset over her spending sprees, being dissatisfied with what she'd bought, going out to purchase more clothes, complaining to Mr. G. about her problems, ta-da, ta-da, ta-da, ta-da! Yes, he'd like to keep matters simple. But I, for one, don't think that's fair. Why should she have it so easy, enjoying life without any questions or doubts while I find life so complicated? I think I'll pay her a little visit."

Mr. S. slunk over to Eve's garden table where she was nibbling on a chocolate chip cookie. Tipping his straw hat, he asked, "Ssssay, would you mind a little company?"

Not startled in the least, Eve smiled and said, "Oh, no, not at all. Could I fix you some tea, Mr. ... ah?"

"Mr. S.," he whispered seductively. "I happen to be a neighbor. And, yes, I would like a cup." As Eve prepared the tea with just a little sugar, he continued, "What a sssplendid sssanctuary you have here."

"Thank you. My husband and I think it's a bit of heaven on earth."

"Sssss," Mr. S. hissed as his face contorted at the word heaven. Then, regaining his composure he gushed enthusiastically, "Those are mighty nice fruit trees. The fruit looks sssimply sssumptuous! I bet you've sssampled them all?"

"Not quite," she answered. Rising to her full height, the graceful curves of her body now highlighted in the morning sun, she pointed to a tree at a spot where the inscription, "Middle of the Garden," was carved on a marble slab. "Mr. G. told us we may not eat the fruit of that tree," she dutifully observed.

"Wha...?" Worldly-wise as he was, even Mr. S. blushed as she stood there, completely unaware that being naked had implications for onlookers.

"Why are you looking at me?" she asked innocently. "The tree is over there."

Perspiring, Mr. S. murmured, "Oh, yesss, yesss, over there," as he strove to focus on the one tree whose fruit the couple were ordered never to eat. "Why that's the topbanana tree!" he noted approvingly. "Topbanana sends me up a tree. It's marvelous!"

"Topbanana?" The name was news to Eve. "Mr. G. never mentioned its name. Only that we had better not eat it if we didn't want to become topa ... topa?"

"Topbananas."

"Yes. Topbananas."

"Really? Becoming topbananas? What's so bad about that? I'm surprised at Mr. G.," he exclaimed, affecting a disappointed tone.

"I never dreamed Mr. G. would forbid anyone from eating topbananas."

"Why?" Eve's curiosity was aroused.

"Well, confidentially, Eve...." Sliding a finger slowly down Eve's back, Mr. S. continued in a hushed voice, "Topbanana has got twice as many vitamins as other fruit; it's high in potassium and iron, low in cholesterol, reduces chances for cancer, heart failure, arthritis, and lung disease, takes care of irregularity, and ..." he paused as he prepared himself to deliver the winning line, "... just one bite of a topbanana will put you in complete control of your life."

"Gee, does it really do all that?" Eve marveled.

"Most certainly," he reassured her, dancing the fingers of his right hand on the nape of her neck.

"But Mr. G. said we'd die if we ate it."

"Die? Oh never, never. You solve all your problems with sssucculent, sssavory topbananasss. You wouldn't need anything or anybody to tell you how to run your life. Yes, you'd really be topbanana. In fact, you'd be able to tell others what to do."

"Wow! We'd become like, like ... Mr. G!" Eve danced spritely over to the tree in the middle of the garden and fell on her knees. "To think it would take care of irregularity! Adam would like that. He hasn't been himself lately. If topbanana is all that you say it is, then Adam and I would be pretty much on our own. I'm fond of Mr. G. but...," she paused, then added resentfully, "it unnerves Adam and me to have someone always telling us what's good and what's bad for us."

Eve could no longer contain herself. She rose and plucked a topbanana while Mr. S. looked on triumphantly.

"Good, good, go ahead! You'll love it!" he urged.

Eve sunk her teeth into the fruit. "Weeee! Really bitter!" Her lips puckered up. "It looks better than it tastes. I hope there's no aftertaste."

"Oh, no, no," Mr. S. assured her, crossing his fingers behind his back.

At that moment Adam appeared from the other end of the gar-den. "What are you doing?"

"I'm eating a topbanana, Adam."

"Topbanana?"

"Yes, it's the fruit Mr. G. told us never to eat."

"What?" he cried.

"Oh, don't worry, dear! This gentleman, Mr. S., has been en-lightening me about its value. One bite and you're in charge of your life. It's your show and you call the shots. You're topbanana all the way."

"Really?" Adam's eyes widened.

Eve strolled over to Adam and dangled the fruit in front of him. "What's more," she whispered confidentially, "it will take care of your irregularity."

That did it! He devoured it greedily, though his face registered the same sour displeasure.

"I know, I know. It's bitter. But Mr. S. assures us there's no aftertaste."

"Ha! Ha! Ha!" Mr. S. laughed ominously. "No aftertaste! Ha! Ha! Ha! Wait and see if there's no aftertaste!"

"What are you laughing at, Mr. S.?" Eve puzzled.

"Look at yourselves!" he sneered.

"Adam, turn around! Don't look at me," Eve pleaded as she attempted to cover her whole body with her hands. Since this was impossible, Eve ran off to find anything available to hide her na-kedness. Adam stood there dumbfounded.

"Ha! Ha!" Mr. S. pointed to Adam's body.

Adam's face flushed. "What's the matter? Don't you think my equipment is adequate?" he asked defensively.

Mr. S. rubbed his hands together. "Now I know you've di-gested the topbanana. Your question sssmacks of the ssour after-taste you and your sssons will always know. You'll never feel ad-equate again. Ever!" he shouted. Abruptly, he resumed a chatty tone. "Well, I have to be on my way. I'm sure we will be seeing one another again, Adam." He slithered into the foliage as Adam puzzled over what Mr. S. meant about the aftertaste.

Adam began to feel more and more uneasy. The garden which moments earlier had been home now appeared strange and ominous. He wanted to run away, but every direction he turned seemed equally hostile.

Spotting a vine climbing a nearby tree, he grabbed several of its shoots, tied them together, and draped them over his body. No sooner had Adam finished than he spied Eve several feet away. She had covered herself similarly. For a moment they stared at one another, two persons not only aliens on their own land but also to one another.

"Adam?" Eve called softly as if she were speaking a stranger's name.

"Eve?" He found her name foreign too. Warily, as if meeting for the first time, they inched towards one another until they were standing face to face. There was an awkward silence. Finally, Adam spoke. "Why, why did you make me eat the topbanana?"

"Make you eat? I didn't make you do anything," Eve said, folding her arms, ready to stand her ground.

"You practically shoved it down my throat," Adam persisted.

"I did not. Mr. S. was behind it all. He kept telling me how great it was."

"Oh, come on ... don't pass the buck! I...." Adam stopped, waited, and checked himself, sensing things were escalating into a huge argument. "See what's happening? We're arguing and acting horribly. I thought the topbanana was supposed to do away with all our problems. We...."

"It will! It will! We'll manage! We'll call the shots ... oh...." Eve remembered promising Adam that eating the fruit would enable them to "call the shots." Then the words seemed liberating; now they appeared to be charged with responsibility.

"We can manage?" Adam laughed bitterly. "If Mr. S. is correct, I for one am never going to feel adequate again. I'll be trying forever to prove I'm adequate. Isn't that what being topbanana is all about?" Then, looking directly into Eve's eyes, he continued somberly, "We are on our own all right! But I'm not sure this is what we had in mind."

"What are we going to do, Adam?" Eve asked fearfully.

"What are we going to do?" Adam repeated slowly. "We're supposed to know the answer, aren't we?" He paused and continued, "And all we really know is just how helpless we are without Mr. G. What do you say we go and share that bit of knowledge with him? And let him do what we could never do — save us!"

Reflection

Are we satisfied to participate in the light or do we want to be the Light? There is a considerable difference between the two. This becomes apparent if we think of people who get carried away by "light" inflation. For example, a football team wins and the team members, cheerleaders, and fans all shout, "We're number One! We're the best!" Or we get a Ph.D. in Philosophy and lay claim to being The Philosopher. The expression, "A little knowledge is a dangerous thing," implies "light inflation" and all the problems it presents. We know a little but get inflated and think we know everything. We are all light and in us there is no darkness! We think we can make no mistakes, do no wrong, and never get hurt.

But these illusions are generated by light inflation. We aren't really the Light. One day we discover, through an accident or an egregious error or a bad choice, that we are not pure Light but contain quite a bit of darkness. If we are lucky, we might also be ready to call upon the one who is Light to save us from any future light-headed illusions.

Were there times when we felt giddy about our accomplishments? Did we ever think we had it made and could do no wrong? That we certainly knew more about whatever ... than the people around us? And how did this influence our behavior towards others?

Junior

*The father said to his servants, "Quick! Bring out
the finest robe and put it on him; put a ring on his
finger and shoes on his feet. Take the fatted calf
and kill it. Let us eat and celebrate because this
son of mine was dead and has come back to life.
He was lost and is found." Then the celebration
began.*   — Luke 15:22-24

Dressed in red running trunks, a blue Down-On-The-Farm
sweatshirt, baseball cap, and sneakers, Junior gazed steadily at himself in the full-length bedroom mirror. He assumed several poses:
charming; witty; sexy; business like; bon vivant. Junior sighed. He
was compelled to conclude the world was waiting to see him and it
was time to strike out on his own. All he needed was to convince
his daddy he was making the right decision. But that didn't promise to be easy. Daddy would never understand his need to get away.

After all, Junior had the run of a mansion large enough to hold
conventions. He had three squares a day, a sizeable monthly al-
lowance, and, of course, a daddy who doted on him something
awful. True, not everything was perfect. Ralph, his older brother,
spent all his time working and expected Junior to do the same. But
generally Junior had nothing to complain about. Still, he agreed
with the figure in the mirror that his time had come to make his
move. Then and there he decided the best time to approach Daddy
was during Daddy's morning ritual in the chicken coop. Daddy's
spirits were always highest when he was gathering and counting
eggs.

The next morning Junior showed up at the coop, and seeing Daddy was in a happy, egg plucking mood, he made his move. "Daddy, I want to split!" Looking around briefly, Junior grinned, "I gotta fly the coop, if you know what I mean!" Daddy dropped the large basket of eggs in the chicken poop. He didn't know what Junior meant. "You wanna leave this?" The old man puzzled as he waved his hand around the coop. "What's gotten into you?" he muttered as he knelt down to sort out the broken eggs from those still intact. "Daddy," Junior pleaded. "I gotta go. There's a big world out there, just waitin'!" "Waitin'?" Daddy interrupted. "For what?" "For me, Daddy, for me. An' I can't wait. The world can't wait any longer. All I want from you is what's coming to me as if you had already died." Junior brought his hand to his mouth. "Did I say that?" he gasped. Stunned, the old man dropped the basket a second time. Junior thought it wise to help Daddy in retrieving whatever unbroken eggs might still be left. "Do you understand, Daddy?" By now Junior was kneeling alongside Daddy and dropping eggs like bombs into the basket. "No, I don't." The old man shook his head sadly. "But if you've made up your mind, I'm not going to hold you back. But," choked up with emotion, he interrupted himself and lectured, "stop droppin' those eggs like that in the basket. I wanna have at least enough left for an omelet." Then his face softening, the old man practically whispered, "I'll have the servant give you the money this afternoon." "Thanks, Daddy," Junior smiled as he rose to his feet. "I knew you'd understand." Junior pushed open the coop door, threw his baseball cap into the air and shouted, "I'm on my way. I'm on my way." Yes, he was on his way.

Off to a far country — twenty miles away. The first thing he did was splurge on expensive snakeskin boots, a Stetson hat, Levis tight as tight could be, and a red kerchief to drape around the collar of a new white silk shirt. Facing the mirror in his Motel 6 room, Junior primped and preened. Cracking his Dentyne gum, he drawled, "I'm ready for the big time." Strutting to the door he felt the perspiration gathering under his arms. "Damn," he whispered as he felt its tell-tale traces on his shirt, "I'm just a little nervous. Maybe I oughta stay in tonight and work crossword puzzles —

like I do at home," he muttered, retreating a step or two. But he stopped, crossed his arms, and told himself he hadn't come this far just to spend time in a motel room. Staring intently at the door, he said, "The world is out there at my feet. I gotta go. I gotta go." Marching to the door, he turned the knob and pushed it open to the evening air.

Out on the street, Junior's eyes grew big as silver dollars. His mouth dropped open an inch or two. "Wowee!" he cried. There they were. Ladies of the night. Sashaying on one side of the street; striking inviting poses on the other. Leaning on street lamps and lounging in second story windows. All shapes and sizes. "Hi, there, hot buns! Want a little fun?" out of the shadows in an alley a seductive voice beckoned. "Gollee!" Junior gasped. "Someone's there waitin' for me." He hesitated a minute, perspiration beading on his forehead. Then, mustering his determination, he said, "I can't deny her." Junior tipped his Stetson forward, flexed his muscles, flung his shoulders back, whistled softly, and stepped into the shadows.

"Pow! Wham! Bop!" There was scrambling, then the patter of feet fleeing quickly into the night, and finally a low moan. "Ohhh!" Junior crawled haltingly into the light of a street lamp. Gone were his snakeskin boots, his tight as tight could be Levis, his wallet.

Naked, except for blue shorts with the embroidered monogram J, a Stetson covering his ears, and his red kerchief, Junior staggered barefoot back to his room. "Those ladies pack some wallop," he mused as he examined the raccoon rings forming around his eyes. "Daddy never told me it could get so rough! No matter! Tomorrow there'll be time for fun and games. Meanwhile, I think I'll have me some milk and cookies." Junior ordered out and shortly was munching on Oreos dunked in milk — a favorite snack of his at home. "Just like bein' at home," he purred. Having eaten his fill, Junior fell back on the bed and drifted off to sleep.

The following afternoon Junior was ready to go again. "The gamblin' halls are waitin' for me," he persuaded his partner in the mirror. He was modeling new tight as tight can be Levis and new ostrich-skin boots he had purchased that morning. "Now I gotta go and strut my stuff." He tipped his Stetson, popped a stick of Dentyne in his mouth, and swaggered towards the door. But then he halted and scanned the room. "I wonder if there's any old comic books around — like at home." Quickly he answered himself, "What am I talkin' about? I can't stay here. I've gotta show them all a thing or two at the gamblin' hall." Flinging his shoulders back, he turned the knob and opened the door to the world of the gambling halls.

"A shot of your finest brandy. It's what I need to get the juices going," he confided to the bartender at Ben's Big Bucks Gamblin' Palace. "Then you'll see me take the place by storm!" A shot it was and then another and then.... "Who does he belong to?" were the last words Junior heard. And the next thing he knew he was staring at the ceiling from his Motel 6 bed. A milk and cookie man he was; a brandy man he wasn't. "Ohhh," he groaned. "Someone's playin' with my brain." Panicking he felt for his Stetson — it was there; his kerchief — there; his monogrammed shorts — on but backwards; his Levis — gone; his boots — gone. His wallet? Why even check? Resigned, he thought, "Tomorrow there'll be fun and games. But not today." So all that day he slept and in the evening he hauled out a pack of cards for solitaire. "Daddy and I used to have so much fun playin' cards," he thought as he looked longingly out into the night. Setting aside the cards he reassured himself. "I'll be all right. What I need is some milk and cookies." Once more he ordered out for his favorite and ended the evening bingeing on milk and Oreos.

Late the next morning he washed and shaved. "Today's the day I'm really goin' to have fun. I just know it," Junior chortled. Bracing his cheeks with Country Spice, he grinned and winked at the mirror. Then he studied himself: Stetson, kerchief, boots, tighter than tight can be Levis purchased an hour earlier. "That's it!" He passed inspection. Tilting his Stetson forward, he strode to the door, turned the knob, paused, and reflected, "Hmmmmm! If I were home today, I'd be going fishing with Daddy." Then he cut the air with his hand. "No, I can't think about that. I'm off to the races! I'm goin' to show them how to bet. It's my lucky day, I'm bound to be a winner." And he opened the door to the world of the race tracks.

Junior placed his bet on Lucky Legs — a thousand to win! Then he sauntered into the boxes with confidence to spare ... and five minutes later he came running out a loser — minus leather boots, tighter than tight Levis, and of course his wallet. So certain was he Lucky Legs would win, that he had told the fella sitting next to him, "I'll bet my Levis and my boots and all that's in my wallet that Lucky Legs will win!"

"It's a deal, guy," the fella eagerly shook hands.

Too bad for Lucky Legs. No sooner had she cleared the gate than she stumbled like some drunkard weaving home. And it was off to the glue factory for her. "Hey, guy," the fella elbowed him. "Pay up — now!" What could Junior do but strip to his shorts, hand the booty over, and Stetson pulled low, gallop out of the stadium. This way and that he scurried. Finally, he hid himself in a clump of bushes until evening and then high-tailed it back to the room in his shorts.

"What'll I do? What'll I do?" he panicked as he paced the floor. "I've nothing left — not even a pair of pants." Sinking on the bed he scanned the want ads. His eyes fell on a small ad tucked at the bottom of page twenty-one. "Fodder Feeder Wanted. No talent needed. No experience needed." And in very fine print ... "Just a very strong stomach." Junior had no time for small print. "Hmmmm. Fodder Feeder? Sounds pretty good to me. Besides, I've gotta go. I've nothing left." As he lifted his head, he caught sight of the pathetic-looking figure in the mirror. That was all he needed to spur him on. Having plopped on his Stetson, shoulders slumping, he slunk to the door, and asked sadly, "I wonder if Daddy misses me?" Then he opened the door to the world of the fodder feeder.

"This isn't what I had in mind when I answered that ad," Junior grumbled on the second day of fodder feeding. He was ankle deep in pig crap. "Why didn't they say a 'pig fodder feeder'? I call that false advertising." Arms filled with corn cobs, Junior looked the picture of despair as he threw cobs one by one to (or at) the pigs. They in contrast were squealing with delight. "Doesn't take much to make them happy," he grumbled as he stood forlornly in his shorts 'n Stetson. "Fodder feeder indeed! Big success I am! No clothes. Nothin' to eat. And ..." he paused, tears forming in his eyes, "I miss Daddy." Junior wept quietly for a couple of minutes.

"What am I doing here? I want to go home. Yes, home. But how can I? After all I've done. Still, I've got to. What'll I do? What'll I do?" Tapping a cob against his furrowed brow, Junior thought and thought. "I know," he exclaimed, lifting the cob high in the air. "Maybe Daddy will take me back. I'll just tell him, 'Daddy, I've messed things up. I've done you wrong. Please take me back. I'll do anything ... help out in the chicken coop, clean the cow barns, anything!' " Reflecting on his words, Junior stood there a minute and carefully rehearsed what he wanted to say. Then he flung the last cob to a startled pig in the corner of the pen and cried, "That's it! I'm leaving."

Walking home in his shorts 'n Stetson, he spied the old man in the distance. Junior quickened his pace and cried out. "Daddy, Daddy, I've messed things up right good. Please, please take me back. I've done you wrong. I've...." "It's okay; it's okay. No need to say anything," Daddy broke in as he hobbled down the path with outstretched arms to embrace Junior. However, Junior had memorized his message and there was no stopping him. "I'll do anything — clean the cow barns, clean the chicken coop...." "No! No!" Daddy put his hands over his ears. His anxiety level shot up. He was overjoyed to see Junior; but the one favor he wouldn't grant was having Junior work with him in the chicken coop. "You're home. That's all that counts." By this time the servants had joined Junior and Daddy, their arms around one another. Daddy said to the servants: "Quick! Bring out the finest robe and put it on him; put a ring on his finger and shoes on his feet. Take the fatted calf and kill it. Let us eat and celebrate because this son of mine was dead and has come back to life. He was lost and is found." Then the celebration began. Junior was home to stay.

Reflection

Junior thinks the world is waiting for him and he fantasizes himself living out different roles in that world. We laugh at his posturing and wonder how he could be so foolish as to think the world is breathlessly waiting his appearance. The truth is Junior is living out the myth we are all called to live, namely, the myth of the hero.

All of us need to know we are called to do something and be someone. Attractive fantasies of the future energize us to overcome whatever obstacles might prevent us from realizing our dreams. One of the obstacles is leaving home. This can be too overwhelming for some people. The secure, known world of the home appears preferable to the unknown, uncertain world a person has to explore in order to live out the dream or vision. And unless that person feels strong enough to do this successfully, he or she will not even take the first step out of the nest.

Junior's fantasies lead him to explore different worlds. Invariably he is unsuccessful in doing what he sets out to accomplish. Of course many heroes do achieve their goals; they are successful in slaying dragons or rescuing maidens. In this regard they are unlike Junior. But ultimately all heroes have to die and be reborn. Die to what? To the sense of self-sufficiency. No one is able to go through life without experiencing failure of one kind or another. And when this happens the hero dies to the self-perception of invincibility. Pictured variously as going into the tomb, the belly of the whale, the desert experience, the night sea journey, etc., this dying leads to a rebirth or a new perspective on life. What is this new perspective?

A person comes to recognize his or her neediness and reaches out to be helped, e.g., Junior reaches out to his daddy and Jesus relies on his Father. We all hope to gain insight from our mythic journey as we move through life: born to be heroes; heroes undergoing death; heroes reborn. The prodigal came back to life all right but not as the boy who left home. The hero was reborn.

Narrow Door

He went through cities and towns teaching — all the while making his way toward Jerusalem. Some-one asked him, "Lord, are they few in number who are to be saved?" He replied: "Try to come in through the narrow door. Many, I tell you, will try to enter and be unable." — Luke 13:22-24

"It appeared in *Haute Couture!*"

"And *Entre Nous!*"

"Not to mention *Pour Nous Seulement!*"

Sipping Darjeeling tea in Mildred's sitting room, the three women were breathless. And why? Each had read in their exclusive magazines about the elegant party which the king was to host at the palace the following month. "It's obvious to me," Mildred sniffed, "that not just anybody is getting in through the palace doors that night."

"Of course not," Marcella agreed. "Otherwise, why would the announcement have appeared in our magazines? Who but our kind get *Haute Couture* or *Entre Nous?*"

"Not to mention *Pour Nous Seulement*," Marlena mewed. "Besides the announcement clearly states that any of us who wants to attend should submit our names to the arrangements committee. What else could that mean except that the arrangements committee is actually a screening committee?"

"And that our kind of people are the only kind who will get through the palace doors," Mildred assured them. "Which means those who have our kind of color: skin, hair, and eyes; who practice our kind of religion: sweet shepherd-Jesus-of the-sweet-talking sheep; and of course the kind of people who live in our kind of homes on our side of town and who wouldn't think of receiving third class mail in their boxes."

"As well as those who love in our kind of way ... which is loving our kind of people," Marcella instructed. Folding her hands, eyes lifted, she whispered, "And who share our ambition to ensure more and more blessings for our kind."

Mildred raised a finger, "Yes, indeedy, very few are going to get through the palace doors!" she purred. "I'm going to write to the screening committee straight away and let them know that Marvin and I are available. I'll let them know we're the kind of people they're looking for."

"Well, Melvin and I certainly know we're two of the right kind," Marlena huffed, "and we thank each other and God for that every night!"

"Girls," Mildred announced, "I'm ready to write to the committee that I am in complete agreement with their policy of being very selective. What kind of an example would we be giving our children if we let every thrill-seeking Tom, Dick, and Harry through the door? Hummph!" Mildred rose to her feet and declared, "Let's write our letters!" The others nodded and each went home to write to the committee.

The letters they produced contained complete profiles of themselves and their husbands: country clubs, credit cards, expensive restaurants, department stores, and banks they frequented, important people they knew, schools their children attended. Satisfied they had sufficiently informed the committee of their virtues and that they deserved an escort through the palace doors, they sent their letters to the palace.

Within a couple of days, each received an invitation to the party. They were ecstatic! Obviously the committee was impressed with their credentials because the invitation read, "The king is especially delighted to have your kind of person at our party." The invitation confirmed everything they had discussed earlier in the week.

The night of the party the women wore evening gowns purchased from Our Kind Of Gown Boutique. Their husbands, Melvin,
Mervin, and Marvin were also dressed to kill. The three couples
stepped out of their plush homes and got into their chauffeur-driven
limos. They formed a mini-caravan passing through the streets of
their suburban far, far eastern neighborhood populated exclusively
with their kind of people: skin, hair, eyes, and cash. Finally, they
reached the magnificent palace doors. "Ah! We've arrived," they
chortled and then broke into a chorus of "The king is my kind of
guy ... the king is my kind of guy...." But their good humor turned
to horror at what they saw when they stepped out of their limos
and looked towards the ancient portals.

People had driven up in old jalopies, Pintos, Vegas, and other
bug-size cars; some had come on bikes, trikes, motorcycles, and
rickshaws. A few even came on mules and horses, while a long
assortment of bag ladies were pushing shopping carts towards the
doors. And the people! They were white, black, yellow, red, spot-
ted, and striped. Dressed in bib overalls, granny dresses, miniskirts,
kaftans, dhotis, or wearing shawls, boas, babushkas, beads on their
heads, they all marched proudly towards the large palace doors.
About the only thing they had in common was the postcard which
they presented to the doorkeepers.

"But I don't understand," Mildred protested. "How can they
get in? Surely they didn't go through the screening committee?
How could they? They don't have special invitations like we do!
Doorkeeper, what is going on?"

"Ma'am, the king sent out invitations on postcards to everyone in the realm. See!" The doorkeeper showed Mildred a postcard on which was printed the invitation and it was worded exactly
the same way as was hers: The king is especially delighted to have
your kind of person at the party. The doorkeeper continued, "Well,
you know what happens to third class mail. Sometimes people just
ignore it! So, after the postcards had been sent, the king decided to
publish the announcement in a few magazines and requested that
anyone who wrote to his arrangements committee be given an invitation. That is the kind of invitation you are holding."

"But ... but, the king is letting in people who aren't our kind!"

"Our kind? I'm sorry I don't understand what you mean," the doorkeeper answered. "Are you coming in?" he asked.

The three couples wailed in unison, "But they're not our kind! They're not our kind! How can we go in when they're not our kind!"

By now people were streaming in — from the inner city, the countryside, the suburbs, the farms. In order to accommodate the crush, the doorkeepers opened the huge palace doors even wider and admitted the guests without requiring them to show their postcards. From outside it was possible to see into the grand ballroom. Everyone inside was dancing, singing, feasting, and enjoying one another. The king stood in the middle of it all, laughing and kicking up a storm! Still Mildred, Marlena, and Marcella and their husbands Melvin, Marvin, and Mervin chanted, "We can't go in! We can't go in! Not with any other kind but our kind!" Pounding their fists, they refused to go through the doors either because they didn't want to go in or because it had now become impossible. Had they locked themselves out?

One thing was very evident that night, they were truly spending the evening with their kind of people!

Reflection

Some people's understanding of being special is being superior to and therefore better than everyone else. As a game it is known as One Up.

One Up can be inoffensive. If we say to a friend that we caught a fish twelve inches long and, winking mischievously, our friend says that he caught one fifteen inches long, he is one up. Or, if we say that all of our brothers and sisters graduated from college and our friend says all his graduated with honors, our friend is one up. However, if we quickly add that the members of our family went to Yale when we know our friends' family all went to Dogpatch U., then we are one up. The game becomes nasty when we tell our friend that our mother makes great meatloaf because she doesn't use cheap meat like some mothers we know. That is being one up by cruelly putting down another. It's a more serious thing when we find it necessary to put down another's point of view, eating habits, dress habits, religious convictions, etc., in order to be one up. The game creates division. Why, then, do we play it?

Are we are afraid of losing our individuality — that which makes us who we are? If we are no different from others, then who are we? What is our worth? Our value? Instead of establishing our uniqueness, playing the game of One Up turns us into PODs — Possessive, Offensive, and Defensive. PODs are dependent on what they own for self-definition and so they become increasingly possessive. They attack others' integrity and grow offensive. They think others are out to get them (just like they are out to get everyone else) and this makes them defensive.

How do we ever stop playing One Up? How can we escape the destiny of a POD? It only stops once we realize that being unique doesn't mean being completely independent from others, and then acknowledge our interdependence. We are most ourselves when we relate to others in ways which emphasize our mutuality. A model is beautiful because there is someone to admire her. What is a doctor without a trusting patient, or a teacher without a docile student, or a preacher without a receptive congregation?

Letting the light shine doesn't mean outshining others so much as highlighting and being highlighted by others as in a colorful rainbow of light. Attempts to outshine others are just another way we hide the fact that we are still in some ways possessive, offensive, and defensive — PODs, and not persons of light.

Do we understand that we stand to gain by acknowledging our interdependence with all of creation? Do we realize we risk losing everything if we insist on establishing our light as the only light?

Fun

*The father said to his servants, "Quick! Bring out
the finest robe and put it on him; put a ring on his
finger and shoes on his feet. Take the fatted calf
and kill it. Let us eat and celebrate because this
son of mine was dead and has come back to life.
He was lost and is found." Then the celebration
began.*   — Luke 15:22-24

"It's my turn now. I've had to put up with a lot of crap over the years, but now that Junior's home he can take over." Ralph was simultaneously removing moth balls and shoving whatever clothes were within reach into his suitcase on the bed. The wide-eyed servant listened in astonishment as Ralph continued. "Do you know how many years I've had to listen to Daddy talk about Junior?" Ralph stopped packing momentarily as he shouted at the servant.

"Well, I...." the servant tried to answer.

"More years than I can remember! And do you know how many years we kept an empty plate at the table?"

"Well, I...."

"More years than I care to remember." Ralph was thoroughly worked up. "But now I'm going to live it up. Oh, yes, I am! I guess you've already gathered that, haven't you? Why else would I be wearing these outrageous clothes? You've never seen me with a plaid shirt, plaid pants, and plaid shoes before, have you? Or sporting really outlandish looking suspenders, have you?" Ralph snapped his multi-colored suspenders and strutted back and forth in front of the servant.

209

"Well, no," the servant had to confess. Ralph's ensemble was quite a switch from the bib overalls, the large straw hat, and army boots the servant was accustomed to see Ralph wearing. He wanted to add that he hadn't heard shoes squeak as loudly as Ralph's plaid shoes did whenever Ralph made the slightest move.

"No, you've never seen me dressed outrageously, and you certainly haven't ever seen me act outrageously. Not ole Ralph. Oh, no! I've done everything according to the book ... fed the cattle, milked the cows, taken care of the chickens, and everything else I was told to do. But that's over. Now it's fun time. F-U-N. Junior is home. So let Junior take over." Ralph wrestled his suitcase to the floor and knelt on it to secure the latches. No sooner had he finished than someone was knocking at the bedroom door. "Who is it?"

"It's Daddy." Ralph motioned the servant to open the door. A little man with a long white beard stood in the doorway.

"Is that a new bedroom outfit you're wearing or are you modeling some new drapes I don't know about?" the old man wisecracked.

Ralph ignored the old man's disparaging remarks. "Look, Daddy, I know what you're here for. But I'm not changing my mind."

"Reconsider, son. You know all I have is yours. Really."

"I've heard that line before, Daddy. It didn't work then and it isn't going to work now. I want what is mine to be all mine now!" Ralph's words sounded vaguely familiar.

"And I think I've heard that line before too," the old man quickly added.

"Junior said that, not me," Ralph reminded him.

"Maybe we can sit down and talk it over," the old man pleaded.

"No, no, no," Ralph insisted.

"What do you think you're going to do when you leave here?" the old man wondered.

"I'm going to have fun."

"F-U-N," the servant unintentionally blurted out and immediately brought his hand to his mouth. "Sorry, sir," he said as both men glowered at him.

"I've never had any fun. But now I'm going to live it up. Just like Junior did." Ralph's eyes shown wild as he spoke.

"But you don't like fun. You never have. You've always wanted to work. When you and Junior were kids, I wanted you to play and have fun. Do you know what you said whenever I encouraged you to play?" The old man shook his head recalling Ralph's response.

"No," Ralph puzzled.

" 'I wanna work. I don't wanna play and have fun.' "

"Well, now I'm going to make up for lost time. He had fun. So now I'm going to have fun even if it kills me. Fun, fun...."

"F-U-N," the servant broke in a second time and once more brought his hand to his mouth as the two men glared at him.

"Okay, son. Go ahead." The old man relented.

"Do you mean it?"

"Sure. Go on and have your fun. By the way, Ralph, what's the first fun thing you're going to do?" the old man feigned disinterest.

"The first fun thing ... um." Ralph brought his hand to his forehead. He hadn't thought far enough in advance to determine what the very first fun thing was he would do. "The first fun thing I'm going to do is ... live it up with loose women." Ralph beamed.

"Loose women?" The servant rushed his hand to his mouth to prevent himself from laughing.

"Loose women?" the old man repeated. He too tried to stifle a laugh by pretending to cough.

"Yes, loose women. What's so funny about that?" Ralph looked from the servant to his father and back again. The servant began to open his mouth but then decided he had better let the old man handle this one.

"What are you going to do with loose women, son?" the old man said as he stroked his beard.

"What does anyone do with loose women?" Ralph shot back. "Loosen them up more, of course!"

The servant immediately grabbed his handkerchief and immediately shoved it into his mouth to muffle another laugh. Ralph took a few steps towards the servant. However the squeak, squeak of his shoes momentarily caught them all off guard as they listened

intently to the alien sound. The servant signaled to Ralph by pointing to Ralph's shoes. Ralph muttered, "Thanks," under his breath
as he tried to recall what he had just said.

"And what else are you going to do, son?" the old man asked
slyly. "Besides loosening up women, that is?"

"Get debauched," Ralph mumbled.

"What was that?" the old man cupped a hand to his ear.

"Get debauched," Ralph repeated uncomfortably.

"Debauched?"

"Yes, debauched, just like Junior got debauched." Ralph was
determined he would get every bit as debauched as his younger
brother had.

"And how are you going to debauch yourself?" Once more the
old man challenged him.

"How? How does anyone get debauched?" Ralph was now
flailing his arms in the air as he searched frantically for an answer,
like a drowning man thrashing for a life preserver.

The servant's hand shot up with the confidence of someone
who knew firsthand what it meant to be debauched.

"I know," he waved.

"Forget it. Forget it." Ralph dismissed the servant's offer of
help. "But you can all be sure of this much," Ralph said slowly and
deliberately. "However I get debauched, I am going to have fun,
fun, fun. I'm going to have fun if it kills me. I deserve it and you're
not going to stop me," he said defiantly.

"Son, if you want to have fun, you go ahead. Loosen all the
women you want and get debauched. I can't stop you. I wouldn't
want to stop you. Nor have I ever tried to stop you from having
fun. I just want you to know that Junior and I will be here if you
decide to come back home. And when you get back we'll have a
party that'll knock your socks off. You'll have more fun than you
ever bargained for."

Ralph's mouth dropped open. "Really? You really mean it?"

"Of course I do." The old man's eyes twinkled.

Ralph scratched his head, squeaked his way to the window
and peered out into the distance beyond the farm. After several

seconds, he turned and faced the old man. "I'm not sure I want to leave here at all, Daddy. I was wondering...." He hesitated, then continued, "Could we have a homecoming party now without my having to go away?"

The old man's eyes teared up. He looked for a minute at his son, then turning to the servant he said: "Quick! Bring out the finest robe and put it on him; put a ring on his finger and shoes on his feet. Take the fatted calf and kill it. Let us eat and celebrate because this son of mine was dead and has come back to life. He was lost and is found."

Then the celebration began and ... did they have fun!

Reflection

"Try to enjoy yourself" is harmless advice if it isn't taken seriously. However, if it is directed at people who are always trying to do something, it can be dangerous. To try is to "work at" and how can a person work at enjoying? It is a contradiction just as trying to do nothing and trying to relax are contradictions. Still, we pursue contradictions with an erstwhileness that is remarkable.

We read in "Fun" that Ralph is intent on having fun as Junior did. Undoubtedly, Ralph resents his younger brother who expresses the playful side of himself which Ralph has never lived out. Daddy reminds Ralph of his chronic need to be working. Given that addiction, how can he now have fun? "Living it up with loose women" and "getting debauched" are new work projects Ralph will undertake, not occasions for having fun! When Ralph goes on the road, he will be dragging his work bench along with him. In this respect he isn't unlike tennis players, golfers, joggers, etc., who are deadly serious and grimly determined to enjoy themselves.

Can Ralph get out of his bind? Can we, as we try to enjoy, relax, not worry, etc.? Ralph's saving moment is being caught off guard by Daddy's offer of a party. Ralph is disarmed and moved because the party will happen whether he leaves home or not. Not only doesn't he have to do something to enjoy himself, he is unable to try to do anything! Daddy's gracious offer catches him off guard and in that instant joy happens.

Moments of joy like moments of relaxation happen; we can't produce or force them. But we can become aware and savor them when we are caught off guard. Of course we may continue with our old habit of working to duplicate or manufacture similar moments of joy. But we only discover once again that it is in the moment when we are disarmed and caught off guard again they can "happen" to us at all.

What does all this tell us about trying to pray or trying to have faith? Does it tell us we ought not to assume sole responsibility for carrying the burden of being a person of prayer and faith? That, like moments of joy, prayer and faith happen to us and are given as gifts, not as something earned by trying hard.

Daddy

A man had two sons. The younger of them said to his father, "Father, give me the share of the estate that is coming to me." So the father divided up the property. — Luke 15:11-12

"Junior, you've done it again! Putting Exlax in the chocolate chip cookie batter for Ms. Purdy's baking class. What am I going to do with you? Your brother Ralph never did that. He's responsible. Tell me, son, how much Exlax did you use? And did they have to call off classes?"

"Junior, you owe Reverend Duffy an apology. He was kind enough to visit and give us Sunday school literature. Why'd you drop the water balloon on his head from your bedroom window? Your brother Ralph wouldn't do that. He's responsible. What I'd like to know is ... what was the expression on the reverend's face when he got drenched?"

"Junior, how many times have I told you I don't want any egg throwing contests in or out of the coop! It puts the chickens off schedule for a week. I never saw your brother Ralph and his friends do that. He's responsible. Just the same, who hit the target most?"

"Momma, I don't know what we're going to do with that boy," Daddy pondered as he brought the cup of coffee to his lips at the breakfast table. "He's a hell raiser!" he added with thinly veiled praise.

"Mmmm," Momma studied Daddy's face carefully as he shook his head over Junior's latest caper. She was more interested in how Daddy would handle it than with the incident itself.

"Imagine, running off with the girls' clothes while they were skinny dipping in the river," he muttered with feigned indignation.

"Yes, imagine...." Momma repeated, not taking her eyes off Daddy.

Leaning back in his chair, he sighed, "My goodness, that must have been some sight ... ten girls trying to decide which one would scramble up the tree to get their clothes back." Barely disguising his admiration, he added, "And with Junior watching from the top of the tree!"

"Sounds like you wish you had been there," Momma remarked as she took another sip of coffee.

Too quickly dismissing her observation, he protested, "Oh, no, no, Momma. I simply want to get a clear picture in my mind of exactly what happened so I can deal with the situation. What Junior did was wrong. He'll have to be punished. We don't want to put up with any of that nonsense again."

"Just like we punished him in the past?" Momma's voice had a touch of scepticism.

"This time it'll be different! You'll see, Momma," he tried to assure her by shaking his finger indicating he meant business. "He's got to learn to be responsible ... like his brother. Ralph never did anything like that when he was Junior's age. He was careful and didn't need us to look after him. In fact we didn't even notice him half the time he was so quiet." Daddy sat up straight in his chair as he continued his assessment of his older son's character.

"He's a hard worker," Momma added.

"And serious," Daddy contributed. "Maybe too serious," he mumbled.

"What was that?"

"Nothing, nothing," Daddy didn't care to pursue the matter further. He admired Ralph's business acumen, work habits, and his sense of filial duty. Moreover, he had routinely praised Ralph as a model of responsibility to his younger son especially when Junior acted irresponsibly. Daddy wondered if that was a mistake. Hadn't Ralph repeatedly told him, "You expect too much from me," and didn't Junior suffer by comparison? Yes, maybe that was why he didn't care to think too deeply about his relationship with his sons. He was pained to realize how unjust he had been towards both of them.

"So, what are you going to do this time that will be different? What kind of punishment do you have in mind?" Momma inquired.

"I realize now I was too harsh on Junior. So...."

"Too harsh?" Momma interrupted. She couldn't believe he meant what he said.

"By always comparing him with Ralph," he tried to explain.

"By simply mentioning Ralph's sense of responsibility? And then immediately doting on Junior, asking all about his exploits! And you think you've been too harsh on him? Who are you trying to fool?" Momma's face was flushed.

"Who am I trying to fool?" Daddy was taken off guard. "I'm not trying to fool anyone," he protested.

"No?" Momma continued the offensive. "You just might be trying to fool yourself!"

"What do you mean? Why would I want to fool myself?"

Just then the kitchen door swung open, and there was Junior. Smiling with a conspicuous innocence, he strutted into the room and grabbed a handful of cookies from the cookie jar. "Hi, Momma. Hi, Daddy."

"Sit down, Junior," Daddy ordered in a manner signaling to Momma he was taking the matter very seriously. However, Junior chose to stand and Momma was not impressed. Embarrassed, Daddy continued, "I've been wanting to talk to you about that incident at the river ... I...."

"Daddy, I'm sorry about that. It was dumb of me to do a thing like that," Junior confessed with less than total candor.

"You are?" Daddy was both relieved and surprised.

"Yeah, but I've got something else that's on my mind. Daddy, I'm leaving here. I got to split!"

"You what?" Momma and Daddy stood up simultaneously.

Admiring himself in one of the well-scrubbed pots hanging over the kitchen sink, he addressed his reflection, "It's time for me to move on. I've been raisin' a lot of hell around here, and I think I can fare better somewhere else." He didn't sound very remorseful.

"Junior," Daddy pleaded, "maybe we can talk. I've been thinking. Maybe I've been too harsh on you. What are we going to do if you leave? You're our son!"

Junior turned to face Daddy. "No need to worry, Daddy, Ralph is here."

"I don't care if he is here, Junior, you're my son. I love you. I want a son here I can love. I...."

"Daddy!" Momma was horrified.

"I didn't mean that...." Daddy replied weakly as he slumped back into his chair.

"Daddy," Junior came to the point, oblivious of Daddy's confession, "I need money. I need plenty of money. I want my inheritance now!"

Tears filled his father's eyes. "My sons, my sons!" he cried. "Yes, yes, they are both my sons and I will divide the inheritance between them. I will treat them equally. But, Junior," and here Daddy reached out to embrace him, "you I love."

"And I love you too, Daddy," Junior said matter of factly as he gave Daddy a quick hug, "but I gotta go. And I don't have any more time to talk about it. You'll be okay. Ralph will be around." Junior walked to the door, opened it, winked at both of them, and said, "After all, he's so responsible." The door slammed shut.

"He's so responsible," Daddy repeated slowly, "he's so hard working and honest. I admire him but, but...."

"But what?" Momma asked gently.

"But the son I love is leaving. And I don't know what to do."

"You'll have to settle for a son you admire and respect," Momma concluded as she got up and began gathering the breakfast dishes.

And indeed there was nothing he could do except hope for the return of the son he loved and continue to respect the one who remained at home.

Reflection

In a day when so many parents would love to see their grown children finally leave home, we can ask why did Daddy hate to see his son take off for a foreign country? Would he have felt equally bad if his older son had gone instead of the younger? The question becomes more interesting if we look at it in terms of our theme of light.

Did the father dote on his youngest son because he rejoiced in his son's light, or did he delight in him because his son bodied forth his own light in ways which he had never been able to live out? Daddy seemed to take a vicarious pleasure in hearing his son's exploits. He seemed to experience some unlived dimensions of himself coming to light in his son's life. When Junior decided to leave home, was Daddy grieving for Junior or because his sole medium for letting his own light shine would no longer be available? His other son had the fortune or misfortune of not being the vehicle of light the younger son was. Perhaps he had been more like his father had always been: sober, responsible, businesslike. If that were the case, he was dispensable, but Junior, who was Daddy's unlived light, was not.

We don't know what happened to Daddy between Junior's leaving home and his return. Possibly the old man was able to live out for himself that playful, childlike side of himself that he had never done while Junior was at home. Possibly, but we aren't certain. We do know that as many overly-serious men mature, they are called to integrate their neglected, playful side. Wisdom comes from accepting the old and the young in ourselves.

"Old Boy" is the designation for the Chinese sage Lao-tzu to whom the classic Tao Te Ching is attributed. Only with Junior gone could Daddy's light side shine in full splendor. Only then could he love Junior in his own light and not as an extension of himself.

Are there times in our lives when we have to "let go" of others if we and they are to discover whose light belongs to whom? Painful as this letting go is, it might be the first step we take in letting be — letting each other's light shine in each's own unique way.

The Dime

What woman, if she has ten silver pieces and loses one, does not light a lamp and sweep the house in a diligent search until she has retrieved what she lost? And when she finds it, she calls in her friends and neighbors to say, "Rejoice with me! I have found the silver piece I lost."   — Luke 15:8-9

"So, I've lost the dime. It's only ten cents." Freeda tried to dismiss the loss as trivial. "What can you do with a dime these days anyway?" she muttered scanning the table where she knew she had stacked ten dimes but now could find only nine. "Buy a pack of gum? Xerox one page of the *Jerusalem Gazette*? Get a second rate postcard at one of the flea markets on David Drive? So who needs a dime?" She shrugged her shoulders and cut the air with her hand, signaling to herself that the case was closed.

Freeda marched across the room to the easy chair and sat down. She closed her eyes for a little rest before continuing her chores. However, after a couple of seconds her eyes had involuntarily opened and focused on the table where the nine coins lay neatly stacked. She shook her head, tapped her left foot softly on the rug and wondered, "But what happened to it? Where could it have gone? It's not important, of course. I don't need it. Plenty more of them in the bank." Once more she closed her eyes, all the time tapping her foot. Soon she noticed her finger restlessly rapping the arm of her chair. "That's it," she sighed as she got to her feet. "It's not important but it's got to be here somewhere. And I'm going to find it." Freeda wasted no time retracing her steps to the table.

"It will only take a minute. I'll find it," she said confidently. "Most likely it's on the rug beside the table. Maybe even underneath the table." Her eyes narrowed as she brought her forefinger to the side of her nose and paused before making her descent. Then she slowly got down on all fours and lowered her head close to the floor, squinting as she scanned the rugged terrain of the shag rug while she carefully ran her fingers over its surface. She stopped, studied the rug again, and repeated the maneuver. Then her right hand halted, her eyes lit up, and she started to say, "I found it!" But she had barely blurted out the word "found" when she realized that her discovery was a paper clip, hardly what she was looking for.

"It isn't worth it. It isn't worth it. It isn't worth it," she declared over and over as she got to her feet. Then seemingly unaware of what she had just resolved, Freeda cried out, "Now where are you? I am going to find you! Wherever you are!"

Obviously, Freeda was no longer in any mood for games. Hands on hips, she surveyed the whole room like a field marshal preparing to attack. She swept the floor with her eyes and continued her gaze right up to the ceiling. The sleuth in her knew perfectly well that the chances of finding the dime on the ceiling were highly unlikely but this didn't prevent her from inspecting each of the wooden beams and every inch of plaster between them. For a minute she paused as she noted cobwebs in the corners. "I've never seen those before." There was alarm in her voice. "I've got to get rid of them." She hesitated. "Later, later," she added as she resumed her investigation and examined the four walls. Her eyes rested on a picture. "No, that's ridiculous. It couldn't be there," she laughed as she took down the picture of her late husband and looked inside the frame between the picture and the cardboard backing. No dime but a love letter lodged there for years. She had forgotten about that letter and her fingers caressed it as tears formed in her eyes. "I'll read this tonight," she promised herself tucking the letter in her apron pocket and straightening the picture in its frame.

"I bet the dime is under the cushion of that chair. It has to be there." She removed the cushion from her favorite chair. There were a couple of kernels of popcorn, two rubber bands, and a fifty cent piece. "Fifty cents!" she exclaimed. "But I don't want fifty cents. I want that dime. It's not important but I want it." Plopping the cushion back on the chair, Freeda buried the popcorn, the rubber bands, and the fifty cent piece for another undetermined length of time.

She looked out the window and wondered if she could have lost the dime on her porch. Highly unlikely she thought. She had hardly stepped outside since her husband died. But she felt she would have no rest until she checked out the porch. Freeda cautiously opened the front door, peeked outside, put one foot and then the other on the well-worn porch. As she quickly swept the porch with her eyes, she spied a couple of forget-me-nots waving gently in the breeze alongside the porch. "How lovely," she thought as she leaned forward to get a closer look.

"Beautiful, aren't they?" a voice rang out.

"What?" Freeda was startled as she saw two women from the neighborhood standing on the walk in front of her house. "Oh, yes! They're beautiful."

"It's nice to see you, Freeda. We haven't seen you for such a long time."

"Well...." Freeda didn't know what to say.

"Are you looking for something?" one of the women asked.

"As a matter of fact I am," Freeda confessed. "I lost a dime. I know it's unimportant but I want to find it."

The two women came closer. "Where did you lose it?"

"I'm not sure."

"Can we help?" And without waiting for an answer the two women started looking alongside the porch in the grass that had grown unattended for weeks. One of the women started pulling weeds so the forget-me-nots had greater visibility and more breathing space.

"Really, it isn't all that important." Freeda was apologetic.

"We don't mind. We really don't. Even if we don't find the dime, I have an extra one in my purse," one of them volunteered.

"Oh, no!" Freeda interrupted. "The dime I'm looking for is very important. It...." Freeda caught herself. "Important? I said, 'Important'?"

"Well, if that's the case ... by all means, let's find that dime," the other woman added.

And so that whole afternoon they looked and looked. They went through Freeda's yard, straightening overturned garden chairs, pruning back overgrown window vines, retrieving abandoned garden tools, and generally putting the yard in order as they searched. The three women even moved into the yard next door and picked a few weeds growing in the flower bed of an elderly gentleman whose arthritis had him confined to a rocking chair on his porch. As other neighbors walked by, the two women enlisted their support. Since the search continued into the evening hours, some of the neighbors volunteered to bring sandwiches, pretzels, and coffee for the workers. Freeda and the others were very tired when they finally retreated to her porch late that evening, forced by the growing darkness to suspend their efforts.

"I don't think we'll ever find that dime," Freeda said as she munched on a pretzel. "I just don't know why it became so important to me," she puzzled. "Why that dime?" she asked the others. They shook their heads. They didn't know as they all ate and drank their food together under the stars that night. They simply didn't know.

Freeda sighed and put her hands in her apron pockets, and ... "What's this?" she gasped as she felt a small round thin object in her right apron pocket. It couldn't be, but it was ... what she had been looking for ... what they all had been looking for since morning. It had been with them from the beginning. Freeda smiled broadly.

As she looked around her and all that had happened that day, she knew now why that dime of all dimes was so important. She relaxed, settled back among her rediscovered friends and the party continued.

Reflection

Freeda's search for the lost dime is limited to a day's time. But this story is about much more than a single day's search; it prefigures the quest for meaning which, like Freeda's search but on a much larger scale, involves us in a struggle we hadn't anticipated. The struggle finds expression in the phrase "still searching."

When someone goes through a period of intense questioning, we can be very understanding at first. The person might be confused about his or her identity, sexuality, life career choice, education, etc., and this may lead to drifting and exploring a variety of lifestyles. But once that person is forty or fifty, and still hasn't settled down, we may be inclined to be more judgmental. "You're still searching? When will you ever settle down?" Maybe a word or two is in order on behalf of those still searching.

Settling down, setting in, rooting, getting grounded, finding one's niche; knowing who we are, what we want, and where we are going are all the opposite of "still searching." But while having arrived sounds appealing, the dark side of having arrived is complacency and stagnation. Settling down and in, our curiosity and wonder disappear. And relationships can suffer because in our complacency we think we know all there is to know about friends, relatives, lovers, and yes, even God.

So from time to time we need to become exposed to the unsettled, confused, searching, still searching side of ourselves which rescues us from the side that has settled in. That still searching side makes us pilgrims again, restless questors, merchants in search of the pearl of great price. The sign of the kingdom is as much in the searching as it is in the object of the search, the pearl. And seeking after the pearl necessarily involves us in getting lost and confused about our direction.

It is true that our "still searching" can be a sign of irresponsibility rather than of our commitment to searching for the kingdom. We have to ask ourselves whether in our still searching we become more open and aware of fellow pilgrims along the way? Do we reach out in greater compassion and understanding to others who are lost or confused or broken? That distinguishes a holy quest from an exercise in self-indulgence.

The Party

As he moved on, Jesus saw a man named Matthew
at his post where taxes were collected. He said to
him, "Follow me." Matthew got up and followed
him.   — Matthew 9:9

"Parties? The last thing I want is a party. They're a waste of time and you can't make money at a party." That's how Matt responded to any suggestion of a celebration. And his distaste for parties was no recent acquisition. As a youngster he learned this attitude from his parents.

"We don't believe in parties!" That's what they told him when he asked if he could have a birthday party like his friends. "Parties cost too much. Besides, you should spend your time doing something profitable!"

"Like what?"

"Like making money."

Matt felt cheated. He wished that he could be special at least one day of the year like the other kids. Their birthdays were times for presents, balloons, paper hats, colorful plates, and napkins. But his birthday was just another day. And he was so ashamed when his friends asked why his parents never gave him a party.

As the years passed, he learned to hide his hurt on birthdays by reminding himself of his parents' counsel: the value of thrift and the wastefulness of parties. Of course he made certain to remember their advice on all the other special days his parents didn't celebrate: holy days, national holidays, graduations. Clearly the lesson

225

he learned was that nothing in life was worth celebrating. And since he didn't celebrate anything in his life, he decided not to celebrate anything in anyone else's life either. All parties were out! Better to concentrate on doing what he had been told repeatedly by his parents: making money.

And when he grew up? Well, at age twenty-four he got a job that paid well all right! But it wasn't the kind of job his folks had in mind. He became a tax collector — a profession which horrified them and made him a traitor in the eyes of others.

"How can you work for the Romans? Robbing us to fill their pockets and your own?"

"I'm making money. Isn't that what you wanted?"

"But no one will want you in their company. You won't be invited to their homes. You...."

"So what? Since when is being with others so important? I don't need them!"

What his parents didn't realize was how Matt felt relieved that he had become a hated tax collector. Now his isolation wouldn't feel so personal. Now he was alone because of his job, not because he was Matt! Yet, in a strange way the attention Matt got as a tax collector met a need that his parents had never met. Collecting tolls on the border between Capernaum and Bethsaida, people had to notice him as he determined how much they owed on goods they were transporting. As an obstacle they couldn't ignore, he became at least for a few moments the center of someone's attention. Of course he never would have admitted this need to himself. He thought he was simply doing what was expected of any good tax collector.

Day after day he sat at his desk interrogating the travelers who came through his doors. One day a young man entered his office, sat down and declared the few items he had to carry over the border. Matt made his computations and concluded, "That will cost fifteen dollars."

"Fifteen dollars? But I don't have fifteen."

"Then you can't cross the border."

"But I must...."

"Fork over the money or forget about your little trip!"

"Well, I don't have the money. But I do have food."

"Food. For what?"

"For a party." The man smiled broadly.

"A party? You must be crazy!"

"Don't you like parties? Haven't you ever had one?"

"Well ... I, I ... No, I've never had a party," Matt stammered, "and I don't intend...."

"You've never had a party? Well, Matt, it's time you had one; we'll throw it in your honor. It'll be a birthday bash!" he laughed.

"But ... how do you know my name? And ... it's not my birth...." Matt stopped, brought both hands to his mouth and said, "My God, today is my birthday! How ... how?"

"It doesn't matter how I know. What matters is you deserve a party! And you're going to get one." Before Matt knew what was happening the man had taken a white tablecloth from his knapsack, cleared the money table and spread the tablecloth on the desk. Then he leaned out the window and cried to his friends, "Fellas! In here!" Four other young men entered the room. Their arms were loaded with cheese, fruit, wine, salami, and bagels. One of the men had balloons and streamers which he promptly strung from the beams.

Matt was too dumbfounded to protest. "I don't believe this," he murmured. Nor did the other travelers who crammed Matt's little office to pay their taxes.

"What's going on here?" they asked.

"Matt's party! Come and join us," the young man answered. "Okay, Matt?"

"Why, why, yes," Matt answered. "I guess it is."

"But what about the tolls?" the travelers asked.

"The tolls?" Matt had completely forgotten his job. For the first time in his life he was enjoying his own birthday party and he didn't want anything to spoil it. "Forget the tolls. Enjoy yourselves," he cried. Matt looked at the young man. He was amazed at how lavish this man had been towards him. No one had ever treated

him to a party — with balloons and streamers, no less! He didn't
want the party to end.

The young man smiled warmly. "Great party, isn't it? You ought
to throw a few parties yourself! Why stop a good thing! Right?"

"Right!" Matt laughed. "Why stop a good thing!"

"Oh, I know!" the man said, "Why not join us? You could be
in charge of throwing parties and inviting others who have never
been to any. Wouldn't that be great?"

Matt's eyes filled with tears. "I'd love it!"

"Good! Come and follow us! Oh, I almost forgot ... my name
is Jesus. Welcome, welcome to our party."

Levi belonged.

Reflection

As children, some of us were forced to become adults before
we were ready. Our playful childlike side was suppressed in favor
of the serious adult side. The reasons why many adults as children
shouldered the burden of adults are many. In some cases children
had to parent a chemically dependent adult. In other cases they
become surrogate spouses for a parent whose real partner was no
longer physically or emotionally available. And some parents em-
phasized work so highly that there was no time for play.

Work was Matt's parents' priority, and so it became his. There
was no time for celebration, not even on birthdays or holidays. But
celebration is essential to growth. There are times in our lives when
we need the playful celebration of our light. Celebrations make us
more aware of the gifts our lives are to ourselves and to others. We
all need to shine, and celebrations afford those opportunities. Without celebrations during which we can admire another's light or be
admired, shame can flourish. "I am inadequate and inferior," is the
feeling response to a light never celebrated.

That shame can be so painful that our work becomes a com-
pensation for our sense of the inadequacy of our own light. By

throwing ourselves into our work, we try to razzle dazzle others and ourselves into believing we are adequate. And we can never stop this razzle dazzle because we fear there'll be only darkness once the show of light is over.

From time to time all of us need to reevaluate the place of work in our lives. For some of us this stepping back is the first step forward. Only then can we realize our light isn't shining because of what we do but because of who we are! Is that the step we need to take?

Blabbermouth

A leper approached Jesus with a request, kneeling down as he addressed him: "If you will to do so, you can cure me." Moved with pity, Jesus stretched out his hand, touched him, and said: "I do will it. Be cured." ... Jesus gave him a stern warning and sent him on his way. "Not a word to anyone, now," he said. "Go off and present yourself to the priest and offer for your cure what Moses prescribed. That should be a proof for them." The man went off and began to proclaim the whole matter freely, making the story public. — Mark 1:40-45

"Blabbermouth!" His mother was enraged. "You're nothing but a blabbermouth! Prattling to the neighbors about my new front teeth." "Blabbermouth!" His brothers wanted to kill him. "Blabbing to Mom and Dad we were smoking pot last night." "Blabbermouth!" His friend felt betrayed. "Tattling to Ms. Hocum I was making faces behind her back!" He had become a blabbermouth at an early age and now at seventeen he was even more the blabbermouth. Who was he? Little Benny Schwartz. "Benny the Blabbermouth" they called him. How did he become a blabbermouth? He had been a quiet baby who played by himself for hours at a time. Naturally, everyone assumed he was happy because he seemed to need no attention. Not like his brothers who were always up to something and needed constant surveillance. Yes, he played by himself, but he wasn't happy. He was lonely and he gradually discovered the only way he could win others' attention was by trading this or that bit of gossip for another's interest in him. Unfortunately, their interest lasted only as long as Benny had something spicy to tell about others or to the extent they felt they were the objects of his interest.

Benny went to any lengths to get the dope on anyone at any time. Sometimes hiding under tables while friends traded confidential comments; often perched precariously on a limb overlooking lovers exchanging intimate secrets; even deciphering notes scribbled on paper scraps he'd scavenged.

And no sooner had he pieced some bits of information together than he breathlessly broadcast it faster than the airwaves. Benny'd stop perfect strangers on the street and gossip about what they did or didn't care to know. "Wait till I tell you ..." or, "Excuse me, but did you know ..." or, "Have I got news about ..." and then he'd tell who slept with whom, who was getting operated on, or losing a job, or having mental problems, and so on. Benny couldn't keep anything to himself. He had to tell it all, and all because he craved attention. However, as soon as the high wore off he'd have to get the latest scoop for another fix of blabbering.

Benny blabbered so much that naturally no one trusted him. Everyone kept a respectful distance. Even inquiring minds avoided getting too close for fear of being inquired about themselves. So Benny grew more and more isolated. And as is often the case with loners, others began regarding him as quirky or strange, and spread strange stories about why he was always alone.

First it was, "He's a blabbermouth. No wonder no one talks or listens to him. No wonder he's a loner...."

Gradually, however, the stories about Benny got wilder. "I think he's hiding something: a rash nobody knows about," someone somewhere speculated. "The blabbermouth bit is just a cover. He doesn't want us to know the real problem."

"A body rash? C'mon, c'mon," someone somewhere else challenged. "The truth is his skin is silky white beneath his tunic. Notice how he hides his arms — keeps them hidden deep in sleeves a

size longer than he needs. A rash indeed! There's more to it than
that. Believe me!"

Rumors built on rumors flared up everywhere. The word was
out — Benny the blabbermouth had leprosy! The town was buzz-
ing as cliques of people chattered over coffee and imagined Benny's
leprosy slowly consuming him. Benny picked up vibes that something wasn't right. But what?

Walking down the street, he strained to catch the drift of strangers as they spoke. "Leper! Unclean," they conspired underneath
their breath. Benny cocked an ear and listened intently for the mention of a name. "Who? Who's a leper? Who's unclean?" "Benny,
Benny the Blabbermouth's a leper," the word filtered in from somewhere somehow. "Wow! Benny the Blabbermouth," Benny echoed thoughtlessly. "Benny the Blabbermouth's a lep...." Realizing
the judgment he was passing on himself, Benny was horror stricken
and froze on the spot. "Benny?" he gasped. "They're talking about
me! No, no, you must mean someone else. I'm not a leper," he
protested. Voices from all directions assaulted him with warnings.
"Keep your distance! Come near and we'll stone you! Unclean!
Unclean! Leave us!" Stunned, Benny walked the streets for days
and nights. One afternoon, studying himself reflected in a store
window, he tried to convince himself. "It isn't true. I'm not a leper.
Gossips! Rumor mongers! Blabbermouths. They're all blabbermouths, just like...." He stopped, looked long and hard, pointed
slowly to himself, and said, "... like me?" He let the words sink in
one by one. "They're blabbermouths like me ... like I've blabber-
mouthed to others." Benny sunk to the curb overwhelmed by what
he had discovered. He hadn't been sitting there long when he felt a
hand on his shoulder.

"Have they been saying things about you too? Things that
haven't been true?" "Who?" Benny turned to look up into the eyes
of a man smiling down at him. "Hi. My name is Jesus. It's mad-
dening, isn't it?" He sat down next to Benny. "I mean having people
talk behind your back about you. Saying things that aren't true."

"Why, yes," Benny answered. It had been so long since anyone had spoken directly to Benny, he was at a loss for words.

"Makes you feel so alone you want to cry. It might even make you determined not to do that kind of thing yourself. Right?" Jesus looked directly into Benny's eyes as he waited for an answer. Benny's face flushed. "Do you know me?"

"No, but I'd like to know you. Not what others say about you, but the real you." The man had a warmth about him which disarmed Benny.

"I feel so lonely," he confessed.

"I know the feeling," Jesus assured him.

"Can you help me?" Benny pleaded.

"Maybe we can help one another," Jesus responded.

Benny remained silent. Then slowly, "I want you to know right off I've got a reputation for being a blabbermouth. Nobody trusts me."

"Tell me more about yourself, Benny." And Jesus was genuinely interested.

"About myself?" Benny shook his head. "You wouldn't want to hear about me. But I can tell you about others. I can tell you lots about others ... who slept with whom, who...."

"No," Jesus waved his hand, " I want to hear about you." Benny scratched his head. No one had ever asked Benny to talk about himself. He had never thought of himself as being interesting. Others, yes. But not himself and now this man wanted him to talk about himself. And that he did. He told his life story and poured his heart out — his fears, his hopes, his growing isolation. As he opened up more and more, he felt cleansed, purged, strangely different. More importantly, Benny didn't feel isolated. He was not a leper anymore.

After Benny had finished, Jesus put his arm around Benny. "There is one thing I have to ask of you. Don't tell anyone what has happened between us. Or at least keep my name out of it. Do you think you can do that?" Jesus winked at Benny and rose to his feet.

"Oh, yes, yes," Benny assured him.

Jesus laughed warmly, knowingly. "I've got to go. My friends are waiting for me. Perhaps you'd like to join us later at the park?"

"Yes, yes," Benny answered enthusiastically. Jesus waved and was on his way.

Benny was elated. He jumped to his feet and ran down the block, crying to anyone within hearing distance, "He listened to me. He really did. I'm cured! I'm cured! I don't feel alone anymore." Benny repeated his message over and over until he reached the corner. He shouted to passersby, "I don't need to talk about anybody else anymore. I just want to tell you what's happened to me."

Soon, one, then two, three, four, and finally about fifteen persons had gathered to listen to Benny. They had never heard him speak about himself so openly before. At first they had cautiously kept their distance. But then a hand reached out and patted Benny on the back. Before long others did the same. "Benny's no longer a leper!" someone cried.

"Or a blabbermouth," another added. "Three cheers for Benny!" "Hip, hip, hurrah!" the crowd yelled. Benny's eyes filled with tears. Actually, he had blabbed again, but his news was good news and he knew Jesus would forgive him. And from that time on good news was the only news he ever blabbed.

Reflection

"Once a blabbermouth, always a blabbermouth!" True, but Benny the blabbermouth at the end of the story isn't the same Benny the blabbermouth we read about at the beginning. He is a blabbermouth with a difference. And that difference points to a very important fact about conversion experiences. People who undergo a change of heart aren't brainwashed. They don't stop being themselves. Benny's change is a change in direction. His talent for broadcasting is redirected, not annihilated. Jesus didn't want him to blab and in that sense Benny didn't change. However, the blabbing he did was on behalf of the good news and not simply out of his need for a "fix." But Benny got his fix proclaiming the good news in a way similar to recovering alcoholics at an AA meeting get a high on witnessing to their recovery. Something of the old makes its appearance in the new but that doesn't mean the experiences are not genuine conversion experiences.

It ought to be consoling to people who have lived fifty or sixty years to realize the hot temper or impatience they had at age twenty and continue to have at age sixty need not mean they haven't changed or matured. The hot temper and the impatience might signify indignation over injustices perpetrated on others rather than adolescent pouting or earlier self-centered tirades. It is the entire gestalt or context which we need to understand when we speak of a change of heart and not the eradication of this or that peccadillo. And of course it is only through being converted over and over that change becomes lasting. After all, a recovering alcoholic is recovering, never recovered. Accepting the ongoing nature of the change rather than worrying about the presence of an undesirable trait promotes a deeper appreciation of the place of conversion in our lives.

In Praise Of Ourselves

The reign of God is like the case of the owner of an estate who went out at dawn to hire workmen for his vineyard. After reaching an agreement with them for the usual daily wage, he sent them out to his vineyard. — Matthew 20:1-2

"Two hundred bucks for a day's work! That's fantastic!" Bert marveled.

"Oh! Oh! We don't deserve it! We don't deserve it!" Elmer wept with joy. "What a boss! What can I say about him? I'm at a loss. I am at a loss. He's...."

"Beyond compare," Bert bellowed.

"A man of vision," Elmer prophesied.

"The best in my book," Bert tapped his chest. "A man for all seasons!"

Elmer extended his arms. Neither Elmer nor Bert had been employed for a month and they were almost broke. The owner of The Bottom's Up Winery had come to their rescue by hiring them. "And wait till the fellas in the other vineyards hear what we're being paid! They'll be green with envy." Elmer rubbed his hands with glee.

"Yeah," Bert chuckled. "I can hear them now. 'How do you guys rate? What's your secret?' I'll tell them that we don't rate. We've got no secret. We're not special. It just happened this way. The boss saw us and liked us!"

" 'Liked us.' Be sure and add that," Elmer cautioned. "We don't want to make it look like we had nothing going for us, now do we?"

"You have a point," Bert said. "We wouldn't want them thinking that the boss was into his own hootch when he chose us to work. Speaking of work, we'd better stop our gabbing and earn our keep." So the two day-laborers picked grapes alongside the regular workers. At noon they stopped for lunch.

Sitting in the shade offered by the leafy oaks, they noticed about eight old men coming through the gates. Dressed in thread-bare, oversized suit coats and baggy pants, they looked like they hadn't shaved for two or three days. Shuffling into the vineyard, some of them held beer cans in one hand while supporting one another with the other hand.

"What's this? What's this?" Bert muttered. "Look what we're getting now! A bunch of old drunks. I wonder where the boss got them? Probably hiding in some bar, drinking up their welfare checks! I know those kind. The boss has saddled himself with some real losers. I hope he gives them what they deserve. Lucky he's got us."

"Yeah," Elmer agreed. "You don't find our kind in bars or cheap motels. I bet he's singing our praises after picking up those guys. Let's go back to work. I can't stomach watching their kind come in for a free ride." And back to work they went.

Around midafternoon they took a break. Munching an apple, Bert's eyes widened as he saw four or five men and women hobble through the gate on crutches while three or four others who were blind tapped their canes as they inched along. They were followed by a few paraplegics who wheeled their way towards the vines. "Do you see what I see?" he cried. "This is incredible! He's hired a whole hospital ward of cripples. I wonder if he knows what he's doing. I hate to say it but ..." he whispered, "I think the boss is a little balmy."

"Out to lunch," Elmer whispered back.

"And dinner," Bert sniggered. "The boss can thank God he's got us! We're keeping this place going. I bet he's singing alleluias and offering incense because he met up with us. Two hundred bucks is a small price to pay for the likes of us. Right?"

"Roger," Elmer said. Saluting each other, they scanned the vine-yard that the boss had gratefully entrusted to them. Then they went back to work.

It was late afternoon when Bert happened to look in the direction of the gate. "Nooo," he gasped. "It can't be! Elmer, Elmer! Look!" This time about nine laughing children ran, skipped, and cartwheeled through the gate. Clapping and dancing on the field, they then tugged the vines.

"Kids don't know the first thing about work," Bert snapped. "All they can do is play."

"Now I know the boss is daffy," Elmer said. "No business sense! Doesn't understand that we all have to get money the old-fashioned way — we have to earn it! I'm surprised he hasn't gone under. Well I guess he can thank people like us for the fact that he stays afloat. There, but for the grace of us, goes he! He's indebted to us! He doesn't deserve us!"

"We're beyond compare!"

"The best in our books!"

"Men for all seasons!"

"What a paycheck we'll be getting," they sang as they danced in a little circle and then continued working.

When the work day ended, Elmer and Bert rushed to the pay office and stood first in line, pushing aside all others. "He'll want to see us first," Bert said.

"Undoubtedly," Elmer agreed. But a voice over the loudspeaker indicated otherwise. "Workers who were hired late this afternoon please come to the beginning of the line and those hired early this morning go to the end!"

"Wha...." Bert's mouth dropped open. "What's happening?"

"I guess when everybody else has left," Elmer confided, "the boss will be throwing a big party in our honor. And he certainly doesn't want them hangin' around. They don't deserve it."

"Yeah, that must be it," Bert said.

After they had gone to the end of the line, the voice over the loudspeaker continued. "Now I'll begin giving two hundred dollars to each of the workers. Please step forward!"

"They're getting two hundred bucks and they've only worked an hour!" Bert blurted. "Those kids are getting two hundred bucks! For doing nothing!"

"Don't worry," Elmer said as he wiped the perspiration gathering on his forehead. "Can you imagine what he's going to give us? I know it won't be what we're worth but you can be sure we'll be able to live very comfortably. Wait and see!"

When they reached the office, an elderly gentleman sitting at a desk smiled and handed each of them two hundred dollars. Bert and Elmer looked at the money, then at one another, and then at the boss. "This is it?" they asked.

"Yes," the old man said.

"But, but ..." Bert stammered, "we're worth more. You, you owe us much more."

"Yes," Elmer added. "We let you hire us. Is this how you thank us?"

"I beg your pardon," the old man said as he cupped his hand to his ear. "Am I hearing you right? You let me hire you? I ought to thank you?"

Ignoring his questions, Elmer pressed on. "We deserve more than two hundred bucks, much more. You're indebted to us."

The man laughed. "I'm indebted to you? Ha! Ha!" Scrutinizing their faces, he said, "I thought I recognized you boys. Every time you're down to your last cent I hire you. You sing my praises for an hour, and then your own the rest of the day. Don't you?"

"Why, I'm...." Bert scratched his head.

"You can't accept the fact that I like to help people because I get a kick out of it, can you? I do it not because people are so darned good that I have to pay them but because I enjoy paying them!" The old man shook his head sadly. Embarrassed, Bert and Elmer stood silently with their heads lowered. They were there ready to walk out of the office when the old man raised a hand and said, "Wait! I suppose you expected me to throw a party for you too, didn't you?" More silence. Winking, he said, "Well, you're not going to get the bash you probably expected, but we can go into the back room and share a cup of wine and some cheese and crackers. You think you fellas can settle for something 'less' than you deserve?" he laughed.

Bert and Elmer swallowed hard, nodded and followed the old man. For the moment they were grateful they had something to eat.

Reflection

Talk to physicians or lawyers or clergy or social workers! They'll tell you. Before they've given their services, clients are desperate for their help. "We need you. Tell us what to do," they implore. They're mighty grateful and willing to pay whatever is necessary to get well or settle some legal dispute or get some kind of intervention in a marital or family dispute. But once the crisis is over, well that is a different matter. "I could have done it myself," he says, or, "Why do I have to pay you so much money for the operation or the counseling or the legal fees? You people owe us a lot. If it weren't for us, you'd be out of business!" The predictable course of events for many clients is from deep indebtedness to contempt for services rendered. Why?

As in our story, people conveniently forget what they have received and then they rationalize their lack of gratitude by attacking the very people who had helped them. "We deserve what you did for us," is the assumption. Deserving all too often cancels out gratitude. The trees, the birds, the air, people — they are all there for us. We deserve them!

But we not only take others for granted; we take ourselves as well for granted. In other words we no longer rejoice in our own light. But a light taken for granted might just as well be hidden under a basket because it is no longer noticed. Remembering is essential in being grateful and gratitude helps us be aware of the gift which each light is.

Do we appreciate the gifts of light shining in our presence? Or have we forced them in hiding by taking them for granted? Are we no longer even aware of them?

Talents

The case of a man who was going on a journey is similar. He called in his servants and handed his funds over to them according to each man's abilities. To one he disbursed five thousand silver pieces, to a second two thousand, and to a third a thousand. — Matthew 25:14-15

"Hi!" Louie smiled and waved at people in expensive cars, beat up jalopies, taxis, school buses, eighteen-wheelers, and pickup trucks. It didn't matter whether the passersby were seniors, teenagers, school children, or hefty truck drivers. Louie had been greeting people on his street corner every day for forty years. That is all he did!

When he first started, people called him Screwy Louie. "Why's he doing that? What's he smiling for? Who's he saying hi to?" they asked as they craned their necks for a better view. "You're mental! They ought to lock you up," were the cruelest comments a few ignorant people hurled at him as they sped by his corner. But gradually those who regularly drove past Louie began to anticipate his familiar greeting. Sometimes a husband and wife who had been arguing called a truce just long enough to wave and comment on Louie's greeting. Chubby-cheeked boys and giggling girls waved wildly on their way to school in yellow buses. Occasionally a matronly-looking woman stopped her car and handed Louie a box of chocolate chip cookies.

Yes, Louie had been saying hi for forty-four years. Brain damaged as a baby when he fell out of a crib, he had spent his childhood playing quietly with his toys. And when he became a teenager he did nothing else but rock away his time and look at pictures in comic books. Louie's parents had long ago despaired of Louie doing anything constructive. "Let's face it," his dad harped whenever the subject came up, "Louie has no future. He'll be looking at comic books forever."

Louie's parents were grateful they had at least one son who showed real promise. Lenny, their youngest, had brains and good looks.

"I'm gonna be a lawyer. You wait and see," he promised his folks.

"Our son's going to be a lawyer. Just wait and see," they bragged to relatives, neighbors, and anyone who cared to listen. There wasn't much they could say about Louie, and they felt embarrassed describing his preoccupation with comic books. Nor were they interested in discussing their middle son, Larry. "We hope he grows up some day. All he does is sit around, talk for hours on the phone to his girl friends, and raid the refrigerator," they sighed. "Oh, yeah," they added as an afterthought, "Larry likes to go into Louie's room, wave, and say hi to him." Then they'd laugh. "He thinks Louie is actually going to answer him some day. What a pair of losers!"

One day when Larry was bounding past Louie's room, he leaned in, smiling and waving and, as usual, cheerily bellowed, "Hi." Then, as he turned to split, he thought he heard a quiet "hi" come back to him. Wheeling back, Larry cried, "Louie, you said, 'Hi!' " This time Louie smiled, waved, and said more loudly than before, "Hi!" Larry was beside himself. He dashed over to Louie, hugged him, ran out of the room, and told his folks.

They were pleased, but certainly not elated. "Isn't that nice," they agreed. "Our son can say, 'Hi,' at last. Let's hope he can learn more — complete sentences." They were happy for him but of course a wave, a smile, and a hi didn't come close to what their son Lenny would accomplish one day when he became a lawyer. Larry, on the other hand, marveled over Louie's accomplishment and his role in getting Louie to respond. He decided then and there to make a career out of helping people with problems similar to Louie's.

"Well, of course, it's better than doing nothing," his folks conceded when Larry told them what he intended to do. And in the privacy of their bedroom they observed, "He'll never succeed like Lenny, but there isn't anything we can do about that." Lenny had the brains and the looks all right. He also had the gift of gab. "I'm gonna be a lawyer. You just wait and see!" And everybody waited.

Louie, on the other hand, wasted little time using his new-found talent. He took his next big step when he put his comic books on a shelf, walked to the front door, opened it, and stepped out onto the porch. There he waved at letter carriers, kids delivering papers, bill collectors, neighbors — making them all feel welcome. Pleased with his success, he finally strode proudly to the corner of his block where a new world eagerly waited his presence, his talent.

And among the many persons who waved every day to Louie was Larry as he drove to the hospital where he worked as a physical therapist for children.

As for Lenny, if anyone cared to look closely enough, on any afternoon he could be seen muttering from a swing on his porch, "I'm gonna be a lawyer some day. You just wait and see!"

Reflection

Lights don't need to be floodlights in order to illumine. Children need parents who facilitate the emergence of even the smallest light in their children. Parents who either discourage their children from shining or who expect them to be the whole stellar system produce similar results: their children's light remains hidden.

This story illustrates what happens when a child's feeble light is not appropriately recognized or mirrored by the parents. Since the child's sense of self depends on affirmation, a failure to notice means the child experiences a deficient self. Thus Louie sits in his rocker day in and day out. What little he had to offer was never affirmed until his brother Larry consistently acknowledged him.

Expecting too much, however, also places too much of a burden on a child. When we brag about our children's gifts, we want to bear in mind that affirming their achievements isn't the same as imposing unattainable goals on them. This generates anxiety instead of self-confidence. None of us ought to have to bear the burden of being the best of anything. It is enough that we be who we are. In being that, we discover what kind of light we really are and not just what kind of light our parents had intended. Lenny's failure is that no one was around to affirm him in his limitations as well as in his successes. "You don't need to be perfect and that is fine," is the message which he needed to hear and didn't.

But what Louie heard from Larry sustained him, and the first steps he took, though small, were his first steps out from under the basket. Once he was out, Louie's flickering match light became a beacon of light to all the travelers who passed his way. Can we recognize that very small steps are very important ones in coming out from under the basket?

Who's Lost?

"Who among you, if he has a hundred sheep and loses one of them, does not leave the ninety-nine in the wasteland and follow the lost one until he finds it?" — Luke 15:4

He returned to the house with them and again the crowd assembled, making it impossible for them to get any food whatever. When his family heard of this they came to take charge of him, saying, "He is out of his mind." — Mark 3:20-21

"Every family has one!"

"And he's ours...."

"Without a doubt!"

"The black sheep!"

The black sheep? Who were Jesus' cousins talking about as they sat fanning themselves on the porch that hot afternoon in Nazareth?

"Yes, Jesus is our black sheep," Joses nodded gravely. "He doesn't take after his mom or his dad. I don't know of any of us who are as crazy as he is. I'd say John comes the closest. He's really weird — eating insects, into leather, and a real hell raiser with the authorities!"

"But that's Mary's side of the family, not ours. I'm worried what people will think about us," Jim said.

"Right!" Joses waved a hand. "I've already had total strangers come up to me and say, 'You're Jesus' cousin, aren't you? What's he up to anyway?' What can I say? What can any of us say? That he's running around the countryside giving pep talks to losers about some pie-in-the-sky day when they'll all be winners?"

"Or that he wastes time telling stories and hanging out with guys who are out of work like himself," Jim added. "And if that isn't enough ... that Jesus parties with pretty shady characters, doesn't have a place of his own, and wears the same outfit his mom gave him two years ago!" "Yeah, I know he got a kick out of the fact that it's a one piece tunic, but enough is enough already!"

Joses shook his head. "What bothers me most are the wild stories I'm beginning to hear about him acting like some faith healer: laying hands on the crazies and trying to touch others' hurts away."

"You'd think he was some heaven-sent masseur!" Jim interrupted, his voice tinged with sarcasm. "Let me tell you, these stories worry me too, but not half as much as the reports I'm getting about his run-ins with the authorities. Seems he doesn't like the way they keep shop. He scolds them for preferring their pocketbooks to the poor; chastises them for endlessly primping and preening in public; and lashes out at them for saddling who he calls 'the little ones' with oppressive laws. I tell you if he keeps undermining their authority, you and I, and the whole family are in for trouble," Jim concluded ominously.

"Yes, they'll send a team down here to snoop around and dig up dirt to implicate all of us with trumped up charges," Joses warned. "We've got to do something before that happens. We've got to go to Capernaum where they say he's hanging out and bring him back with us."

"I'm not certain he'll listen to us," Jim said. "I don't think he trusts us. But if we can get Mary to come, he may give us a hearing. She hasn't seen him for a while, and we'll tell her we'd like to visit Jesus and we'd like her to join us."

"Good idea," Joses said. "Remember, no talk about him being a problem child. She thinks the world of him — like he's God's gift to the world and all that. We'll just try to convince her while we're walking that maybe Jesus needs a little rest and we'd like him to come home for a while. She'd like that. Maybe she'd even make him a new tunic!"

"Yeah, might even get him to cut his hair and shave!" Jim said.

"Now you're talking! Well, let's get at it! We can't lose any time," Joses said.

Jim and Joses persuaded Mary to come along with them to Capernaum. She seemed puzzled by their sudden solicitude for Jesus since they had never seemed fond of him when he lived at home. As Mary remembered it, Jesus had often tried to be their friend, but they always had excuses for not spending time with him. Even at the family get-togethers Jim and Joses avoided Jesus. But then those two tended to go their own ways, avoiding most of the other family members as well. "I wish I could reach them," Jesus had told his folks on several occasions. However, now the two wanted to visit Jesus, and even though Mary had reservations about their intentions, she decided to give them the benefit of the doubt.

They arrived at the public square in Capernaum just in time to see a large crowd gathered around a man who was speaking to them. Shading his eyes from the noonday sun, Joses squinted and cried, "It's Jesus!" The three walked as quickly as possible to the gathering. As they stood at the back of the crowd Mary tapped her finger on a big, burly man's shoulder. After she had gotten his attention, she told him she was Jesus' mother and asked if he could muscle his way through the crowd to tell Jesus she and his cousins were waiting to see him. The man grumbled, hesitated, but finally angled his way through the crowd and disappeared.

A couple of minutes later he returned. Laughing, he told her, "Jesus says we're all his relatives if we act like family and care for one another like God wants us to do."

"Now what's that supposed to mean?" Joses asked angrily.

"Hey, buddy, I'm just giving you the message. Interpret it any way you like. If you're his cousin, you oughta know what he's talking about. You've always cared about him, haven't you?"

"Of course I...." Joses was going to say he had always cared, but he noticed Mary's eyes fixed on him and he said nothing more.

Pressing the point, the man directed his comments to Jim, "I mean you'd try to reach out to him if you thought he was in trouble. Right?"

"Well, I...." He too caught Mary's eyes and sputtered, "I ... I ... I ... of course, of course!"

By this time the crowd had thinned out and the two men took advantage of the situation. Joses elbowed Jim, "Let's get away from this guy! He's getting to me." They practically carried Mary as they shoved their way to the center of the crowd. "He's telling a story," Joses whispered.

"Who among you, if he has a hundred sheep and loses one of them, does not leave the ninety-nine in the wasteland and follow the lost one until he finds it? And when he finds it, he puts it on his shoulders in jubilation. Once arrived home, he invites friends and neighbors in and says to them, 'Rejoice with me because I have found my lost sheep.' I tell you, there will likewise be more joy in heaven over one repentant sinner than over ninety-nine righteous people who have no need to repent."

After Jesus had finished, his face lit up as he caught sight of Mary and his cousins. "Mom," he cried as he ran over to her and gave her a big hug. "Jim, Joses, what a surprise! I was just thinking about you. I've found you at last!"

"Thinking about us?" Joses puzzled.

"Found us?" Jim muttered. "Why...." Jim couldn't finish the sentence since Jesus was embracing them both like long-lost brothers.

"You're going to stay for a while, aren't you?"

"Well...." The brothers looked sheepishly at one another. "We ... uh...."

"Of course you are. We've got so much to talk about. And nothing is more important than being with you ... and Mom, of course," Jesus laughed.

Tears had formed in the two brothers' eyes as they put their arms around Jesus' waist. They had come to bring the black sheep home with them and for some strange reason they felt they were being welcomed back into the fold ... where they belonged.

Reflection

"I'm lost! I hope I can find my way," could as easily be the cry of someone who finds no meaning in life as it could be the complaint of a frustrated driver in a strange city. Yet the simple admission that we are lost is essential if we are ever to find our way. Unfortunately, we do not make these admissions easily. Just as we can insist that we know where we're going as we drive around in circles in the strange city, so we can also insist that we know where we're going in life when we really don't. Mindlessly watching television, endlessly having affairs, or working nonstop day after day are a few of the ways in which we get lost and lose all sense of purpose and meaning in life.

However, once we recognize we are at a loss about what to do with our lives then we are already beginning to walk in the light. No one is so far gone as the one who is completely unaware of being lost. Rather than despairing of finding our way once we have seen the light and admitted to being lost, we might regard that very insight, intuition, or recognition as a first step in coming out from under the basket.

How do we react when we discover we have been lost? Do we despair or become depressed? Or do we see that "seeing" is itself light, a gift from the Light?

Index

Lectionary Texts And Liturgical Days

Note: The index lists the scripture texts used, title of the story written on each text, and the corresponding liturgical day for each text in Cycles A, B, and C. When RCL appears in parentheses, it means the passage doesn't apply to Roman Catholics for that day, and when RC appears in parentheses it means the passage applies only to Roman Catholics for that day.

Proper 19/Pent. 24	Short On Memory	Matthew 18:21-24
Proper 20/Pent. 25	Eleventh Hour	Matthew 20:1-2
Proper 20/Pent. 25	In Praise Of Ourselves	Matthew 20:1-2
Proper 23/Pent. 28	Big Daddy	Matthew 22:2-3
Proper 28/Pent. 33	Talents	Matthew 25:14-15

Cycle B

Advent 4	A Modest Proposal	Luke 1:26-28
Epiphany	Favorite	Luke 1:26-28
Epiphany 3	Fishers	Mark 1:14-20 (RCL only)
Epiphany 6	Blabbermouth	Mark 1:40-45 (RCL only)
Lent 3	Broom Bristles	Matthew 21:12
Palm Sunday	The Man Who Would Not Be King	Mark 11:2
Easter	Broken Promise	Luke 24:13-14
Easter 3	Fishers	Mark 1:19-20 (RC only)
Easter 6	Blabbermouth	Mark 1:40-45 (RC only)

Pent. 24	Junior	Luke 15:11-33 (RC only)
Pent. 24	Fun	Luke 15:22-24 (RC only)
Pent. 24	Daddy	Luke 15:11-12 (RC only)
Proper 20/Pent. 25	Giveaway	Luke 16:1-4
Proper 20/Pent. 25	The Chocolate Man	Luke 16:1-4
Proper 25/Pent. 30	The Sinner	Luke 18:9
Proper 26/Pent. 31	Tree Climber	Luke 19:1-3

(These stories have either no exact references or no references in the Common Lectionary)

The Topbanana Tree	Genesis 3:1
High Hopes	Matthew 20:20-21
Our Kind	Mark 5:1-9
Speechless	Luke 1:13
Tradition	Luke 1:57-61
Maggie	Luke 8:1-3